THE PILGRIM

THE
PILGRIM

MICHAEL SERAFIAN

LONDON
MICHAEL JOSEPH

First published by
MICHAEL JOSEPH LTD
26 Bloomsbury Street
London, W.C.1
1964

Set and printed in Great Britain by Tonbridge Printers Ltd,
Peach Hall Works, Tonbridge, Kent, in Bembo eleven on
twelve point, on paper made by Henry Bruce at Currie,
Midlothian, and bound by James Burn at Esher, Surrey

This book is dedicated to His Holiness Pope Paul the Sixth as a pledge of the author's devotion to the interests of Christ's Church and the great cause to which His Holiness has consecrated his life.

MICHAEL SERAFIAN

CONTENTS

INTRODUCTION

The second session of the Second Vatican Ecumenical Council lasted sixty-seven days, from September 29 to December 4, 1963, and the title chosen for this study might well have been *The Sixty-Seven Days of Paul VI*. For these were the days of his personal and pontifical drama, as Bishop of Rome, as Patriarch of the West, the 263rd successor to Peter the Fisherman, as the Vicar of Christ, as Giovanni Battista Montini.

Yet the official capacity and performance of any human being depend largely on the fibre and the stuff of which he is made. Because the actions of any man in Paul's position have results that not only go beyond his original intentions but are caught up in the web of history-in-the-making, I have preferred to entitle this study *The Pilgrim*. This is, perhaps, the only way in which we can perceive Paul at work and gain some insight into the deep causes of his decisions and his significance for history. For he has already entered history.

Someone has said that to understand history, it is not sufficient merely to know single events or to recount them. This is what the chronicler does but not the true historian. It is rather the conjunctural significance of two or more events which constitute history, which manifest the inner logic of human events and breathe with the ever-restless spirit which moulds and vivifies. By destiny and by historical position, Giovanni Battista Montini became Pope at a moment which was an axial point for centuries of Christian and of human development. By the votes of the cardinals gathered in the Sistine Chapel on June 21, 1963, the hands of Paul VI's very definitely patterned character were placed on the huge fulchra of absolute rule with power to direct the vast edifice as he desired and judged best. Herein lies the conjunctural significance: the hands of Papa Montini at the controls of a two-thousand-year-old organism at a turning-point in history. This is the object of our study.

It is not merely the decision which he made and the direction which that decision has taken in recent months. Nor is it Paul's particular way of implementing it. All these elements do enter into the texture of our subject. But it is this man at this moment, at grips with a certain historical conjuncture. For by his decision and its implementation, Paul has inevitably taken a stance in history, has made history, and committed himself to a flow of events which he cannot stem any longer and for which he must bear final responsibility.

Pope Paul spent almost three full months preparing for the second session of Vatican Council II. From September 29 until Friday, November 8, he rode with the steady, irresistible, sometimes febrile flow of mounting conciliar activity. By Tuesday, November 12, it was all over: Paul had stood aside from a current which he had been taught to suspect and learned to fear. By December 3, an entirely new twist had been given to conciliar events by every means at the power of Paul's Roman dicasteries and by the communications media at his personal command. The Council of Trent was solemnly commemorated. The two documents on the Liturgy and Communications Media were solemnly promulgated but compromised in their execution. There had been 45 general congregations or working-sessions of the Council, in which a total of something like 612 speeches had been delivered. The Council Fathers departed with the Apostolic blessing. All eyes were fixed on the lands of the East and on Pilgrim Paul.

On the surface and as isolated actions, these events seem to refuse any rational structurization, any coherent interpretation. Without an insight into the character of Paul and his real pilgrimage, we will never make sense of what happened. Nor will the future be any clearer to us. The character of the present Pope must be understood.

The antecedents of Paul VI and the external events of his life are well known and do not need repetition here. At present he is 66 years of age, slight of build, delicate in appearance, measured and deliberate in his gestures. The impact of his mere physical presence and personality in the Vatican, coming, as they did, after the figure of Papa Giovanni, had an almost catalytic effect: 'This is John twenty years younger and with a brain,' was a typical formulation of the general reaction.

On the one hand, there was a certain continuity – felt or imagined – between *borghese* Montini and *contadino* Roncalli. But it was the continuity between a respected elder son and beloved father. It was the advent of a very brilliant star in the wake of a celestial comet. Where John had burned like a steady prairie fire, kindling warmth and light in the darkest and most remote regions of modern man's spirit, Paul glinted like the steel-blue flame of a blowtorch, bespoke efficiency, foretold purpose, advertised caution. John was the chosen instrument of nature and grace, fashioned almost independently of human ingenuity. Paul was a product of the system, rubbed and polished by advancement, adversity, preferment, schooling, until he scintillated like a precious stone from the hand of master-jewellers. 'Papa Giovanni created the necessary conditions which made possible the brilliant functioning of the efficient and fully-fledged instrument which Papa Montini is,' said *cognoscenti* in the inner circle. This too was the impression of Vaticanologists looking in from the outside.

The fatherliness of Pope John, it was noted, was replaced by the papal presence of Paul. To the papal attendants who bore him on their shoulders John's weight on the *sedia gestatoria* was a continual reminder of his own comic remarks to them on the subject. Paul's weight on the same mobile throne was a sacred thing and a reminder of high duty. Pope John's infectious humour, the resistant tonality of his reactions, the innate charm of his personality revealing native simplicity, his dislike of formalism, the obviousness of his emotions, all this was succeeded by the correct smile of Paul, the tortuous tone of his reactions, the cultivated habits of someone schooled to regulate the impression he produced on others, his obvious adherence to the mannerisms and behaviourisms of standard diplomacy, his obvious need for reverence and quiet in his presence, for respect, for undivided attention, the apparent absence of spontaneous emotion.

The striking, sometimes laughter-provoking, vociferous gestures of John – the stubby forefinger stabbing a point or hammering an argument, the sudden kicking or stamping with his tough columnar legs, the unrestrained swaying of his bulky torso, the ploy of spatular hands to convey expressions of irresistible blessing, enveloping love, or genuine welcome, were succeeded almost exclusively by two conventional oft-repeated gestures of Paul's, the *pacellist* acknowledgement of gratifying *vivas* from the masses – palms turned upward, curved arms moving vertically, or the *pacellist* stance of dignified approval – hands joined one on the other, the body slightly turned, the face solemn.

The difference between the two men was emphasized by the total diversity of face-structure. Roncalli's face presented a monolithic unity as if carved *in toto* and in one burst of forceful inspiration from nature's material. Everything was massive and all the traits harmonized. The whole posed no questions, was rather a strong affirmation of power, of solidity, of affectivity, of big perspectives. Montini's face was a mosaic of composition, the result of refined skill, of hidden processes, a combination of ambivalent elements, contrasts, differentiating parts, subtle unities. The whole physiognomy aroused queries, provoked the idea of a mystery, warned of unsuspected power, hinted at schematic structures and an inner mysticism. To use theological terms symbolically: Roncalli's face was an incarnation; Montini's face was a sacrament.

Roncalli's broad expanse of forehead raftered on prominent brow-ridges was in perfect accord with the solid presence of his chin and walled cheek-line. Montini's curving dome-like head and smooth temples overhung the rest of his face as if already too heavy a burden, as if containing secret power too spiritual to find expression in his brows and receding mouth-piece. On the contrary, the solid nose toppled over and out, was affirmed by the protruding lower lip and sharply jutting chin. Hence the posed mystery of his forehead and skull, the sensitive appreciation of his lower lip, the thin definite mouth-line, contrasted with the sudden protrusion of nose, the intangible question-mark of chin, the cheek-wall sloping away indefinably into a delicate neckline. In short, Roncalli enveloped because of manifest strength, won because of an embracing presence. Montini imposed himself because of abiding mystery, instilled respect because affirmation walked with question across his countenance. The steady brown eyes of natural intuition were replaced by the now-blue, now-hazel eyes of intellectual assessment and enquiry.

But the spirits housed within these tenements of clay were even more diverse. John had no pretensions or valid claims to any intellectualism, to profound historical scholarship or learned grasp of theological and philosophical intricacies. He found it hard to follow any argument which depended on theoretic premises or mental acrobatics. He rarely conceptualized. He never felt the need to protect himself by formulations or by conscious refuge in the parapets of dogmatic verbiage. The spirit that burned in him supplied him with a directly penetrating force that went to the core of any problem. His solutions were never the conclusions of a syllogism. They were the concrete formulations of his intuition. Consequently, there was no fission between his understanding and his action. He was, to use the apt French expressions, both *malin* and *intelligent*. Above all, he had the hallmark of all genius, originality. He could create an event and exploit it.

His very handwriting was, graphologically, an expression of this character: the middle zone of his letters stood out betokening one occupied with the here-and-now, while the upper zone with its intellectual connotations was restricted to the barely necessary, roofed in by the horizontal bars on the 't', restricted to the shapely but limited loops of 'l' and 'h'. The hand as a whole rushes forward steadily, with no trace of studied restraint or effort at effect.

Paul's character is marked, firstly, by a need for schematic representation, for intellectual formulation, for clear outlines and sharply etched parapets not to be approached but always to be watched. For his spirit, however, this 'schematism' is not sufficient; such intellectual sketching contains its own arid dangers, because it is inclined to presume on the old weakness of the intellectual and interpret words as acts. His spirit, then, is balanced by a mystical side, a constant penchant to envelop intellectual formulations and theoretic behaviourisms in the inspiring veils of a mysticism: to soften rigidity, or use inspiration as a substitute for the concrete action which his words do not comport. When we speak of *mystique* in connection with Paul, we are not referring to spiritual mysticism such as one associates spontaneously with the names of people like St Teresa of Avila or St John of the Cross. Much less are we remarking on the literary style and terminology of Paul: he is fond of Italianate phrases like *disegno immenso e misterioso; arcanum consilium; celsissimum finem; mysterium novi temporis; consilium inscrutabile.** But this is not the mysticism we speak of here.

He will avoid, if possible, the stark formulation of hard verities, and will seem – both for his own spirit and for others – to overcast all formulations with a trans-world, trans-word, trans-subjective aura. As a weakness, he can at times lapse into expressions as hard as a whip-lash. As a final refuge, he can withdraw to mystical ramparts. If ever he comes into his agony, it will be when no mystical overflow is available to clothe the schematic outline of his thought. As a constant condition for his smooth functioning, he requires the theoretic and the practical side – but both illumined by his inner mysticism.

His is the studied approach backed up by a naturally subtle spirit. He is neither veritable humanist nor truly intellectual egg-head: he will quote the language of the one and employ the structures of the other. He is pragmatist and mystic. And his mysticism is nature's balancing for the drabness of the pragmatic. He has neither global vision nor intuitive force by nature. He would not be able to create an event. He would be able to use the creations of others. He has a studied handwriting in which the upper zone indicating intellectual leanings preponderates.

* 'Immense and mysterious design'; 'arcane counsel'; 'loftiest end'; 'the mystery of the new time'; 'inscrutable counsel'.

All his letters are perfectly formed, the arcade ligatures of each letter are studied and deliberate. There is no sign of haste; each formation is a joy in itself, is meant to convey schematically its value. And the lines of writing are graceful formulas of presentation, softly flowing garments of his approach. Roncalli's handwriting was communication. Montini's handwriting is a formulation.

Thus, just as Papa Giovanni appeared on the stage of papal power and strode uninhibited and guided by touch, feeling, intuition, Papa Montini walked gently but firmly back to the Vatican and to the papal throne, his body slightly turned in the attitude of someone listening for a voice no one but he can hear. There was a noted contrast in the physical reactions observed in both men at the moment that the papal tiara was placed on their heads during their individual coronation ceremonies. Roncalli bent his head, the open eyes registering his physical reactions to find the metallic, encircling clasp of papal responsibility being fitted on his temples, his lips apart but relaxed, seemingly absorbing the towering length and weight of the tiara into the already massive lines of his head, neck and shoulders. Montini had his eyes firmly closed, his lips tightly shut to a thin line, his bent head and tense face-lines bespeaking the burdened spirit, the mystical communion, the acceptance of Gethsemani for the sake of future glory. Roncalli seemed to speak confidently and look directly ahead, Abraham-like, at the Eternal. Montini's eyes were covered by an angel's hand so that the passing glory of the Most High would not kill him.

The reactions of the two men on these occasions were replete with symbolism. John accepted the ancient order of things, the seven-tiered pyramidal tiara symbolizing papal power, Romanism, and the juridical form of the Logos incarnate; he accepted it and bore it as it was. For Papa Montini there was a new model of the old one, the gift of his former Milanese subjects but designed by himself, still seven-tiered, but streamlined and reduced in weight. He accepted it as a weight of mystical agony which he was destined to carry at the top of the juridical pyramid and overlooking the vast scarred plain of the contemporary world. There was a positive reaction and a common-sense touch to John's acceptance. There was passivity and an aura of mystical communion in Paul's bent tenseness. Symbolically, two different reactions to the Pyramid on the Plain.

If I have dwelt at some length on Pope Paul's character and traits, it is with a definite reason. It is impossible to understand the present Pontiff's actions and decisions with regard to current situations unless we keep in mind the area of his appreciation and the fullness of the gifts with which he has been endowed. There is a *boutade* attributed to Papa Giovanni (like every other one of its kind, it is impossible to substantiate but very quotable), underlining this thought. '*Come va il vostro vescovo amletico?*'* Roncalli was supposed to have asked an old friend from the Milan diocese where Montini was then Cardinal Archbishop. Carlo Falconi, writing in the Roman weekly, *L'Espresso*, at the time of the conclave from which Montini emerged as pope, popularized the expression: *l'amletismo di Montini* ('the Hamlet-like character of Montini'). Both before and after the conclave one heard in Rome comments that Papa Montini was afflicted with a certain ambivalence, that he could not make up his mind, that he changed it rapidly or even suddenly once he had made it up, that he was capable of quick twists and turns in actions, that he could contradict today what he affirmed yesterday.

I think that the entire concept of *amletismo* or a Hamletic element in Papa Montini's character is both inaccurate and unfair. Those closest to him now would be the first to repudiate the idea in all honesty and objectivity. The charge is a dangerous one, however: it can imperil our understanding of the second session of the Council. For we can easily take refuge in it as a portmanteau concept to explain the apparent contradictions, the sudden tangential attitudes of Papa Montini, the apparent inconsistency between some of his words and actions. As I hope to point out, he has been quite consistent throughout, consistent, that is to say, with his outlook and formulation of the central problem besetting him as Pope.

Besides, such an attitude betrays an already formed judgement about Paul VI. If true, it should embrace his entire story. Not without reason have I entitled this book *The Pilgrim*, for Paul is on pilgrimage, as the Church which he heads is in pilgrimage. The Church of Rome as a corporate organism in time is a pilgrim. Therefore, resisting the temptation to pass ultimate judgement on him is the wisest of counsels at the present moment. As in the case of Papa Pacelli and Papa Giovanni, we are too near him in time to attempt any ultimate assessment.

At most, we can view him as a man called by destiny and God's providence to act his role against the double backdrop of the Vatican and the twentieth century. We can estimate his capacity, evaluate his achievements and assess his future possibilities. To assume that *amletismo* explains everything is to be deceived by the innate gentleness of this

* 'How is your Hamlet-like bishop?'

Pontiff, and not to hear the high-frequency overtones of his character and historical office, overtones which are too subdued, too understated, too muffled, like drums covered with velvet, to be perceived by a superficial attention. We will not be able to see how he worked on the summits of darkness, nor to understand the compulsive forces which called him down to traverse the valley of decision, nor to correctly focus on the perspectives of the pilgrimage ahead of him and his Church.

For Paul will never cry out in exasperation, never indulge in angry words, never give way to disillusionment. He may leave the stage of contemporary history with sadness, but when the full story of his life is written, it will be seen that this Pope made a definite decision, that he opted for one type of development, and that he then departed to the silence of eternity, having momentarily illumined his historical situation against the background of the surrounding darkness.

One final word about the division of our material. No pope springs from a historical vacuum. Each new occupant of Peter's chair has a complicated genealogy and, unlike the biblical Melchizedek, we can name his father and his mother: the womb in which he was formed, the paternity from which he derives his hereditary traits as man, as churchman, as pope. Over and above this, it is true, there is the stamp of individuality: a particular complex of characteristics that make him this, and not that, personality. These considerations have led me to arrange the material at hand in a certain way.

Properly speaking, we should deal with Paul VI in three chronologically tidy periods: from his election on June 21, 1963, to the start of his agony on November 8, from November 8 to November 23 when his decision to change was made and implemented, from November 24 onwards to New Year's Day 1964, at which point our consideration stops.

Yet for reasons which are explained later, I divide the material as follows: Part 1 sketches the main outlines of the position occupied today by the Roman Catholic Church in the world; Part 2 is a consideration of the Joannine era; Part 3 deals with Paul VI from his election to September 12; Part 4 discusses events between the latter date and November 23; Part 5 rounds out our study with a discussion of the period from November 24 to the beginning of 1964.

ONE

THE PYRAMID ON THE PLAIN

1. The Bearer of the Keys

The image which the Roman Catholic Church evokes in the minds of most of its adherents, as well as those outside its fold, is that of a monolithic edifice, resting on a broad human base and tapering up through a complex system of priest, bishop, archbishop, patriarch, cardinal and Pope. Very little about this composite and compact structure is generally known. Indeed it appears as a 'riddle wrapped in a mystery inside an enigma' to use Churchill's one-time description of the Soviet Union.[1] Despite every rent torn in its unity throughout two thousand years of chequered history, it appears to have well survived all vicissitudes. In the twentieth century, within a space of five years, it has been able once more to direct the eyes of the entire world to itself and to the solemn meetings of its leaders in St Peter's basilica in Rome.

Many people, on the other hand, for want of a more detailed knowledge, and under the influence of popular representations of the Roman Catholic Church, are inclined to think with Harnack[2] that 'they cannot doubt the justifiability of this world-wide institution (the Roman Catholic Church) which goes right on nourishing saints and at the same time it teaches the rest of its children "to hurl their spears and honour the gods," that is, to take religion as the masses have always taken it and as the masses require it.' With him they would conclude that the Roman Church is both necessary and useful because 'it disciplines the common man and still gives delicate consciences what they want.' Yet to accept this assessment of the Roman Catholic Church would be as faulty as to accept the assessment of it made by the American Institute of Management in 1960. Neither concern the inner dynamism of Catholicism. And neither render the pyramid transparent to the enquiring onlooker.

The stresses and strains, however, which exert simultaneous centrifu-

[1] W. S. Churchill, *Blood, Sweat, and Tears*, Putnam, New York, 1941, p. 173.
[2] Adolf Harnack, *Lehrbuch der Dogmengeschichte, III*, Tübingen, 1932, p. 903.

gal and centripetal pressure on the architectonic balance of this vast edifice, can be underestimated on a vast scale. This Christian Communion is now flung to the four quarters of the globe, can claim adherents among all peoples, is in touch with minds imbued with every variety of human culture and civilization.

Let us deliberately leave aside the error of interpretation which for want of a better term we can describe as *maximalism:* the childish, harmful, unrealistic presumption that 'all is well,' and that the very enumeration of peoples and languages and cultures involved suffices to dispel any doubt about the progress of Roman Catholicism and its future expansion. The error is as old as patristic times; Basil of Ancyra (a fourth-century Christian writer) in his *Treatise on Virginity* asserted it; Tertullian in his *Contra Marcionem* presumed it; Cyprian of Carthage in one of his letters to Demetrianus merely echoed the same persuasion as we find in the *Commentary on Daniel* by Hippolytus of Rome. Biblically the idea was based on the parallel drawn between the Tower of Babel on the plain of Shin'ar. There, human unity was fractured and men suffered the loss of a destined universalism. The Lord confused their search,[3] so that they no longer understood each other and each went his own way.

Now in the dispensation of God's salvation, Christ the Messiah was conceived by Christian writers as coming to repair the loss of universality and restore again what was lost on the biblical Shin'ar in a welter of identities. The restored identity of speech was that of the children of God; the restored Tower was the *cælestis urbs Jerusalem*, the Church, the blessed vision of peace. And this triumphant parallel was immortalized in medieval drawings of the Pyramid, of the *Ecclesia Christi:* located on the Plain of the world in sight of the earthly Paradise, solidly and squarely based on the 'people' and tapering upwards and inwards through the successive strata of religious orders and priests, of bishops and Roman dignitaries, to end in one single indivisible, pre-eminent apex, the Pope.

The Pyramid in the Plain, to which streams of white, black, yellow people flowed joyously at the New Pentecost, 'Parthians and Medes and Elamites and residents of Mesopotamia, Judaea and Cappadocia, Pontus and Asia, Phrygia and Pamphylia, Egypt and parts of Libya belonging to Cyrene, and visitors from Rome, both Jews and proselytes, Cretans and Arabs, telling in their own tongues the mighty works

[3] *Genesis*, 11:1-9.

of God.'[4] It was left to Bishop de Smedt of Bruges to excoriate this ever-ancient, always revived *simplisme* during the first session of the present Vatican Council, when he scathingly referred to the *clericalismus* and *juridicimus* and *triumphalismus* afflicting the modern Catholic mentality.

A deeper misinterpretation of the forces undermining the pyramidal structure can arise from an ignoring of the centuries old elements in the edifice, the accretions of two thousand years, which make for dissolution. The peculiar configuration of present day Church conditions must be carefully read in the light of these perennial components. And the reading must be on a world-wide scale. The mass of individual phenomena must be polarized on the principle which both the late Pope John XXIII and the present Pontiff have declared to be the guiding principle for Church policy today: namely, *aggiornamento*. The word is derived from the Italian word for 'day,' 'today,' and signifies in Italian, updating, bringing-up-to-date, modernizing. As both Pontiffs clearly saw, the Church's problem today is not the extirpation of heresy or the condemnation of fresh errors; it is rather the *balzo in avanti* (John XXIII), the communal and organized effort of the Church to get out of an intellectual, terminological and religious ghetto, and to meet the contemporary world with intelligible language and suitable twentieth-century gestures.

This necessary polarization leads us to the following considerations. The process of *aggiornamento* should be one of 'defrosting' long frozen blocs formed and perpetuated by historically caused tensions. This seems to be the basic first step. Roman Catholicism today is still characterized by such obstructive tensions. Still more serious: acceptance of these historical residues is regarded as normal and lies at the heart of the Roman Catholic dilemma today. This could lead to a harmful explosion tomorrow.

In the remainder of the chapter, we shall examine briefly the meaning of the Pyramid and the Plain. In the Pyramid, the prime source of interest is the power-structure, those who are invested with the keys of authority, granted to Peter and wielded for him by his 'right arm,' the Roman Curia. Then there is the composition of the broader parts of the Pyramid, the traditional Catholic countries and the places where Catholicism is suffering. There are many streams on the plain. Some of the original masonry forming part of the Pyramid has broken off: the Protestant confessions and dissident Oriental Churches. There are religious streams which are not Christian: Judaism, Islam, Buddhism,

[4] *Acts*, 2:9–11.

Hinduism and the other great religions of the East.*

Contemplation of these elements reveals a series of tensions within Catholicism, tensions which naturally flow out to the world around it. Finally, a last consideration is fundamental to our study: the nature of Roman Catholicism as an ethic, a way of life, based on a revelation, which has, over the centuries, adopted certain forms, put on certain garments. To understand the Second Vatican Council, to grasp clearly the historical role and significance of Paul VI, we shall have to acquire some notion about these forms and garments.

Above the laity, priests, bishops, archbishops, capping the age-old sloping sides of the pyramid of authority and jurisdiction, we find the Pope with his papal government and court. This government and court is called the Roman Curia, the *Curia Romana*. Theoretically, the Pope is the apex-point, the centre and the source of power for all others. Yet, it would be naïve to suppose that any other but a Pope who combined organizational genius, complete ruthlessness, intimate knowledge of human nature, and a far-reaching vision, could hope to wield the power that nominally is his. In point of fact, a Pope is as dependent on his government as the apex-point is on the support of the sides of a pyramid. And no man reaches the top of the Vatican system without having been conditioned by, and assimilated to, that system. It is a matter of speculation as to who wields the fulcra of power in the Vatican administration. There are certainly centres of power and those who occupy these centres can work their will on the whole mass, Pope, clergy and laity.

The Pope has twelve ministries which in Roman parlance are called Congregations.[5] He also has three courts (tribunals) and six executive bureaux or offices. He has several other supplementary bodies, two of which are of special significance to our analysis, one for the administration of the property belonging to the Holy See,[6] the other for managing Vatican monies. I shall call them, respectively, the *Normal* and *Extraordinary Administrations*. An examination of the constitution, component

* Cf. Appendix, where a conspectus is given statistically of Christianity and the other world religions.

[5] Supreme Congregation of the Holy Office; Congregation of the Consistorial; Congregation for the Oriental Church; Congregation of Sacraments; Congregation of the Council; Congregation of Religious; Congregation for the Propagation of the Faith; Congregation of Rites; Congregation of Ceremonial; Congregation for Extraordinary Ecclesiastical Affairs; Congregation for Seminaries and Universities; Congregation for St Peter's Basilica. I shall refer to these in an abbreviated form throughout the text.

[6] Administration of the Possessions of the Holy See.

members, and functions of these Curial organs can be most confusing: the multiplicity of functions and functionaries, the overlapping and interlocking system of membership, can blind one to the real method of government. Cardinal Cento, for instance, belongs to eight of these Vatican ministries,[7] and Cardinal Antoniutti belongs to seven.[8] Yet Antoniutti wields more power. Cardinal Ottaviani is called *Secretary* of the Holy Office, while several other cardinals like Marella, Agagianian, Larraona, are called *Prefects* of Congregations. Yet the Secretary of the Holy Office dominates all three cardinals.

Basic to the power structure and functions of the Curia is the Congregation known now as the *Supreme Congregation of the Holy Office*.[9] The ground-law of the Roman Church[10] declares that this Congregation has jurisdiction throughout the world on matters of Faith and Morals. Because Faith and/or Morals enter into every human act, the Holy Office actually enjoys competence in the fields belonging to all other Congregations, can interfere, block or reverse decisions, decide. Its proceedings take place in absolute secrecy. There is no trial for accused men. Condemnation and punishment are communicated to the individual in question, who is frequently admonished not to say that he has been condemned or for what reason (*if* the reason is communicated to him). The cardinals of this Congregation are ten in number.[11] Ottaviani is Secretary, Parente is Assessor.[12] The principal officials are seven in number.[13] At least one member of the Holy Office has an official status in every one of the remaining Congregations and in the all-important *Secretariat of State*, (the Vatican 'State Department'). The other Congregations are, therefore, held from within.

The Holy Office maintains its grip by an intimate control of the five most powerful Congregations: the *Consistorial* (which names bishops and regulates dioceses); the *Extraordinary Affairs*, which deals with all questions relating to the politico-religious status of the Church and its members; the *Council*, which deals with the discipline of secular

[7] Consistorial, Oriental, Council, Religious, Propagation of the Faith, Rites, Extraordinary Ecclesiastical Affairs, Seminaries and Universities.

[8] Holy Office, Consistorial, Oriental, Council, Religious, Propagation of the Faith, Extraordinary Ecclesiastical Affairs.

[9] Originally known as the Sacred Congregation of the Roman and Universal Inquisition. It is commonly known as the Holy Office.

[10] Canon Law, as it is called.

[11] Antoniutti, Agagianian, Bea, Cicognani, Ciriaci, Confalonieri, Micara, Ottaviani, Pizzardo, Testa.

[12] The Pope is nominally Prefect.

[13] Carpino, Dell'Acqua, Palazzini, Parente, Principi, Samorè, Staffa.

priests and the laity; the *Seminaries and Universities*, which deals with matters of Church education, the training of priests, ecclesiastical studies, etc., and the *Secretariat of State*. In fact, the head of each of these central Congregations is a member of the Holy Office.[14] Not only are the heads of these Congregations *Holy Office* men, but the next-in-command in each of those five is also a member of the Holy Office.[15] This double control means, in effect, that no decision on bishops and dioceses, on the relations of the Holy See with foreign states, on how the ordinary clergy or laity should comport themselves, on the Church's educational programmes, or on the Church's foreign policy, can be made without the consent and approval of the *Holy Office*.

The last, essential element in this intricate 'Chinese-box' of administrative surveillance involves the organs we called *Normal Administration* and *Extraordinary Administration*. They are chiefly concerned with Vatican finances.[16] The first group, the *Normal Administration*, handles funds and properties in possession of the Holy See. The monetary value is impossible to calculate: it includes priceless works of art such as the *Sistine Chapel*, the *Pietà*, the *Moses* (all by Michelangelo Buonarotti), as well as lands, houses, apartment buildings, churches, monasteries, libraries, hospitals, etc. It administers *Peter's Pence*,[17] the yearly contribution to the Vatican by the Catholic world; this exceeds several million dollars yearly. The *Extraordinary Administration* manages the monies conceded to the Vatican in 1929 by the Fascist Government of Benito Mussolini after the signing of the Lateran Treaty.[18] This

[14] Cicognani (Extraordinary Affairs, Secretariat of State), Ciriaci (Council), Confalonieri (Consistorial), Pizzardo (Seminaries and Universities).

[15] Carpino (Consistorial), Dell'Acqua (Secretariat of State), Palazzini (Council), Principi (Extraordinary Affairs), Staffa (Seminaries and Universities).

[16] It is difficult to say precisely where and in what amounts Vatican monies are invested. Pius XII made Enrico Galeazzi his financial adviser. The latter proceeded to invest Church funds throughout the whole Italian economy. Galeazzi was aided by the three Pacelli nephews (Pius XII made his nephews princes), Giulio, Carlo and Marcantonio, by Giovanni Battista Sacchetti and Massimo Spada. Banks in which the Vatican holds important stocks are: Banco di Roma, Banca Commerciale, Banco di Santo Spirito. Monies are mainly invested in banking and credit, iron and steel (Finsider), building (Instituto per l'Edilizia economica, Italcementi), public utilities (Società Acqua Pia), real estate (Immobiliare), foodstuffs, insurance (Riunione Adriatica di Sicurtà, Finelettrica), electricity (Società Romana di Elettricità, Centrale Group), chemicals (Romana Gas, Montecatini), tourism (Compagnia Italiana Turismo).

[17] Originated with a contribution made by King Ina of Wessex, England, in Anglo-Saxon times, and revived in 1854.

[18] The accumulated balance of a yearly $750,000 which in 1870 the Italian Government offered to pay to the Vatican for the loss of the Papal States.

amounted to one billion and a half pre-war Italian lire.[19] At first, this was administered by a layman, Bernardino Nogara. After his death, in 1958, a board of eight cardinals was set up,[20] to govern both the *Normal* and *Extraordinary Administrations*. In spite of World War II, Nogara, by skilful financial wizardry, left on his retirement a fund of half a billion dollars; the major portion is deposited with J. P. Morgan & Co. (New York), with Crédit Suisse (Switzerland) and with Hambros Bank (London).[21] In spite of Vatican investments, it is still true to say with the American Institute of Management report of 1960: 'In the final analysis, the greatest wealth of the Church is the resources of its members and their willingness to provide on call.' The Vatican Bank, which is used only by the clergy, religious orders and a limited number of laymen, means that the financial restrictions of the Italian State do not apply. Banking secrecy is absolute, of course.

The only non-members of the Holy Office involved here are Marella and Di Jorio. The latter was appointed by John XXIII, the former is in charge of the upkeep of St Peter's basilica. All other six members of the two boards are members of the Holy Office and have a single president, Cicognani. It is not difficult to guess what the basic power-centres in the Vatican administration are. The situation is clearly shown in the table on the next page.[22]

This shows a closely-knit, closely-woven phalanx of an interlocking directorate. It would be a mistake, however, to underestimate a young

[19] About 83.9 million dollars.

[20] Cicognani (President), Ciriaci, Confalonieri, Di Jorio, Marella, Micara, Pizzardo, Testa.

[21] Not only does the Vatican have the best advice from the financial world as such, it also benefits from its steady stream of contacts from all over the world, clerical and lay. The quantity of Vatican monies must, of course, be seen realistically against the background of Vatican expenses and outlay. The Vatican maintains literally thousands of institutes, institutions and establishments all over the world. In the majority of cases this means paying the yearly bills for every expense and meeting the bills half-way in the remainder. In Rome, the cost of maintaining the papal institutions (universities, colleges, libraries, monasteries, convents, seminaries, orphanages, churches, etc.) is enormous. In addition, there are the salaries of Vatican officials. At least 90 of all 310 Italian dioceses are not solvent, and Rome must perforce help them out each year.

The papal works of social assistance in Italy alone employ 150,000 persons; in 1959 they handed out 21,459,901 kilograms of foodstuffs, 2,869 parcels of shoes, 16,267 packages of clothing to over 5,148,200 needy persons. Each year, about 1,300,000 children are cared for. The mission countries claim most; in them, dental, medical, clinical centres, leprosaria, schools of all kinds and at all levels, social welfare organizations have to be maintained.

[22] The numbers in brackets after certain names indicate the head (1) and the second-in-command (2).

HOLY OFFICE	CONSISTORIAL	COUNCIL	EXTR. AFFAIRS	SEM. & UNIV.	SECRET. STATE	NORMAL & EXTR. ADMINISTRATION
Cardinals Antoniutti Agagianian Bea Cicognani Ciriaci Confalonieri Micara Ottaviani (1) Pizzardo Testa	*Cardinals* Antoniutti Agagianian Cicognani Ciriaci Confalonieri (1) Micara Ottaviani Pizzardo Testa	*Cardinals* Antoniutti Cicognani Ciriaci (1) Confalonieri Micara	*Cardinals* Antoniutti Agagianian Cicognani (1) Ciriaci Confalonieri Micara Ottaviani Pizzardo Testa	*Cardinals* Bea Cicognani Ciriaci Confalonieri Ottaviani Pizzardo (1) Testa	*Cardinals* Cicognani (1)	*Cardinals* Cicognani (1) Ciriaci Confalonieri Pizzardo Testa Di Jorio } Marella
Officials Carpino Dell'Acqua Palazzini Parente (2) Principi Samorè Staffa	*Officials* Carpino (2) Dell'Acqua Palazzini Parente Principi Samorè Staffa	*Officials* Palazzini (2) Parente	*Officials* Samorè	*Officials* Carpino Principi Staffa (2)	*Officials* Dell'Acqua (2) Samorè Staffa	

Structurization of the Roman Offices, and interlocking directorates of the *Holy Office* cardinal such as Giuseppe Siri (aged 58). To be a cardinal at his age, to become the Archbishop of Genoa, to be President of the Italian Episcopate, to enjoy the position of pre-eminence he does in Italian Catholic circles, are not achievements to be tossed off lightly.

To complete the picture of how Roman administration works, we must note that every week a central group meets, the first and second in command of the *Holy Office* (Ottaviani, Parente), of the *Consistorial* (Confalonieri, Carpino), of the *Council* (Ciriaci, Palazzini), of the *Seminaries and Universities* (Pizzardo, Staffa). No appointments are made in the City without being discussed here. No attitudes of the Curia as a whole are adopted without confirmation by this group. Here major decisions affecting the Roman mentality are reached.

Much has been written and said of a denigratory nature about the Curial mentality, mainly by people who do not know what the Curia is. It is impossible to affirm that the majority of these Churchmen are in bad faith and are not acting from true zeal. If the contrary were true, a normal law for the conduct of human relations would no longer hold true.

The truth and reality are quite different, and more ghastly. The majority of these men are convinced 'conservatives.' There is no question of bad faith or viciousness on their part. It is a question of human blindness and historical ignorance. The mentality is somewhat as follows: As regards the *Church:* The Church consisting of Pope, Curia, bishops and religious orders, is there by divine appointment to take care of the people who *belong* to the Church. The Vatican Congregations, especially the *Holy Office*, are the organs of the Holy Father, and they share, therefore, his infallibility. The pillars of this Church are her universal canon law, her universal language – Latin. Since the first Vatican Council (1869) there is no further need for ecumenical councils; the Pope can decide for himself what is best for the Church. Collegiality is not based either on Scripture or Tradition. As regards those who belong to other *Christian* denominations: they are in grave error; they have but one alternative, namely, to renounce their errors and return to the fold of Peter. Submission is the condition for admission. Humility precedes unity. As regards other religions in general, whether Christian or non-Christian, error has no rights, and the erring person is in an inferior position.

As regards the *State:* the ideal arrangement is a state which acknowledges the Roman Catholic Church as the true Church, a confessional state. In the concrete order, the Church must temporize, but her doctrine remains intact and inviolate. As regards the *Jews:* the latter were guilty of crucifying God, and God put a curse on them for all time. Their sufferings and misery through the ages are but a divine recompense for their initial error and refusal to accept Christianity. As regards the *Bible:* modern attempts to interpret it in the light of archaeology, the literature, the languages, the culture, the civilization, the psychology of ancient peoples are tendentious, false, and lead to error.

With a sheaf of such principles in hand, there would be no difficulty in condemning anyone who appeared to err. And a denial of a fair hearing or trial or, indeed, of any word but that of condemnation, is logical, can even be holy. The refusal to go halfway to meet non-Catholic Christian brethren can be absolutely justified: return and submission are first required. It would be absolutely obligatory to ally oneself with the traditional, right-wing political forces in any given country. The reason: the latter hold out hope of a return of the confessional state, and error must be combated by all good means.

Finally, this Curial mentality would and does inevitably lead to a frozen historical ghetto outlook which promotes increasingly a sense of irrelevancy and indifferentism. The whole affair of religion just does not seem to matter or be relevant to a world trying to solve concrete problems and which has been offered such ill-adapted instruments for this purpose. There is, finally, a kind of aura of glory around the Vatican administrative centre, a *mystique* of history, a feeling of timelessness, of continuity with past generations of two thousand years, of immediate relationship to countless generations to come. This is the glowing heart of *romanismus.*

We must remember that the all-important Congregations which we have been discussing (in addition to others) are the product of the Tridentine and post-Tridentine period; they were and are the answer of the juridical, Roman mind to the onslaughts of the Reformers; they are also, in part, the answer of the same mentality to the problem of grappling with the modern age ushered in by the Industrial Revolution of the eighteenth century. Thus, the Holy Office was founded on July 21, 1542 by Paul III, and its procedures have remained the same since that date. The *Consistorial* was founded in 1591 by Gregory XIV. The *Council* on August 2, 1564, by Pius IV, the *Seminaries and Universities* in 1588 by Sixtus V, the *Extraordinary Affairs* in 1793 by Pius VI. This last owed its origin to the Vatican's difficulties with Revolutionary France. The *Propagation of the Faith* was established in July 1568 by Pius V, the *Oriental* in 1862 by Pius IX (by detaching a section from the *Propagation of the Faith*). The *Secretariat of State* dates from the time of Martin V (1417–31).

Small wonder that the traditions, customs, and mentality of these institutions have hardly changed and hardly befit the modern conditions of the Church. Originally Italianate in membership and outlook, they were and are also Romanist in the full sense of the word. *'Qui pensiamo in secoli'* is an oft-repeated phrase in the corridors and offices of the Roman dicasteries ('We think in terms of centuries'). The Eternal City.

We are here at grips with a true *mystique*, a group mentality that has never found adequate expression but which nevertheless is part of the very atmosphere in which Romans live, work and die. Rome overflows its Seven Hills, piling up layers of eternity and of time on top of each other, still refusing to be identified with any one epoch or period or culture. It stands apart even from the bones, marrow, essence of the ecclesial group to whom Christ promised eternity in time, His Church. Indeed this Church, the living organism that weaves dry dogma, dusty scholarship, imperious clericalism, prescribed rites, institutionalized sanctity, sinners, saints, all into one pulsating living thing, the Church, is not seen in Rome, nor is the glowing centre of the Roman mentality. If Christ came back as He was two thousand years ago, He would not be at home here; He spoke no Latin; He did not wear satin slippers. And this is admitted by these Roman minds. No, the *mystique* is as much that of the Roman Emperors as of Roman bishops, as much the elegance of Roman Diana as the supernatural beauty ascribed to the Virgin. And when Greek hymns, Coptic songs, or Latin chants swell up beneath the spanning arch of the Roman basilica, it is impossible to hear the melodies of Moses and Miriam, the Voice of Yahweh on Sinai, or the gentle tones of the Sermon on the Mount. For Romanism is a human expression of an historical garb the Message has assumed. The essential lines of that garment are divinely ordained: Peter is to have successors in perpetuity, the priest is to consecrate, minister, the bishop to rule, the faith to be kept alive, the moral rule to be observed intact.

It would be a distortion of reality, however, to be misled by the trappings and names of Roman institutions and to think that their preoccupations were exclusively or even principally spiritual or otherworldly. We spoke before of the Romanization of the Christian ecclesial idea. Now, this Romanization has involved an absorption in politics down through the ages. The politics of Italy, first of all. Pius

XII did not hesitate to affirm that 'it has always been one of the essential tasks of the Holy See to see that, throughout the entire world, there reign between Church and State normal and, if possible, friendly relations.'[23] To cope with the world situation, the Vatican developed a diplomacy which is 'the science and art of regulating, through official representatives, relations between the Church and the States.'[24]

First as to Italy. The kingdom of Italy was proclaimed on March 17, 1861, at Turin. Venice and Rome were added by 1870. The Pope, Pius IX, decided to make himself a prisoner in the Vatican.[25] He rejected the Law of Guarantees and an offer of financial compensation. He ordered the faithful not to take part in the new State. The unification of Italy was achieved without any reference to the masses of people and was the work of Piedmontese moderates and radicals like Mazzini and Garibaldi. Cavour and the succeeding prime ministers belonged to the political Right (*destra*) and were definitely conservative-minded. They preferred limiting the suffrage to the upper classes. They believed in a separation of Church and State, and practised the doctrines of the bourgeois world. Italy received a Piedmontese Constitution which was modelled on the French Constitution of 1830 and provided for a centralized state. This centralism corresponded to the tastes and fears of the aristocracy and upper classes who ruled. There are many Italian churchmen today who would prefer to see such a government of this type installed in the Quirinal.

From 1876 onwards, men of the political left (*sinistra*) directed the government of Italy. They extended the electorate (universal suffrage only came in 1918), and while neglecting education, housing and social welfare, they concentrated on the armed forces (navy and army), the merchant marine, railways and public works: Italy must appear in the eyes of the world as glorious and fully developed as France and Germany. Heavy industries were emphasized and protectionist policies were adopted in order to further these ideals. Gradually the liberal principles of a former generation became corrupted. Gradually too, the distinction between the Right and the Left became blurred.

Trade unions developed, on the Left, almost simultaneously with the rise of industrial capitalism, especially in the northern triangle of

[23] Allocution of May 12, 1953.
[24] P. Savino, *Diplomazia ecclesiastica, I*, p. 10.
[25] The Popes remained thus until 1929 when Pius XI concluded the Lateran Treaty with Mussolini. The prisoner mentality was so extreme that it cost Pius XI a severe struggle to come out and give his blessing from the balcony of St Peter's on the day of his election.

Genoa, Turin and Milan. The Socialist party came into being in 1892. World War I was followed by severe unrest. The Socialists grew bolder. In the 1919 general elections (by this time Catholics could vote in the state elections without committing a mortal sin) a hybrid party emerged, composed of Catholics and radical groups. The Socialists were the largest single party (165 deputies). Don Sturzo's Popular Party came next (100 deputies). In 1921, the extreme Left-wing Socialists split away to become the Communist party of Italy.

The way was open for Fascism which came more as an answer to a question than as something progressive. On October 29, 1922 the King asked Mussolini to form a government. By 1925, the Vatican had disavowed the Popular Party and accepted Fascism. Many ecclesiastics saw in it a possible secular right-arm for the Roman Church or, at least, viewed it as a good bulwark against Communism. This illusion persisted into the late 1950's in certain ecclesiastical circles in Italy.

Mussolini abolished the parliamentary regime as such. The Left went underground. The Right was reduced to silence and impotence. The Vatican, tacitly or openly, approved of his interventions in Ethiopia and Spain. His adoption of racist laws in 1938 finally soured relations with the Vatican. He declared war in 1940. By 1944 Mussolini was dead, and his Roman Empire was no more. He had been unable to challenge the supremacy of certain power-groups such as the Church, big business, the financial monopolies, the civil bureaucracy. The Communist party which he suppressed had but 10,000 members. The monarchy was voted out of office by popular plebiscite in 1946. The new Italian Constitution took effect in 1948. It was new in the sense that it was drawn up by the deputies elected in a general plebiscite. It was old in that it embodied a mixture of Catholic, liberal and Marxist principles. Out of this *mélange* has come a very unstable political situation.

The instability is due to many factors: the lack of education at all levels, dating back to the nineteenth century, the lack of identity between the individual Italian and the Italian nation, the inherent Italian tendency to splinter, the constant play of Vatican interests in the political arena. Since 1948, two characteristics have been noted: the general drift to the political Left, and the continual identification of Church interests with those of the conservative Right.

In 1947, the Socialist party split; Giuseppe Saragat headed a small minority which left Pietro Nenni. By 1952 Nenni had freed himself from the spectre of a united front with the Communists (by now

22·7 per cent of the electorate) and proceeded to move away from the extreme Left towards the Centre: he advocated parliamentary government as necessary for national life and progress, voted for Italy's participation in Euratom, did not oppose Italian membership either in the European Common Market or in NATO.

In the meantime, a wing of the Christian Democrat party drifted towards the Left. In 1954, Amintore Fanfani, Secretary-general of the Party cut short his party's dependence on Catholic Action (an ecclesiastical organization under the direction of Italian bishops); up to that time his party had had no party organization of its own. Both the Vatican and the politico – financial Right saw the danger and engineered his political downfall in 1959, after a brief coalition with Saragat's Sociodemocrats, (between July 1958 and January 1959). And a one-party government (by the Demochristians) followed.

The movement toward the Left has been called in Italy the *apertura a sinistra* (the opening to the left), or *sinistrismo politico*. The Vatican's control over the Demochristians has not choked it off. The Vatican actually supported the interim Tambroni government in 1960 which depended for its existence on Fascist votes. But by November of the same year, in spite of frenzied efforts by ecclesiastical circles, *sinistrismo* had been widely installed on the administrative level. To aid Fanfani and his *centro-sinistra* movement, the new Pope, John XXIII, refused to condemn or tamper with Fanfani's Centre-Left government.

At the general elections in 1963, Fanfani lost control of the government. The Church and the Right-wing financial and economic forces were appalled by the Communist increase in votes, totalling 25 per cent of the electorate. A government by Leone failed to last. President Antonio Segni finally called in Aldo Moro (who had tried once before in 1959 and failed) to form a government.

The result was a government of the Centre-Left, a shaky alliance between Christian Democrats, Nenni's Socialists, Saragat's Sociodemocrats, and the Republicans. The new Government had the blessing neither of Togliatti's Communists nor of the Vatican conservative directorate. On January 14, 1964 a group of twenty-five members of Nenni's Socialists, who had broken with Nenni and formed a new party calling itself the Italian Socialist Party of Proletarian Unity, formally constituted a separate group in parliament. The issue at stake was Nenni's participation in a pro-NATO government. Aldo Moro's coalition government with 361 seats in parliament still tops the required majority (316); in the Italian Senate, six or seven

Socialist senators are expected to swing their allegiance over to the new splinter party. The coalition government will still have a comfortable majority of 184 or 185 (required majority is 161). Nenni's party is still experiencing growing pains; a group of pro-Communist members are remaining with it solely 'to fight the government from within.'

As is clear from the foregoing, the official Vatican line has been to side with any political party except those tinged with a form of Socialism or Marxism. The Vatican and her traditional allies, the upper classes and the industrial concerns, saw in the 1950 elections a foretaste of what could happen in Italy. At that time the total vote of the Socio-democrats (Saragat), Socialists (Nenni), and Communists (Togliatti) amounted to a little over 41 per cent of the total popular vote. This had increased by spring 1963. A tendency to splinter seems to be inevitable among the Socialists.

The Church has always represented Italian voters as having a choice between good or evil, between Christianity or atheistic paganism. It is certain that a large part of this enthusiasm on the part of the Vatican for the political Right is due to a theological principle: error has no rights; any compromise with the erring only leads to irreparable loss. It is equally certain that this attitude contains an equally large dosage of genuinely human, this-worldly fear: the financial and economic strength of the Vatican is tied up with the Right-wing segments in Italian life. To abdicate this, to opt for a neutral position would involve two dangers: loss of financial and economic independence (due to Socialist and Marxist appropriations), the loss of the financial advice, guidance, confidence and collaboration of Rightist financial and econo-mic circles, not only in Italy but in *Mitteleuropa*. For the first time in 2,000 years, the Church would be transposing the central fulcrum of its material life and power. These dangers are real. They are perhaps painful. They would amount to stripping the Church of certain historical and accidental overlays.

Perhaps the ultimate solution to the Vatican's dilemma lies in the nature of the modern world and the type of world in the making. We have moved away from colonialism and empire building. Internation-alism has found expression in the United Nations, a multi-national organization. The plain on which the Pyramid stands is rapidly changing under the blows of unimaginable problems, population explosion, population control, nuclear disarmament, space exploration, scientific progress in genetics, developments in biblical research, the world food problem, Communism, the complexity of Europe uniting, politically as well as economically, the rising star of Communist China. It was in such a world that John XXIII decided to hold his Vatican Council, to achieve *aggiornamento*, to break down barriers, to bring the Church out of her self-imposed ghetto, to prepare the unity of the Christian family which is already on its way.

The solution John offered can be summed up in one word: love, Christian love. To policy-makers, politicians, Vatican financial experts, American diplomats, sociologists, the attitude must have seemed madness. For politics, traditionally, is the art of knowing where you want to go and how to go there. And such a policy left only blurred outlines of the final destination it was to attain and the dangerous curves in the path leading to that obscure goal. 'Love Nikita,' he said one day to a group of political students, 'God loves him.' 'Why should I condemn the Socialists?' he asked when told of Fanfani's alliance with Nenni, 'are they not, all of them, my little sons?' John XXIII's easy-going political attitude, his success with men of all political complexions whether from Moscow, Constantinople, Rome, Washington or Florence, his political manifesto *Pacem in Terris*,[26] sent shivers down Rightist spines in Italy. A statement of John's like: 'Obviously there can be no accord between the Christian religion and materialist atheism, but there can and must be practical co-operation between Catholics and the Communist regimes on the social and political level,' only served to arouse united opposition to the dead Pope's entire policies and outlook.

Called either *giovannismo* (after his death) or *sinistrismo ecclesiastico* (during his lifetime, it was pointed to as the direct cause of the Communist increase in votes in the spring of 1963), this may be partly true. There is certainly a direct, causal connection between the politically harrowing months of the Leone government in 1963 and the sudden veering of conciliar policy and attitude of Paul VI. But more about this later on.

We cannot grasp the essence of the problem posed by this intricate bureaucracy unless we bring out the most important factors; the *functional* aspect of the doctrines of papal primacy and infallibility, and the functional character of the Holy Office. The doctrines of the primacy and infallibility, theologically speaking, amount to the following, in essence. The primacy concerns the power of governing. This power is hierarchic in the Church of Rome, that is, it reposes on a graduated

[26] The main collaborator in its composition was Monsignor Pietro Pavan, of the Lateran University.

series of leaders right up to the Pope who is supreme head. Now, the Pope's governing power and authority are supreme: he has a primacy of authority in that it is universal (over the entire Church), direct (not through any intermediary), and perpetual (will last for ever). Infallibility concerns the teaching office of the Pope. It is a prerogative of his, according to Catholic doctrine, which the Pope can exercise when he fulfills the following conditions: is performing his duty as universal pastor and teacher, exercising the supreme authority given to the Apostle Peter, proposing a doctrine to be held as a tenet of faith by all the faithful everywhere, and proposing a doctrine concerning faith or morals. In such case, the Roman Catholic Church declares, he cannot err. He enjoys the gift or prerogative of infallibility.

The nature of the two doctrines may be more or less familiar to readers already, and it is not on the theological aspects that I wish now to focus attention. First let us look at the functional aspects of these doctrines. Actually, the Pope rarely interferes in the normal government of the universal Church personally. Normally the local bishops govern and submit matters of greater moment or difficulties to the Pope's ministries in Rome. Nor does the Pope often teach infallibly by word or written document. The normal teaching function of the Church belongs to the local bishops and their assistants.

In practice and according to the time-honoured habits of the Roman Curia, when the latter speaks, it claims to speak with the governing and teaching authority *of the Pope* himself. While none of these officials would claim supreme governing authority (primacy) or supreme teaching authority (infallibility), their decisions are presented as the decisions of the Holy Father himself. Their offices are the ministries of the Holy Father. Technically, theologically and ecclesiastically, they have no legislature or mandatory authority of their own; they are merely consultative and executive. In actual fact, however, they regard their decisions as the decisions of the Holy Father himself, and therefore binding on the consciences of the faithful everywhere. This would still be a bearable situation – *if* the ministries confined themselves to a consultative or executive role. But they do not. Now the most glaring example of this encroachment is the Holy Office. This brings us to the functional side of this particular ministry.

It is beside the point to repeat that the Holy Office exercises a legislative and mandatory authority in the Roman Church which is at times at variance with the wishes of the Pope. It has been often said. The present authorities of the Holy Office, Cardinal Ottaviani in particular, have taken great pains to reject any accusations. One of the most frequent phrases on this cardinal's lips at meetings of the council's Theological Commission is 'this is the will of the Holy Father.' What Ottaviani really means to say is: 'I and the Holy Office have decided the matter in this way; the Holy Office is a ministry of the Holy Father. Therefore what we have decided in this matter is the will of the Holy Father.' Anyone who knows anything about Roman dicasteries – and I am not referring to naïve spirits like Monsignor Bandas of St Joseph's Seminary, or Monsignor Raymond Etteldorf, a minor official of the Oriental Congregation, who wrote an emotional defence of the Curia Romana and the Holy Office in the weekly magazine, *America* (September 7, 1963, pp. 234-235), maintaining that the ministries of Rome can do no wrong because it is the Holy Father who acts through them, and *he* cannot do wrong – will readily admit that abuses exist.

The very efforts which the Holy Office and Ottaviani have made to rebut the accusation are significant. Interviews with English-speaking and French-speaking newsmen were granted during 1963 in which the cardinal explained away the accusations. Monsignor James I. Tucek was instructed to comment on an official statement released by the Holy Office last year and to get his story as widely circulated as possible.

It would not be profitable to give a very long list here of instances in which the Holy Office has intervened behind the scenes to have theologians removed, books banned from public sale, public speakers silenced. The names, the issues, the institutions, would probably have no significance for the general reader. The most recent indictment of the methods of the Holy Office is contained in an article by Robert A. Graham, S. J., which also appeared in *America* (September 14, 1963, pp. 257-260). In conclusion he says that a review of the Holy Office's own conception of its function is desirable. Its role is essentially negative – 'that of vigilance over orthodoxy of doctrine; in practice, because of its all-pervasive authority, it has taken over in effect the direction of the progress of research.'

Important to our subject is the fact that the notions of the papal primacy and infallibility have undergone changes. Over the centuries these notions have been deformed to such an extent that Council Fathers, especially during the second session, could roundly denounce them as such. Archbishop Elias Zoghby, Vicar of the Greek Melchite Patriarch for Egypt, stated on October 16 in full Council session: 'The doctrine of primacy was never denied by the Eastern Churches. But as a matter of fact after so many centuries of separation (from Rome) this doctrine has evolved in such a unilateral sense that our Orthodox brothers can hardly recognize it today ... In the form we have it today, even in this Schema *De Ecclesia*, the doctrine of the primacy is proposed in such a unilateral way that it is rather unacceptable to the Orthodox. It represents only one theological view in the West and there is no trace of the Eastern tradition.' Patriarch Maximos IV Saigh of Antioch, was even more explicit, in an interview with the Divine Word News Service on October 9: 'The dogma of the primacy of the Roman Pontiff ... has occasioned abusive interpretations which have disfigured it ... No difficulties for re-union come from the doctrine itself but from these abusive interpretations in doctrine and in concrete exercise.'

The core of the problem of the Vatican bureaucracy, therefore, lies in this, that it purports to wield the authority and infallibility of the Pope himself. This has been done in such a way as to obscure and even deny the ancient doctrine of the Church regarding the collective responsibility of the bishops for the universal Church. This doctrine was opposed in the Council. It will be opposed in the future.

The control exercised by the Holy Office is so extensive, so arbitrary, that in the last analysis one cannot see how any pontiff can hope to rule the Church, hope to rescue it from its present difficulties unless he eviscerates this power, cuts it down to proper size, clears out not only the wielders of hidden power in it, but clears up the function of the Holy Office itself. If a decree on Communism is to be drawn up, the Holy Office must vet it. If any other Roman office is to issue a document, the Holy Office must vet it. Every public document of the Pope himself must even be approved by the Holy Office. The most glaring recent example was that of the *Motu Proprio* issued in the name of Paul in January 1964. This declares what parts of the recent conciliar decree concerning the liturgy are to be implemented. Certain passages in the *Motu Proprio* are incompatible with the original conciliar decree. The Pope's original draft was taken over by the Holy Office and drastically altered. The shocking thing is that a minor office of the Church, run by a small band of men with narrow-minded views, is able to contradict the will not only of the Pope but of the Council. When will the Pope and the Church recognize, and correct, this outrageous situation?

The matter goes farther. The local bishop has not only been ex-

cluded from participation in the government of the universal Church
but, in his own territory, is hemmed about by restrictions and rules
imposed on him by the Roman Curia, rules and restrictions which
make him dependent on them for permission to exercise his own
divinely granted rights which come to him by virtue of his episcopal
consecration. Besides, this upsetting of the divinely appointed hierarchic
structure of the Church and its replacement by a juridical order has
involved analogous evils on the lower echelons of government. A
cardinal who holds a residential see is considered so sacrosanct that a
bishop or priest will rarely resist his will, even when the cardinal is
manifestly wrong.

Cardinal Santos of the Philippines for example, during the first
session of Vatican Council II, forbade his bishops either to leave the
Collegio Filippino where they were staying, or to attend any lectures
given by theologians. Bishops Gonzaga, Olalia, Sison and Brasseur
defied these orders. In the Philippines, the cardinal continued the same
policy; he warned the Catechetical Centre run by the Jesuits not to
speak about the new norms for Catholic worship. He called in one
head of a religious order and told him that ecumenism was not for the
Philippines, only for places like France, Germany, Holland which were
not solidly Catholic like the Philippines, Spain and New York.
Nothing new was expected from the Council, he said, because the
Church cannot change her nature. He alleged that a small group of
dissatisfied bishops from the middle-European countries had tried to
express extreme views, but the bishops were solidly behind Cardinal
Ottaviani. Allied with the Cardinal of the Philippines stand the
Dominicans of the Universidad de Santo Tomos, Manila, who follow
the cardinal's suggestions in all things.

Lower still on the echelon of authority, but acting in the same way,
we have a churchman like Dr J. C. McQuaid of Dublin who forbade
two Council theologians to speak in his diocese at the University and
at theologates. The two theologians were Fathers John Courtney
Murray, S. J. and Gregory Baum, O.S.A. Father Baum was also invited to speak at the central seminary of Maynooth, but McQuaid
wrote to the President to object to the invitation and to state that he, as
the prime bearer of the care of souls in the suffragan territories, had
forbidden this man to lecture. Father Baum lectured there in spite of
Archbishop McQuaid's strictures. During his reign, the Archbishop
has kept up a running battle with Trinity College, Dublin, refusing to
allow Catholics attending it to have a chaplain, forbidding Catholics

under pain of mortal sin to attend it. Recently a Catholic, Fredrick Boland – who gavelled Khrushchev during the famous shoe-incident in the United Nations General Assembly – was elected Chancellor of Trinity College. This fact, plus the new Catholic interest in ecumenism, has left Dr McQuaid's innate hatred of Protestants and his life-long drive against them somewhat at a loss. But in all these actions we discover the same high-minded attitude, the same substitution of juridical norms for the one irreplaceable quality of a Christian – genuine charity.

A further distortion results when a particular interest of the Church in Italy is allowed to influence the entire Church. For example, the normal Italianate attitude toward problems involving Church and State, liberty of conscience, the Jewish question, relations with non-Roman Catholic Christians, or education. It is unfortunate but a fact that the Roman congregations are directed by men who have no other outlook than an Italianate one. As we shall see, not only the inner tensions of Catholicism but the direction of the second session of the Council was manifestly influenced by these defects at the administrative centre of the Church.

2. The Ancient Kingdom

Divisions running through contemporary Catholicism resulting from various tensions reflect no exclusive geographical, national, or cultural pattern. A first bloc of tensions is represented by countries like Great Britain, Finland, Iceland, Norway, Sweden, Denmark, Switzerland, the United States, Canada, Australia, New Zealand and certain new African countries, in which the frozen attitudes of the Church are conditioned ultimately by the calamitous division of Christianity in the sixteenth century. The Church in these countries is characterized by an economic situation that can only be described as prosperous, from the well-heeled Church of the United States to the modest but adequate status of the Church in countries like Finland or Denmark. Churchmen, by and large, are not poor economically, and are considered socially as on a level with lawyers, doctors, and the professional classes. The Church here is not making any sensational strides in conversions: there is a steady flow of converts particularly in the United States, but the numbers do not warrant any undue optimism. The picture is balanced by a corresponding leakage from the Church. Catholicism here is also characterized by a steady increase in the intellectual level of its laity. The intellectualism cultivated is that of the social milieu. On the other hand, the intellectual attainments of priests, and in particular, of bishops and other Church leaders is not commensurate with the intellectual growth of the laity. A bishop in these countries has normally 'arrived,' once he becomes bishop. He now has full ecclesiastical dignity.

There is also evident here a slow but inevitable assimilation of the laity to the cultural, social and ethical milieu. Catholics are induced to think as their non-Catholic neighbours and to become one with the larger society that surrounds them. In Great Britain and America this is of paramount importance; Englishmen generally speaking are Erastian, especially since the Cromwellian Commonwealth, and both they and their American cousins are in danger of being choked by the softness of their national and social environment.

The structurization of the Church here is based on a juridical outlook which regards anyone below a priest or religious brother or nun as *belonging* to the Church and everyone above that stratum as *being* the Church. It is the pyramidal mentality, frozen as regards non-Catholic bodies, frozen as regards the idea of the Church itself, frozen in a kind of rigid intellectual ghetto. The Catholic in these countries is inclined to be indifferent to a Church which seems, by and in its very structure, to be opposed to the democratic way of life.

Lying apart by themselves, a special bloc of tensions is constituted by Poland, Czechoslovakia, Hungary, East Germany, Estonia, Latvia, Lithuania, and Russia. The situation here of the pyramidal hierarchic Church, is not merely precarious, it is to all intents and purposes in danger of extinction. Communist techniques have been very effective in dealing with the hierarchy. The Hungarian bishops signed a declaration of loyalty to the regime in 1957 without any permission from Rome; for a long while Pius XII thought of excommunication, but finally decided against this because 'it would only result in a dissident Church'. Archbishop Groesz spoke out in favour of the collectivization of agriculture in September 1958. There is no contact between the Vatican and the Hungarian bishops except by underground and secret means which do exist, of course.

Czechoslovakia has had a Stalinist regime since 1948 and all the bishops were in prison or under house arrest until 1963 when five were released. As in Hungary, all religious orders have been officially disbanded. Theological schools and seminaries were abolished. There is no Catholic Press. Most of the Yugoslav bishops had been removed by Tito and his government by 1950. In Roumania, only one of the two original bishops survives. In Poland, Communism has not dealt so successfully with the hierarchy, mainly due to the overwhelmingly Catholic population. Under the Stalinist regime and the more liberal government of Wladyslaw Gomulka (1956), the Church has managed to keep its university at Lublin and many of its seminaries. In spite of atheist propaganda, confiscatory taxation, harsh treatment publicly, the masses have not changed in their loyalties. The Primate of Poland, Cardinal Stefan Wyszynski, is courageous and persevering, but he is also autocratic, narrow-minded, less brilliant intellectually than his Western counterparts.

In East Germany where there are some 1.6 million Roman Catholics; the hierarchy is able to function rather freely considering that the

Grotewohl-Ulbricht regime is Stalinist and anti-Party at heart. In Estonia, Latvia (here, Lutherans dominate, with the Russian Orthodox a good second), Lithuania, there is continual harassment of the hierarchy, restrictions on communication with the Vatican, banning of religious instruction. Roman Catholicism in Russia has always been regarded as a local affair associated with foreigners (Poles, Lithuanians, Latvians). There is no openly recognized hierarchic structure, no such thing as a Catholic school system or Press. Russia is overwhelmingly Orthodox. Catholic Churches are open in Moscow, Leningrad, Odessa, Tbilisi. In Russia, Roman Catholicism has had to contend with the hatred of the Communists and the millennial opposition of the Russian Orthodox Church.

It is clear that the tension characteristic of this bloc of Catholicism results more from Communist hatred of religion than from any objection to the hierarchic structure of the Catholic Church as a puppet of Rome. And Communist authorities have in their hard-headed way come to realize that Catholic Christianity cannot be stamped out by persecution, imprisonment, or oppression. Yet the peculiar tragedy of the situation lies in the tradition of total ideological war against Communist Europe and the Soviet Union, and of the Purple Wall erected parallel to the Iron Curtain, inaugurated by Pius XII. The *Soviet Encyclopaedia* article on Catholicism characterized Pius XII as a Germanophile;[27] and it is certain that for a while his closest advisers considered the panzer divisions of Hitler as the right-arm of God whereby the Fatima prophecy of a converted Russia would be fulfilled.

Given the present Communist grip on these countries, given also the irreversible evolution of Soviet Russia from the wild days of the October Revolution to the present, it required a man of John XXIII's vision to remind Catholics that the way to deal with a persecuting enemy is not to erect walls of hate but to love him. John died before he accomplished his work in this respect. The tension continues. The situation will slowly evolve. Not the least complicating factor here is the Pope's position in Italy where the drift leftwards toward Communism is galvanizing into reaction all those forces with which the Vatican, as a temporal entity, has been allied and with whom it stands or falls in the temporal sphere.

Countries like France, Germany, Wallonia (Belgium), Holland, fall into a category by themselves: they belong to the retarded dynamism areas. In them there is a dynamism for change, for adaptation, for

[27] Volume 20, p. 379.

pioneering, for evolution of religious thought, which is retarded by the rigid mentality of the centralizing, bureaucratic government of Rome. And yet the key ideas of conciliarism, of ecumenism, of biblical research, of liturgical renewal, of adapting science, of Catholic piety, of theological research, of social improvement, have all come from these countries. Demographically, the only one to have undergone a radical change is West Germany: after World War II the Protestants of Pomerania and East Prussia streamed into the predominantly Catholic areas of the Rhineland and Bavaria, and the Catholic refugees of Silesia and the Ermland flowed into Protestant Schleswig-Holstein and Lower Saxony. The age-old demographic pattern was thus shattered. There were over 12 million of these refugees. Out of this enforced mixing has come a partnership and a dialogue between Protestant and Catholic. Out of it has come also an increased political influence for the German hierarchy through the *Catholic Bureau* in Bonn, its official lobby.

Significantly, these countries are characterized by a laity increasingly interested in theology, philosophy, and ecclesiological studies. This cauldron of ideas and intellectual unrest could give rise to an explosion which would rock the foundations of the Catholic Church, not only in Europe, but in countries like the United States and Commonwealth countries which are tributary to Europe for their ideas and intellectual progress. Here in Europe, as the ancient interfaith tension appears to be dying away, there is arising a new tension: between the hierarchy and the laity. The Church, officially, is still working with the essential ideas and weapons fashioned at the time of the Council of Trent in the sixteenth century; but these weapons were too late to be effective then, and they are certainly outdated for today's struggle.

The real danger involved in this explosion is not the rise of any new schism or heresy, a renewal of Gallicanism, Jansenism, Josephism, or of splinter churches from the Catholic body. It is rather the danger of indifferentism to Church authority, of ghettoization, of intellectual, social, moral isolation.

The traditionally Catholic countries of the world fall into different groups. Columbia, Ireland, Flanders (Belgium), Mexico and the Philippine islands are in one category. Here the Church is solidly entrenched: 96 per cent of the population in Colombia, 97 per cent in Ireland, 82 per cent in Flanders, 97 per cent in Mexico, 85 per cent in the Philippines. Large numbers are practising Catholics. The clergy are plentiful, drawn from the middle classes, intellectually stunted, conservative in their theological and philosophical outlooks. The hierarchy is fiercely jealous of its dignity and ranks, politically active and influential. There is no intellectual progress of any notable kind. The mentality is of the ghetto kind.

Puerto Rico, the Argentine, Portugal and Italy fall into the disaster-area class of Catholicism: an acute shortage of priests, a very low percentage of practising Catholics, a retrograde clergy, rampant anticlericalism based on doctrinal as well as historical reasons, all characteristics of areas in which the Church is fighting for its life. Spain, Brazil, Peru and parts of Italy (certain southern provinces of the peninsula) and Sicily, are in a category apart where religion is strongly marked by superstition. The bishops here are out of touch with the modern world and the office of priest is not held in honour.

As a unit, South America is an area of maximum danger for Roman Catholicism: an undeveloped economy, a high birth rate, social disequilibrium, subversive influences, hunger, illiteracy are some of the ills plaguing the region. After 400 years, the Church has still not developed a sense of social justice, or a forward-looking laity. In Brazil alone there are dioceses twice as big as Sicily consisting of only one parish. For over 180 million nominal Catholics in South America, there are 35,000 priests, that is to say, one for every 5,000 souls. We should compare this with Italy, where there are 55,000 priests for 50 million souls, but the official figures here include foreign residential priests. In some places in South America there is only one priest for every 30,000 Catholics. The Vatican has organized two groups to study and remedy the situation: the Bishops' Council for Latin America (CELAM) and the Latin America Commission (CAL).

The vast bulk of the Roman Catholic laity have been trained to look at their Church from the viewpoint of an unbridled *theologia gloriae*. They were taught to consider the glorification of the clergy as a tribute to the person of Christ, to accept extravagant legislation and casuistic rulings as proof of the solicitude of the Church, to bow to unhistorical judgements as expressions of the 'Catholic mind,' to attend Mass quietly, respectfully and almost unthinkingly, to make generous contributions to the Church, and leave their salvation in the hands of the local pastor, the bishop, the bureaucracy in Rome.

Nowhere are these remarks more relevant than in the Catholic Church of America. Wherever the Church is established in North America, we find it in a flourishing state. It may be just beginning to grow, as in the diocese of Atlanta, or it may be a long-standing, richly endowed institution like Cardinal Cushing's Boston archdiocese. From being considered, and often treated as, an alien, authoritarian, antidemocratic, backward body, with picturesque rituals, a relic of medieval times, the Catholic Church has attained a social and national status of respectability within the confines of American pluralistic society. There is little social or religious pressure directed against it, no general assault on its character, no social embarrassment in identification with it. It is accepted.

The Church, with its 43,000,000 adherents in America, presents a variegated exterior. In the South, where before 1900 there were only a few churches, the increase in membership is now topped only by the Pentecostalists; the influx from the north and east has substantially changed the situation. Catholics conduct six universities in Louisiana and Texas. They also have organized nineteen Catholic colleges in Alabama, Florida, Kentucky, Louisiana, New Mexico, North Carolina, Tennessee and Texas.

The Midwest has known Catholicism as long as the white man has been in residence. The Church is, therefore, secure in its outlook, all the more so since the frontier mentality melted into one mass all the various elements that arrived from Europe. The Church was influenced by the spread of the public school system; consequently it is more vigorous, fertile in ideas, daring today. Movements for social reform, liturgical renewal, Catholic social action, phenomena like 'Sheil's Enterprises' (as the projects of Auxiliary Bishop Bernard J. Sheil were called), and a willingness to face the exigencies of progress are characteristic of the Midwest Church. Yet, even with educated university graduates and a laity intellectually aroused, the Church remains too conservative and lacking in vision.

In the Far West, the Church seems to be in a Golden Age of brick, mortar and Church-fund drives. This Golden Age is dominated by the strongly willed, financially astute, theologically narrow Cardinal McIntyre of Los Angeles. In spite of much educational progress and church building, the atmosphere imposed by the cardinal and hierarchy is one that tends to stifle intellectual development and Catholic social awareness compared with progress elsewhere on the burning questions of racialism and ecumenism. The cardinal moves very much in the shadow of Cardinal Spellman of New York, sees no real need for social emphasis, wants his clergy to have a good training but not a well-rounded education, has a nineteenth-century outlook towards the laity and its requirements.

The Church in the East became rooted when the laity was immature and composed mainly of poor Irish, Italian, or German, immigrants. Casting a long shadow over this scene stands the figure of Cardinal Spellman, Archbishop of New York. The Church in the East is, *par excellence*, the church of the chancery, the Church of subtle ecclesiastical politics. It is to the rest of Catholic America what Rome is to Europe, nearer to the political heart of things, richer, more refined, certainly more sophisticated. Yet, these very characteristics denote its basic weakness. It represents the exaltation of the juridical, the dimming of the charismatic, the choking off of any real intellectual achievement, the careful maintenance of the essential identity of the 'Church' with its hierarchic forms. Intellectually, as recent difficulties at Catholic University in Washington have shown, the East seems to be going through a state of crisis too. In spite of attempts on the part of authorities to suppress the news, the facts have come out anyway.[28] Even an independent publication like the Jesuit weekly *America* has to handle the situation carefully.

At the heart of the situation in America lies the same factor we noted elsewhere: the Church is composed of groups from Europe; they have been subject to a conservative tradition. But times have changed. Ten years ago it would have been unimaginable to think of Paul Blanshard sitting docilely at a Catholic Press Conference organized by American Bishops in the Via della Conciliazione, Rome, in the shadow of a Vatican Council, or going to consult a council theologian in his Roman monastery. Yet he did both – more than once. Nor would one have expected Bishop Pike of San Francisco to have commented favourably five years ago on the subject of a Catholic Pope and Catholic bishops. Yet he has.

The problem is different today. The trend toward urbanization, the rise in the standard of living, the arrival of Catholics at a point where they can think of something except earning their daily bread, has inspired a thirst for intellectual curiosity and a questioning of existing values. The old answers no longer suffice. Appeal to authority for authority's sake is not enough. The whole mass has been leavened, to a certain extent, by the ferment of new ideas coming from the Old World.

On the other hand, the hierarchy suffers principally from two defects: they are incapable of leadership and they are theologically backward and overly cautious. These two defects are inter-connected. This is seen

[28] Jon Victor, *Harper Magazine*, December 1963.

in the case of the five American cardinals. Cardinals Spellman, Mc-Intyre and Cushing are financial wizards, each in his own way, the last named having a special charisma for charity work. Yet none of them would claim to be called intellectual, nor have they had any deep training in theology. Fundamentally conservative because that is what they were taught in the seminary, they have no endowments that would enable them to become sociological leaders. Cardinal Meyer of Chicago did devote himself to the study of the Scriptures rather thoroughly, but he gave up this study later when the claims of administration became too much. He is not naturally a leader, is rather cautious and timid about taking the initiative. Cardinal Ritter, on the other hand, is a mixture of common-sense and idealism, able to lead, but without the dynamism and factual information to impose his leadership. As one American bishop has commented: 'Leaders? We *could* have a troika: Meyer thinking, Ritter speaking, Spellman paying, but they would all gallop off in three different directions.' A complicating factor as regards cardinals and bishops is the traditional respect for anything above a simple priest. The episcopal and, above all, cardinalitial dignity is so highly regarded that once the cardinal 'has spoken' there is no gain-saying. I have seen perfectly courageous monsignors, perfectly blunt bishops quivering with apprehension when faced with the alternative: tell the cardinal or the bishop that he is not correct, or agree with him even though he is wrong. This is a simple extension of Romanism, of the juridical idea that episcopal consecration or the cardinalitial dignity confers not only a sacrosanct character but a measure of infallibility, a wisdom and sagacity that command unquestioned obedience. The hierarchy cannot be criticized, cannot be contradicted. It is the chancery mentality, the triumphalistic myopia glorying in the Pyramid. It makes each bishop a replica of the Pope.

A part of the broad base of the Pyramid, the American laity, is now beginning to stir. For the Plain itself is moving. To speak of a possible explosion outwards to the detriment of the entire edifice is not mere melodrama. But it is also realism to admit that from the American hierarchy has come no real leadership ecclesiologically, intellectually, or ecumenically. A conscientious Catholic writer such as Daniel Calla-han[29] sees the history of the American Catholic Church falling into two broad periods; from 1830 to 1917, and from 1917 to 1960. In the for-mer, the foundations were laid for the Church as we find it today. But

[29] Daniel Callahan, *The Mind of the Catholic Layman*, Scribner's, New York, 1963.

the Church developed in a ghetto. The rise of the educated layman, increasing participation in social and political affairs by Catholics, have posed new problems. John Cogley, writing a review of Callahan's book, speaks of the 'baffled bishops, puzzled priests, uncertain laymen, and all who are interested in the present mood of the Church in America' – and says that 'Mr Callahan's is the voice of a new Catholic generation.' Callahan's careful sifting of the evidence, his penetrating and telling analysis of the system and description of its faults make it the best account so far of a changing scene.

3. The Broken Masonry

Another tension-bloc which thrusts itself on our notice is composed of those segments of Christianity which owe their existence to the East-West Schism in the ninth–eleventh centuries. Again, the root-cause for the freezing of these segments is a thousand-year-old historical tension. It is tragic enough to reflect nowadays that the break between Rome and Constantinople was in the logic of affairs at the time, a consequence of political ideologies and ambitions, and not fundamentally over a doctrinal issue (although there were divergences over the famous *Filioque** question between Greeks and Latins). More tragic still is the fact that the Roman Church has incorporated into her outlook certain juridical elements which, if maintained unchanged, would preclude all possibility of reunion. By the ninth–eleventh centuries, Rome had succumbed to what is known as Romanism or the imperialistic outlook. It still persists, even if the territorial expression of that claim ceased to exist during the last century.

Thus Greece, Russia, Roumania, Bulgaria and sizeable populations in Albania, in America, in the Near East, have been frozen into a corresponding attitude of opposition to Rome. Their basic trouble is juridical too. The fault of the Roman approach to them, until recently, has been that it was juridically inspired and relegated the evangelical spirit to a secondary place. Dire consequences followed from this attitude.

When the Crusaders took Jerusalem by storm and established a kingdom there, the Latin rite was installed in a territory traditionally belonging to the Greeks, and with the establishment of a Latin Patriarchate, this particular element of tension was complete. To this day, the existence of the Latin Patriarchate in Jerusalem and the presence of the Latins, in addition to the constant and sometimes crude attempts at

---

* *Filioque*, following the words '*qui ex Patre*' in the Credo, expresses the doctrine of the double-procession of the Holy Ghost, i.e. as proceeding from the Father *and* the Son.

wholesale latinization of villages and communities by the patriarchal authorities on the advice and with the connivance of Roman authorities, has exacerbated the situation. Anyone who knows the situation at the Holy Sepulchre and at Bethlehem will realize the utter disregard for the first principles of Christianity that have characterized the relations until recently obtaining between the Latins and the other rites.

The Roman Church set out to undermine, if possible, the unity of Orthodoxy in a juridical way; for over two centuries its avowed policy was to set up rival Churches wherever possible, much the same way as modern petrol companies struggle for control of public consumption of their particular product, by setting up rival petrol-stations in each other's vicinity along the public highways. This, in the case of the Church unity, only compounded the initial errors. Not only does Orthodoxy find that there are juridical difficulties in reunion with Rome; it finds that Rome has created rival Greek Uniats and Russian Uniats, churches which follow the pattern of Orthodoxy but belong to Rome.

The Roman administration did not stop there. For still other dissident Churches, it set up parallel communities, thus creating a mosaic of Churches: Greek Catholics (Melkites) opposing the Greek Orthodox, Chaldeans opposing the Nestorians, Syrian Catholics opposing the Syrian Orthodox (Jacobites), Armenian Catholics opposing Armenian Orthodox, Russian Uniats opposing Russian Orthodox. Small wonder that when the Soviet Union absorbed the Western Ukraine from Poland, the Carpathian Ukraine (Ruthenia) from Czechoslovakia, in 1946, she dissolved the Brest Uniats of 1596 and returned these groups to the bosom of Russian Orthodoxy. The same fate overtook the 1,500,000 Uniat Catholics in Roumania, after the Communist takeover. And the presence at the current Vatican Ecumenical Council of the Ukrainian Bishops in exile (mainly from America) was a constant source of irritation to the efforts of Pope John and of Bea to establish contacts with the Russian Orthodox Church in Moscow and to relax the East-West tension throughout the Soviet Empire. Even so revered a personage as Archbishop Slipyi has proved an embarrassing treasure to Rome: he proposed during the second session of the Council that a new Patriarchate be set up in Kiev, based on a controversial historical precedent of dubious value. This and similar proposals are all that is needed to arouse the old suspicions of the Russian Orthodox Church with regard to Rome.

Furthermore, Orthodoxy has found, up to this point, that any dealings with Rome have to be channelled through the Roman *Congregation for the Oriental Churches*, a dicastery belonging to the Holy See and imbued with the 'proselytizing' mentality so hateful to Orthodoxy. The action of Paul in bringing Cardinal Testa, prefect of the Oriental Congregation, with him on his recent visit to the East, must be judged in this light: it was a mistake but, as we know, imposed on Paul by the circumstances obtaining at the time of his decision to meet Athenagoras, Patriarch of Constantinople. As of now, any relationship with Orthodoxy must, strictly speaking, be handled by the same Oriental Congregation which during the reign of Papa Pacelli so successfully upset the advances of the Orthodox Patriarch of Alexandria.

To date, the ecclesiastical situation in the Near East between the different Christian rites is a mosaic of authorities, conflicting jurisdictions, patriarchs and patriarchates, that would seem to be a comedy of errors if it were not, more properly speaking, a pitiful commentary on human weakness. The ancient city of Antioch has no less than six patriarchs, a Maronite, a Greek Orthodox, a Greek Catholic, a Syrian Orthodox, a Syrian Catholic, and a Latin Patriarch. In Jerusalem there are, in addition to the Latin, a Greek Orthodox, an Armenian, and a Coptic Patriarch. For the cities of Constantinople, Antioch, Alexandria and Jerusalem together, as many as eighteen different churchmen claim the title of patriarch.

When we come to study Paul's policy as of January 1964, we shall see that it was to this morass of conflicting jurisdictions, ecclesiastical rivalries and tensions that he has addressed his efforts more and more. Already he has had a measure of success. In his own way, he is trying to reduce the jurisdictional complexity: he has allowed three old Latin patriarchates to be dropped from the official list. Jerusalem is still included since Patriarch Gori is alive though at an advanced age. It is to be expected that on the latter's death, the Latin Patriarchate of Jerusalem will fall into desuetude and be abolished by Paul.

4. The Streams on the Plains

There is yet another tension which is ominous for Christianity because its roots not only go back to the very origins of Christianity, but involve the historical act of Jesus Christ by which Christianity came into being as a principle. The tension is that between Jew and Christian, the historical act is the sacrifice and death of Jesus himself. The manifestation of this tension on the part of Christians is generally called anti-Semitism or Hebraeophobia. But we are not concerned so much with the name as with the thing signified.

Catholics often quote a sentence used by Pius XI[30] in order to prove that at least officially the Church has no anti-Semitic bias. And officially, it is true, the Church cannot sanction the killing of innocent people, the violation of the human right to choose one's own religion or the victimization of any human being on the basis of race, creed or colour. Anti-Semitism is a more subtle thing when we peer into its very soul.

Yet, if we listen to the chorus of the ages, we find a strangely consistent note of disapproval, sometimes of hate, and always of unmitigated condemnation, for the Jew, as such, echoing down the corridors of time and blending with latter-day sentiments which can be reckoned as nothing else but rank anti-Semitism. And these ancient voices are not merely those of secular or freelance thinkers: they are no less than the Fathers of the Church, an Irenaeus, a Tertullian, a John Chrysostom, an Augustine, as well as an Aquinas, modern theologians and ancient exegetes, an Origen, a Grotius, a Müller.

Somehow or other, the stream of this perennial Christian bias grates on our modern ears, and yet there is hardly any Christian or Catholic who cannot, in spite of himself, hear some echo in his own sentiments. Let us listen to some of these accents. Origen: 'And therefore, the blood of Jesus fell not only on the Jews of that time, but on all generations of Jews up to the end of the world.'[31] Tertullian: 'The whole

---

[30] In an address to Belgian pilgrims, September 1938, he said: 'Anti-Semitism is a movement in which we, as Christians, cannot have any part.'
[31] *In Matth.* 27:25.

synagogue of the sons of Israel killed him.'[32] St John Chrysostom: 'The synagogue is a bordello ... a hiding place for unclean beasts ... Never has any one Jew prayed to God ... They are possessed by the devils ... Instead of greeting them, you should avoid them like a disease and like a pest of human nature.'[33] Augustine: 'The Jews are dispersed throughout all nations, as witnesses of their iniquity and of our truth.'[34] Aquinas: 'The Jews sinned as crucifiers not only of Christ the man, but also of Christ the God.'[35] That lovely medieval hymn, *Victimae Paschales:* 'You should put more trust in Mary, the truthful one, than in the horde of lying Jews.' And leaping the centuries[36] down to the present age, we hear the same accents in different words. *La Civiltà Cattolica*, the Jesuit intellectual publication in Italy, sometimes called the mouthpiece of the Holy See: 'Judaism is a deeply corrupted religion; it is nationalistic inasmuch as it is the religion of corrupt messianism.'[37] Angelo Alberti, as the voice of popular Catholic exegesis and piety: 'The condemnation of the Jewish world will be announced by the Holy Spirit (on Pentecost day) ... They will be condemned to ruin ... wandering through the world in absolute discomfort ... and reduced to a mere collection of business people. Such is the punishment of their erroneous judgement.' This testimony is all the more painful and alarming since we find that no less a person than the then Archbishop of Milan, Monsignor Giovanni Battista Montini, afterwards cardinal, and present Holy Father, commended the book in a specially written and signed preface.[38]

[32] *Adversus Judaeos VIII* 18. Migne, *Patres Lat.* 2, col. 616.

[33] Migne, *Patres Graec.* 48,847–852. There are eight sermons, in all, of this sort against the Jews.

[34] *In Ps.* 58, *serm.* 1,22. Cf. Migne, *Patres Lat.* 36,705.

[35] *Summ. Theol.* Pars 3a, q.47, art. 5.

[36] A full catalogue of ancient statements of this kind would fill more than one sizeable volume. They have never been collected and classified. For catechism teaching of the same kind in our times, cf. Paul Démann, *La Catétienne et le peuple de la Bible*. Cahiers Sioniens. Paris 1952. T. P. Maher, *The Catholic School Curriculum and Intergroup Relations in Religious Education* 55 (1960) 121.

[37] *La Civiltà Cattolica*, April, 1938.

[38] In this preface, Archbishop Montini wrote: 'This work, with its notes full of sobriety and devotion ... the Sacred Word explained in its full sense, which is a unique sense and the sense of Revelation, and not interpreted in a personal way, arbitrarily and thus open to deformations ... This is a kind of paraphrased synopsis with a sober commentary, which will bring clarity and edifying reflections to those who read it.' Cf. *Il Mesaggio degli Evangeli*, by Angelo Alberti, Edit. Massimo, Milan 1958. French translation by Simonne Jacquemard, Edit. Marabout Université, Verviers 1961, pp. 450–451. The notes of Alberti teem with similar remarks, including the ones quoted in the text above.

It is true that we can set down a list of statements by popes, theologians, saints, writers, to show that the extremer forms of anti-Semitism (persecution, oppression, expulsion, mutilation, imprisonment, segregation), are not admissible. But none ever asserted the religious rights of Judaism in itself, nor declared that Judaism was a valid moral outlook, nor has any theologian or theological school courageously re-examined the millennial attitude of Christians and Catholics to the Jews. And no matter how much anti-Semitism was deplored, the Catholic attitude never went beyond tolerance. Tolerance, of course, is not a Christian virtue; it is a natural expedient. Yet this is the most commendable form which the central Christian virtue of love has so far assumed with regard to Jews.

What transforms this most ancient, persistent, compulsive, strident, characteristic trait of the Christian soul into a veritable antimony is the sound of another voice, that of Christian love. 'God is love,' wrote the Fourth Evangelist. There is absolutely no means of understanding anti-Semitism, this most unchristian of all Christian traits, and no possibility of grasping the disruptive force of this deepest of all Christian tensions, unless we clearly perceive the root of it all.

Within the historical ambit of the first four centuries, it was practically inevitable that an opposition should be born between the ancient religion of Judaism and nascent Christianity. After the suppression of the Second Jewish Revolt in A.D. 135, Judaism was everywhere fighting for its life. Christianity, on the other hand, spread throughout the Mediterranean basin, first in isolated pockets, then in openly organized communities, and finally it attained the dignity of the state religion. But such historical oppositions wither away – if they were merely that.

Within the doctrinal framework of both religions lay the seeds of that undying enmity with which the Christian regarded the Jew and the Jew the Christian. It did not take four centuries to germinate. By the end of the first century of our era, the relationship between the two was reduced starkly to one sharp disagreement on matters essential to each one. The Jew stood before the Eternal alone without an intermediary, worshipping the God of Abraham, Isaac and Jacob unseeingly and in faith, his feet guided by the precepts of Sinai. The Christian saw Christ, his Mediator, pleading, in virtue of His Sacrifice, with the Father, worshipped His humanity, claimed to be nourished with His flesh and blood, claimed that He was Messiah and God. Very early in its history, Christianity rejected the necessity of the Law of Moses, the Torah, for salvation. And yet, it would be unhistorical to affirm that such disagreement could of itself generate the tension which did and does exist between Jew and Christian, between the Synagogue and the Church.

The only satisfactory way in which we can explain the birth of this terrible tension is to be found in the option which Christianity made towards the latter half of the first century, the option for dejudaization and for occidentalization of the Christian message. It was the option which led Peter to Rome and which inspired Paul to give a new formulation to the doctrine of Jesus fitted for the non-Semitic minds of the West. It was an option for the Occident. And it was in the logic of human events at that time.

Jesus had been crucified by the Roman authorities at the insistence of certain Jewish leaders. The primitive Judaeo-Christian Church teaching is well summed up by Peter when speaking of the populace of Jerusalem on two occasions.[39] He insisted that the Jews and their rulers had in their ignorance handed over the Innocent One to be crucified, and he urged penitence on them. To take the text at its face value, on both occasions the conversions following on this preaching were numerous. Peter did not speak of a deliberate deicide nor did he mention the rejection or the curse of the Chosen Race. This would have been blasphemy to Peter, as it was to Paul. By about A.D. 90 however, the outlook had radically changed. In the Fourth Gospel, the rulers of the Jews and the people are painted in a different light: the rulers did away with Him in spite of His obvious divinity, the people connived at this crime and therefore drew an eternal curse of blindness on themselves. The fission had appeared between Christian and Jew.

We can perceive in action here a curious selectivity on the part of Christianity, an eclecticism among the data of the primitive Christian tradition in the light of the historical circumstances then obtaining. Paul summed up his own attitude to the Jewish question in very succinct but incomplete lines:[40] the Jewish people were not rejected by God or cursed, on the one hand; on the other hand, a blindness has fallen on them until the full multitude of the Gentiles has entered into the New Alliance of Christ, and then, he concludes, 'all Israel will be saved.' Reading Paul's disquisition on this problem one concludes that the Apostle did not see to the core of the question. For he fell into logical and theological difficulties; he taught that Christianity inherited all the treasures and the privileges of the Old Testament, and

[39] *Acts*, 2:14–36, 3:12–26.
[40] *Romans*, 11:1–36.

the Christians were now the Chosen People, the spiritual seed of Abraham. But, he taught, the original Chosen People had not ceased to be the Chosen People; they were not rejected by God.

Christianity at the turn of the first century by-passed this inherent lack of logic and incomplete theology in the Pauline position and formulated its own position thus: the Jews are blinded and will remain so until the fullness of salvation is attained; this blindness is the result of a divine curse and this curse is the result of their rejection by God. Now God rejected the people of Israel as a whole because they as a people committed the unspeakable crime of deicide. We are thus a long cry from the primitive teaching of Peter the Jew on Pentecost Day, and at the opposite pole from the genuinely Christian plea of the dying Jesus: 'Father forgive them, for they know not what they do.'

It only remained for Christianity to spread abroad, to infiltrate the Graeco-Roman civilization, to find that, historically and socially, the Roman authorities should not be blamed for the death of Christ.[41] Gradually both Judaism and Christianity began to harden in their mutual opposition, the Christian vying for acceptability, opting for adaptation to new circumstances, the Jew everywhere in recession, clinging to the ancient teachings, refusing to change one jot or tittle of his Law. Each one finally crystallized his fundamental objection to the other: the Jew had knowingly murdered God; the Christian had forsaken the religion of his fathers and thereby committed blasphemy. At this stage there was no possibility of a reconciliation. In exposing Christian doctrine, a deliberate process of dejudaization was effected. And those elements were either transformed or dropped into oblivion, which would eventually have shown forth the true relationship of the Church and the Synagogue. The final seal of division was set when Christianity took over and became clothed in what we have called Romanism. It obtained submission and conversion throughout the world – except in the case of the Jews.

From the sixth century onwards, we find that anti-Semitism is an integral part of Christianity. And down to our own day, it has taken various forms. It may assume the form of an accepted racialism with sociological overtones, in business, in social life, at the club, on the beach: one does not marry into Jewish circles or consort with Jews, for

[41] P. Winter brings this out clearly. Cf. *On the Trial of Jesus*. Studia Judaica, Band I. De Gruyter & Co. Berlin 1961, pp. 51–61. De La Potterie evades this point in his review of Winter. Cf. *Biblica* 43 (1962) 92.

they are a different race with different customs and differing mentality. It may take the form of mere isolationism: the Jew is somebody apart, somebody irrevocably separate from the truth. Here there is an instant refusal to treat them like others, a blind feeling that this person, the Jew, is marked out by divine decision as untouchable. It may, though, take on a more mobile form: the Jews are to be reckoned with as active enemies of the Faith, and therefore they must be restricted, watched warily. It may, finally, go further and translate such feelings into action: the Jew must be expelled, must be warned, must be punished, must be dispossessed, must be liquidated.

In these extreme forms, we meet some phantasmagoric developments: the Protocols of Sion,[42] the Nazi Final Solution, the massacres by their Catholic Majesties of Spain, the so-called Judaeo-Communist world plot against Christianity, the unholy alliance between the Grand Lodge and the Synagogue to subvert Christian principles. In whatever form or shade or colouring we meet this anti-Semitism, its peculiarly Christian characteristic is clear. Yet it is safe to suppose that the majority of Christians, who would regard themselves as good Christians, would share the views of Pope Innocent III as expressed in his famous Constitution *Licet Perfidia Judaeorum* of 1199.[43] Legislating against forced baptism of Jews, against physical assault of Jews with sticks or stones (*fustibus vel lapidibus*), against the mutilation of Jewish cemeteries or corpses, the Pontiff unequivocally states his reason, the Catholic reason, for such prohibitions and for this tolerance: 'Although the infidelity (*perfidia*) of the Jews must be condemned on multiple grounds, they must not be gravely persecuted by the Faithful, because by reason of them our Faith is established as true (*per eos fides nostra veraciter comprobatur*).'[44]

We touch the heart of the matter at this point. The Jew never became assimilated to Christianity. He never accepted Christ. He claimed to represent the Chosen People. The Christian, all-victorious in the

[42] Published by Serge Nilus in Russia as an appendix to a book of apocalyptic nature, and called the *Protocols of the Sages of Sion*. He based his work on an earlier phantasy of Maurice Joly, *Dialogue aux enfers entre Machiavel et Montesquieu, ou la politique de Machiavel au XIXe siècle*, Mertens, Bruxelles, 1864. Nilus copied freely from Joly. I have only been able to locate one copy of Joly's work; Bibliothèque Royale de Bruxelles, destination-number III.2151.
[43] This was considered as the Magna Charta of tolerance for Jews. It was reaffirmed by later popes in subsequent centuries.
[44] For convenient quotations, cf. Denzinger-Schönmetzer, *Enchiridion Symbolorum Defitionum et Declarationum*, Freiburg (Breisgau) 1963, §§ 772–3.

fifth and sixth centuries, finally adopted the Jew as an integral element of his world: an element of opposition, a living proof of God's punishment for the blind, a proof that the Messiah had come in the person of Jesus. *Per eos fides nostra comprobatur.* The very existence of the Jews and the very fact of their refusal to accept Christ and Christianity was taken as a proof (a) that Christ had come, and (b) that the Jews had been blinded for their crime. Pauline teaching that the Jews had not been rejected was obfuscated. They had been cursed, that was sufficient. They would be with Christianity as long as Christianity lasted – till the end of the world. Everything else followed logically, oppression, pogrom, expulsion, ghetto, opprobrium, alienation, enmity. From the tolerance of an Innocent III to the attitude of most Catholics towards Jews today, there is a direct line of filiation. Between the burning and plundering of all Jewish synagogues in Mesopotamia in A.D. 388 on the order of the Bishop of Callinicum[45] and the destruction and desecration of all synagogues under the recent Nazi regime, we cannot but see a relationship of origin. And no one conscious of what has made modern Europe can deny that the pyres and the crematoria, the mephitic smoke and stench of the extermination camps in Nazi Germany, were, if not the logical conclusion, at least one extremist consequence of the normal Christian attitude to the Jews. Here we see Christianity standing at the thin edge of self-destruction due to this admitted tension, moving to what Laurence Dobie has called aptly the *anus mundi*, the ultimate in excretion of the badness which Christianity never undertook to extirpate.

A mortal tension, therefore, exists between Catholics and Jews. I say 'mortal,' because, firstly it reaches to the very soul of the beliefs of ordinary Catholics and likewise entails the very essence of Judaism. Secondly, it is mortal because up to now complete *incompatibility* was the keynote of the Catholic attitude to the Jew and vice-versa. Yet, there is a pathetic note of regret for all the bitterness, all the suffering, all the injustice committed in the name of the Man, Who, as God, preached a Gospel of Love. And among the Jews there has been, especially on the occasion of the Vatican Council, a certain attention

[45] For a full account, cf. B. J. Palanque, *Histoire de l'Eglise*, Paris 1956. Fliche-Martin, vol. 3, pp. 510-511. The Emperor Theodosius ordered the stolen goods to be returned and the destroyed buildings to be restored. St Ambrose told the Emperor he would personally excommunicate him if he maintained this order since 'the Jews as the enemies of Christ had no claim to justice or legal support.' Theodosius gave in to the threat of excommunication.

and listening, a certain tendency to re-examine ancient suppositions and recent prejudices.[46]

The next bloc in which an old historical tension afflicts the Roman Church consists of those countries where Islam predominates: Algeria, Morocco, Libya, Somaliland, Sudan, Egypt, Jordan, Syria, Iraq, Iran, Pakistan, Turkey, Albania, Indonesia, Malaysia, and some of the new nations in Africa, to name the most important. Islam as a creed is unique in history: it has neither pope, nor hierarchy, nor official priesthood, nor iron discipline in dogma, nor centralized authority; it has the Book, the Koran, and the Spirit. Yet this religious ideology, born of the undoubtedly profound religious experience of its founder, Muhammad, spread with the speed of mercury and the consuming power of a forest-fire across the whole of the Maghreb, up through Spain destroying the old Visigoth kingdom, across the Pyrenees, and up to the gates of Tours.

In the East, it absorbed the eastern and southern provinces of Byzantium, it swallowed the Persian Sassanian Empire in its entirety, so that by A.D. 750, Abbasid rule extended from Gibraltar to the Indus and the writ of Islam was co-extensive. Today Islam can claim about 500,000,000 adherents and has reached Malaysia and Indonesia in the Far East as well as the new nations of Africa. Islam is unique in other senses: built on the idea of an ultimate revelation made to God's final prophet, Muhammad, it considers Moses and Jesus as genuine prophets whose partial revelations were corrupted by Jew and Christian respectively. Consequently, it assimilated multiple elements from the books and the beliefs of both Christian and Jew.

It canonized the intuitive 'leap' of utterly trusting belief such as the prophets of Israel had intoned for five hundred years, the unquestioning a-rational attachment to a primary revelation and an absolute code of ethics, and thus produced the asymmetrical method of understanding and the collective feeling that characterize Arab thought and practical efforts and have proved so difficult for Western statesmen in our day to reconcile with their occidental way of thinking and acting. The uniqueness and the timelessness of the Almighty, the supra-historical view of human life so characteristic of the Old Testament, were then fused with a personal devotion to Muhammad which paralleled the Christian attachment to Jesus in all things except in the question of divinity.

Historians generally agree nowadays that the tension which sprang

[46] See H. Adler, *Das Christusbild im Lichte judischer Autoren*, in Band II, Symbolon, 1961.

up between Islam and Christianity is outclassed as a historical anomaly only by the tension which Christianity demonstrated in its first contact with a major world power in opposition to it. The weakness of the world position which Christianity assumed after the fall of the Western Roman Empire explains, in the final analysis, the fundamental cause of the tension: Rome and the faith it preached had taken a temporal stance that made the rise of Islam-Christian tension possible. The end result in our day is that there is no reasonable hope of any Christian penetration of Islam, as things now stand. Positions and mutual relations have been frozen to utter immobility. The appeal of Christianity has lost its lustre: its motives for converting Muslims are irretrievably denigrated. Christians and Roman Catholics have for so long acted on the principle that anyone such as a Muslim, who is in error according to their Christian beliefs, has no rights, that even the Catholic mentality finds it hard to break through the thought-barriers. Anti-Semitism, as a name, has been restricted for historical reasons to mean Hebraeo-phobia. Yet there is ample justification for using the term globally to include Islam.

This is the fundamental reason why the Roman Catholic Church is experiencing such difficulties in countries like Egypt and the Sudan where genuine oppression is occurring, and in Negro countries of Africa, like Kenya and Tanganyika, where Islam has made severe inroads. And a review of the progress and activity of the Church in these and other countries where Islam dominates, shows indubitably that the only value Roman Catholic organizations have for the local populations and their governments is their contribution in the fields of social, medical, dental, clinical and educational assistance. In Malaysia (pop. 7 million), the Church spends about half a million dollars on charity alone every year, and during the past eight years has spent a further six million dollars of the Catholic Relief Service of America. The Catholic Schools educate about 100,000 pupils from primary to high-school level. A boy's home and hospital are only two out of several services rendered. Yet the Catholic population increased only from 90,000 (1957) to 115,000 as of today. Compared with the leakage, and the population explosion, this is poor return by way of concrete results. Above all, the vast majority of converts are Chinese. Apostasy from Islam is as punishable a crime in Islam as it is in Roman Catholicism.

In Pakistan, the picture is still more dismal. Conversions seem high (in the 1961 census, for instance, Christians were shown to have increased by 35.7 per cent as against the national average of 23.8 per cent), until one analyzes the situation: very few Muslim conversions take place; many conversions were made from the Untouchable castes who preferred Christianity to Islam and became Christians following the communal killings that marked the partition of the continent; a greater proportion of Catholic and Christian babies survive than Muslim. Actually, there have not been more than fifty converts to Christianity in the last twelve years. Since 1959, moreover, the teaching of Islamayat (instruction in Islam) is compulsory in Catholic Schools for all Muslim children. The Catholics have to bow to this. The right of those differing in faith to have their own instruction was very difficult to swallow.

One could examine the emergent situation in newly free Algeria and Morocco, in the Sudan (where the situation is critical) and in all Islamic countries, and the conclusion is the same: the tension between Christianity and, in particular, between Roman Catholicism and Islam is an operative factor. The historical antecedents have frozen the situation. Yet perhaps, willy-nilly, the Church of Rome has been led by hard circumstances to adopt the attitude of genuine charity and disinterested service which it lacked over a thousand years ago: the servicing of hospitals, clinics, dispensaries, leprosaria, the running of schools and kindergartens. In other words, an ecclesiastical implementation of the biblical admonition to hide from one hand the good one does with the other hand. This is charity in the Christian sense, and by this means, finally, the genuine message of Christianity will be driven home. It is not so much 'See how these Christians love each other,' as 'See how these Christians love all men.'

In the Far East the most impressive tension bloc is formed by the corpus of Buddhist and Hindu believers. Roman Catholics are distributed in the following proportions in the lands of Buddha: India with a total population of 438 million has 2 per cent Christian and 6,480,000 Catholics; Ceylon with a total population of 8,097,000 has 609,938 (7.5 per cent) Catholics; North Vietnam with a population of 12 million has 400,000 Catholics; South Vietnam with a population of 13,000,000 has 2 per cent Catholics; Sarawak and Borneo with respective populations of 700,000 and 500,000 have 23,000 (3 per cent) and 20,000 (4 per cent) Catholics respectively; Burma with a population of 21,000,000 has 200,000 Catholics; Laos with a population of 2,500,000 has only 27,060 (1 per cent) Catholics. The fact is that conversion from Buddhism to Catholicism or Christianity is very slow.

A steady conversion rate in these countries is maintained only among

Chinese residents, whether it be in South Vietnam, Burma, Sarawak or Ceylon. Conversion is impeded primarily by the fact that Christianity is inextricably associated with, and identified as, the religion of the former Portuguese, Spanish, Dutch, English or French conquerors. The recent accession of these nations to a national life of their own, the constant association of the Roman Catholic Church in the past with the colonial powers, are factors which have branded the Church as something alien. In countries like Ceylon this has brought hardship, curtailment of activities, and even expulsion.

Moreover, the colonial Churches did not really bother about the indigenous population until comparatively recently: Sarawak, Borneo, Indonesia, Burma, Laos, were all reached and more or less colonized in the sixteenth–seventeenth centuries. At that time, the ancient capital city of Thailand, Ayuthya, was at the height of its centuries-old grandeur when the Portuguese landed there, and the Portuguese Dominicans followed. Missionaries in these countries attended to the wants of the colonists rather than of the indigenous populations. One would have expected more progress in 400 years of Catholic presence.

The basic reason for this disappointing lack of progress is to be sought in the occidentalization of the Christian message, which was achieved in the West over a period of a thousand years and which culminated in the Aristotelian-Thomistic system of theology and philosophy. By the fifteenth century, the Roman Church had adopted the system of Aquinas as her official and exclusive vehicle for the dogmatic and moral formulations of her doctrine. When presented to the population of the Far East, the entire system of thought used by the Westerners was not merely repugnant, because strange and unwanted; it was unintelligible and in the end, unassimilable to the mind of the East. Efforts, rather desperate at times, put forth by the ebullient Jesuit Order at that time, were quenched and officially forbidden as dangerous and adulterous. Yet the methods of adaptation exemplified by a Robert de Nobili, his knowledge of Tamil, Telegu, Sanskrit, his loin-cloth, his squatting position in cross-legged fashion on a tiger skin, his prayers and fasts, made him a holy man, a *sadhu*, in the eyes of the Brahmins; and undoubtedly these were the methods necessary in order to penetrate the Eastern mind.

As in China somewhat later, the official Church operating from Rome, with its Western mentality, completely misunderstood the situation, and so effectively closed off this legitimate approach to the East that the message of Christianity never really penetrated the Far

Eastern lands over a span of four hundred years. Later imperialism and colonialist oppression, in addition to the real identity of the missioners with the different variations of European culture, French, German, Spanish, Portuguese, Anglo-Saxon only made assimilation more impossible.

And yet Christianity spread like wildfire across the Mediterranean basin to England within the span of four centuries. And the differentiating factor lies certainly in the occidental garb in which the *logos* had been dressed. Competent and realistically-minded authorities in the East today will state two things about Roman Catholicism: the Church is gaining respect for the first time by virtue of a gigantic effort, by its educational services in Eastern lands, but there is no concrete possibility of mass conversions, or even a steady, comfortably generous flow of individual conversions.

A look at mainland China, Formosa, Hong Kong, Macao, and Japan drives home the same lessons. The maximum number of Roman Catholics in mainland China was 3,000,000 (1949) before the Communist take-over. They were served by 6,500 native priests, 4,500 schools, three universities, and thirty-two printing houses, besides numerous other works of charity. Today nothing remains of the original educational structure. Of the original hierarchy eight are in jail, six co-operate with the government of Peking, the rest are dead or expelled. Four churches operate in the capital; about 1,500 priests still work in China. Japan has a population of about 100,000,000. There are about 200,000 Roman Catholics. There are Catholic educational institutions at every level: primary, secondary, and university. Hong Kong has about 140,000 Roman Catholics of whom 95 per cent are Chinese. Again the educational, social welfare and medical services rendered are huge. Formosa has 219,000 Roman Catholics and eats up over 40 million American dollars annually in maintenance of churches, convents, social services, etc. Macao, in Christian hands since 1559, has only 25,000 Roman Catholics out of a total population of 170,000. Again we find a proportionately large Catholic drive on the level of medical and social services.

Basically and apart from the Communist dictatorship in power on mainland China, the same difficulty, analogously speaking, has hindered the Catholic message from being received by the Chinese and the Japanese mind: the garb in which this message has been presented for over four centuries is an alien one. The majority of Chinese, before the 1949 conquest, were Confucianists; Japan was mainly Shintoist (the state religion before 1945), but since the war Buddhism has attracted about 3 million adherents. Both China and Japan stood at the gates of Catholicism in the sixteenth century, when the Jesuit missionaries set about adapting Catholic liturgy and dogmatic formulas to the Chinese language, but its own leaders, occidentalized both in thought and methods, destroyed by deliberate act these penetrating changes proposed by the Jesuits. The painful result is acknowledged by all: sudden and murderous revulsion of the Chinese mind against the 'foreign devils' and the end of what one writer has called the biggest chance history ever offered to the Church of a mass conversion since the first Pentecost in Jerusalem.

At once the most promising and the most forbidding field of endeavour confronts the Roman Church in Negro Africa. Until recently a continent dominated by colonial powers, Africa has become over the space of thirty years a network of infant nations. Its importance for Catholic effort can be gauged, firstly, from the fact that of the 70 million Catholics expected to exist in mission countries by 1970, at present rate of conversion and baptism, 45 million are expected from Africa alone. We rule out of consideration here the Maghreb countries which are essentially and wholeheartedly Moslem. The Republic of South Africa takes its place logically with countries like Switzerland and Great Britain, for it reproduces the characteristic tensions of these countries.

A second indication of Africa's importance in Catholic eyes is the huge effort put forth by the Church to render services of all kinds to the different populations. In Tanganyika alone, the Roman Catholic Church today has 1,161 schools on primary, middle and secondary levels, with a total of 169,131 pupils, 13 teacher training colleges, 2,857 Catholic teachers, 23 hospitals, 31 Catholic doctors, 52 nurse-midwives, 18 midwives, 103 nurses, 4 dentists, 267 medical orderlies, 8 tuberculosis centres. Of Tanganyika's 9,258,000, there are 1¾ million Catholics, 2 million followers of Islam, a small number of Hindus, and more than 5 million others still adhering to the tribal religion of their ancestors. The number of foreign priests is about 850 side by side with about 290 Africans.

In Kenya with a population of 6,668,417 there are 766,792 Catholics, 1,529 Catholic schools, 144 Catholic hospitals and dispensaries and clinics, various schools for the blind, domestic science centres, centres for crafts and technical and trade schools. In Uganda with a population of 6,536,616, 33 per cent are Catholic, 25 per cent are Protestant, 5 per cent are Muslim, 37 per cent are pagan. The Church there has over 3,000 schools, 55 medical units, 33 doctors, 152 nurses and midwives, treats over 10,000 leprosy patients in over 22 villages. Social centres, women's clubs, Catholic guilds, Catholic Action organizations round off the picture. These three countries are show-pieces of Catholic organization and similar efforts are found throughout Negro Africa. And Tanganyika has the first and only Negro cardinal in history, Cardinal Laurean Rugambwa.

This seemingly roseate picture of the Romanization of black Africa is shot through with dangerous potentials and fringed by a black rim of limited expansion possibilities. There is, first, the population explosion which will inevitably and at the present rate of going leave Christians in a very large minority and the white population as an enclave of oddities in the middle of a black multitude. Another threatening factor is Islam; the followers of Ahmadiya register continual successes not only in Kenya, Tanganyika, and Uganda, but in other African nations, and the Muslim minority at Buddu, Uganda, has grown significantly in recent times. Of course, the rise and the antipathy of Islam in Negro Africa is tied to the spread of Nasserism and the Nasserist mentality. Some of the natural markets for Egypt are to be found lying east and south of the Nile.

By far the source of the most promising trouble for Catholicity in Africa comes from a double development: there is, on the one hand, the phenomenon called africanization and there is, on the other hand, the undeniable fact that the Church of Africa has been founded by missionaries from nations who have not yet begun to adapt to local circumstances. Africanization implies opposition to colonialism. It is true that as long as the new nations cannot shoulder the huge social and educational burdens at present borne by Church organizations, they will welcome Church efforts in these fields. If the Catholic organization left Uganda, for instance, tomorrow morning, there would be at least a quarter of a million school-children without teachers and another quarter of a million men, women, and children without medical care.

According as these nations accede to full nationhood and become more self-reliant, according as their populations burgeon at the present rate, the Church's function will diminish in importance, will be curtailed. According, also, as the educational and social services in these countries come under the influence and direction of the various bureaux of the United Nations, the tendency to what Catholics call secularism, that bogey of the nineteenth century Roman Church, will increase.

C

Already on the political plane, the Church is experiencing real difficulty with the Kabat Yekke Party in Uganda (now the exclusive government of the country). If it is true that people like Tom Mboya and Julius Nyerere of Tanganyika, the former Patrice Lumumba of the Congo, and many outstanding political leaders of African nations are Catholic, this is rather so because of the facilities afforded by the Church for education and should not be taken as an absolute guarantee of future predominance or popularity.

By far a deeper cause of discomfort for the Church of Rome lies in the type of church mentality imported by the missionaries. Fundamentally it is conservative, occidental in conception, timid and short-sighted. Catholic churchmen and authorities have not been distinguished as a body in protesting against the near dictatorship in Ghana. They likewise have explicitly refused to condemn a social scourge such as female circumcision, in much the same way as the Church refused to condemn slavery five centuries earlier in other parts of the world. Further and more seriously, the Christian message has undergone no real adaptation, apart from the intermittent use of local languages for partial liturgical purposes (such as Kiswahili which is used in Tanganyika for certain ceremonies) or the cultivation of the Black Madonna in place of Renaissance or seventeenth and eighteenth century representations of the Virgin used throughout the West.

A vicious circle starts here. According as these nations develop a more educated population through the mighty co-operation of Church organization, the more conscious and rationally aware they become of the difference between their national mentalities and the definitely occidental and exterior identity of the Christianity they have been taught. It is not so much that a celibate clergy may become a demographic impossibility in the near future, or that foreign religious textbooks must be translated into local languages; it is the very presentation of the Christian message that is at stake. The African nations are receiving the first backwash of the new civilization of the masses which has been sweeping over the older nations for over thirty years and has replaced the civilization of the élite. They are acquiring the material benefits of Western civilization which developed over a period of three centuries of discovery, research, trial and effort. But they are not going to absorb the desiccated ethics of Western nations and they will become increasingly apathetic to a religious message which is alien in its presentation and conceptualization.

The day must come when these people will say by word and/or deed to the bearers of such a message: 'We do not need your generosity any longer and we cannot understand your teachings.' Religious thought and ceremony, adapted to the African soul, register far more lasting and deeper results. In Zanzibar, with a population of 160,000 the Church has been working since 1860. Yet there are only 2,000 Catholics and these are all Goans or Africans who came from the mainland either to pick cloves or to work as civil servants. Of the ancient Christian Church of the first six centuries in the Maghreb, in Egypt and the north-eastern parts of Africa, of its network of churches, monasteries, schools and hierarchy, nothing remained once the hordes of Islam swept over it, except the Coptic rite in Egypt (to a limited degree) and the special Christianity of Ethiopia. Both were non-Latin, non-occidental forms of Christianity. The Church Augustine knew ceased to exist as such.

In the foregoing section we have spoken about the major tension-blocs. Each one contains two elements frozen historically into a relationship of strain. In the first seven centuries of its existence, the Roman Church developed a tension with Judaism: the Jews were deicides and accursed by God; Christians were the followers of a renegade Jew. In the seventh–ninth centuries, the Roman Church developed a tension with Islam: Islam was a bastard imitation of Christianity; Christians were infidels. In the ninth–eleventh centuries the Roman Church developed a tension with the vast mass of Orthodoxy: the Orthodox were first schismatics, later heretics, and did not belong to the true Church; Catholics had corrupted the true doctrine of the early Councils and the Fathers. In the sixteenth–seventeenth centuries, the Church developed at least two tensions: with the Reformed Churches of the West, with the great non-Christian religions of the East, Buddhism, Hinduism, Shintoism, which it met for the first time. In the twentieth century, a double tension arose: tension with the powerful ideology of Communism, tension within the very heart of Christianity, within the nations traditionally Catholic and faithful to Rome. The tension with the great non-Christian religions was directly due to the occidentalization of the Word of revelation which took place during the first centuries of Christian existence.

5. *The Garb of the Pilgrim*

In order to understand these tensions properly, it is necessary to consider two historical facts which most Catholics, unconsciously or consciously, canonize as parts of the primal revelation of their religion: the occidentalization and what we shall call, for want of a better name, the Romanization of this very revelation. Both have produced a basic antinomy in Catholicism. Both have hindered her from attaining full maturity as the universal Church. Only 'because she belongs to the whole world and not one particular locality, because through her all humanity and all the earth are hallowed, not one particular nation or one particular country'[47] could she fully mature in her universality (catholicity). And both are the basic causes for the historical tensions that strain Roman Catholicism today.

First let us see what occidentalization has meant. The founder, Jesus Christ, was a born, circumcised Jew, who spoke Aramaic and exercised the trade of a carpenter in the hinterlands of Galilee. In Catholic thought, He was the first truly human being Who, in virtue of His Godhead, had a human concept of God's plan for the world, its cleansing, its salvation, its final destiny. He handed on this concept to His first witnesses; it is through the eyes and minds of these fishermen, tent-makers, tax-collectors and peasants of the Augustan Age that Catholics knew what Christ was like, how His message ran. All were Jews. Their primary function at the start was as witnesses of Christ's resurrection. They were quite few. For Catholics the linch-pin in their work was their testimony to Christ's bodily presence among them after His execution on Calvary.

They did not concentrate on His bodily characteristics but discerned in His person and risen presence an ecclesial element. The kerygmatic news they handed on of the risen Christ was a first exposition of ecclesial practice.

Historically, however, we find that this kerygmatic news became enmeshed with the events of the time. Theology is the wrong word to use here. What happened, according to Catholicism was that the

[47] Words of the Russian theologian, Aleksiei Khomiakov.

68

Logos, the Word of God, His revelation of Himself, had taken a human form, first in the figure of Jesus, then, after Christ's disappearance, in the ecclesial grouping that handed on the news of salvation, of deliverance from iconoclasms and solipsistic fixations. Three centuries later, this ecclesial group emerged as a single, dynamic, victorious community feared by Diocletian and acknowledged by Constantine. We cannot take refuge in a nineteenth century rationalist prejudice and attribute this merely to what we choose arbitrarily to describe as the messianic and eschatological delusions of a Galilean fisherman, or to some intrinsic weakness in the Graeco-Roman civilization under the hegemony of the Julio-Claudian dynasty at Rome. Nothing but the faith of Christians and Jews and the unreason of invading hordes survived the destruction of an entire civilization. The Word of God had become incarnate. Theology had not yet begun to reign.

The first telling sign of future greatness for the limited and hunted Judaeo-Christian ecclesial group came about in the middle of the first century. The story is told in the Acts of the Apostles[48] and recounts what is often called the first Council of the Church. The issue at stake was, simply expressed, between individualism and universalism, between exclusively Jewish Christianity and catholicity, between an in-group idea of the revealed word and an idea of the world.

To grasp the difficulty which Peter himself experienced and which Paul solved through his experience and to which he and Peter and James led the nascent Church, we must remember the individuality, the human colouring which Christ as man took on Himself. His temperament, behaviour, bodily proportions, manner of walking, tone of voice, vocabulary, very concepts, emotions, sickness, pains, death, all were as highly individualized as any other Galilean Jew of Nazareth where He grew up. He must have had a corresponding set of mannerisms, of peculiarities, habits. Any attempt to make of the historical Christ a universal man to distinguish in Him two egos, to isolate the divinity from the humanity, ultimately leads to heretical doctrine from the Catholic point of view.[49]

---

[48] *Acts,* 15:1–35.

[49] This was the reason for the condemnation of Seiller's book (on June 27, 1951), *L'activité humaine du Christ selon Duns Scotus,* Paris 1944. In the same sense the following theologians wrote: Deodatus de Basly, Antonius de Villico, J. Rivière, A. Gaudet, J. Gross; and against these ideas: Diepen, Parente, Druwé, and others. The question was discussed by Peter Lombard (III, Dist. 6), Peter Abelard (cf. Cavallera, *Thesaurus,* nº 763–764), Thomas Aquinas (*Summa Theologica* II,2,6), Tertullian (*De Carne Christi*).

On one of his earlier missionary journeys, Paul of Tarsus stood up in the synagogue of Antioch in Pisidia (in modern southwest Turkey) and declared that his doctrine was destined for both Jew and Gentile. This bold statement finally decided his expulsion from Antioch, and it stirred up some Christians from Judea to attack Paul's doctrine. A meeting was called in Jerusalem at which Paul, Barnabas, Peter, James, some other apostles and the senior members of the group were present. The account in the Acts hints at discussion and dissensions.[50] They were to be expected. The single pregnant word *zētēsis* (investigation) used by the text to describe the first part of the proceedings is replete with overtones. The hard core of resistance to any change was to be found at the centre of Judaeo-Christianity and among the senior members and elders of the young church.

It is hard for us to realize the dilemma of those early Christians. Jews all of them, observant ones, they looked on Jesus as the fulfilment of the Law, the keystone in the vast edifice of revelation begun with Abraham and concluded with Christ. Had they not been told by Him they would sit on twelve thrones judging the twelve tribes of Israel? Had not Jesus gently but firmly refused to see those Greeks who wished to talk to Him?[51]

And when the Jews wished to think of a complete disappearance, a renouncement of their *Sitz-in-Leben*, they said of Jesus: 'Where is He going to go? Is He going to go out to the Gentiles and teach them?'[52] And was not the Law of Moses part of revelation? Why, then, were Paul and Barnabas dispensing newly converted Gentiles from the main precepts of that Law, from the obligation of circumcision and the other precepts? Outside the Law and its implementation there was no salvation.[53] And a favourite and oft-quoted *logion* of Jesus ran: 'Do not think that I have come to abolish the Law or the prophets; I have not come to abolish but to fulfil. Solemnly I tell you: not one bit or scrap of the Law will become null, until heaven and earth pass away. Whoever, therefore, abolishes one of these smallest precepts and so teaches men, he shall be called the least in the Kingdom of heaven. But whoever accomplishes them and so teaches others, he will be called great in the Kingdom of heaven.'[54]

It is almost certain that Peter, had he not received special illumination from on high, would have maintained this strict line of approach.[55] Paul tells us that in this matter he resisted Peter to his face because 'he

[50] *Acts*, 15:10.   [51] *John*, 12:20–23.   [52] *John*, 7:33–36.
[53] *Acts*, 15:5.   [54] *Matt.*, 5:17–19.   [55] Cf. *Acts*, 10:9–48; 11:11–18.

was reprehensible.'[56] Peter had been covertly eating with Gentiles (against the precepts of the Jewish Law) when none of the Jerusalem Judaeo-Christians were present. Conversely, he 'kept himself away' from such things when these Christians were present because 'he feared them.' Worse than that, Barnabas and other Christians practised the same deception, following Peter's example. 'I spoke to Peter before everybody,' said Paul, 'because I saw that he was not proceeding according to evangelical truth.'

As it was, Peter had been converted by a heaven-sent vision. His speech is reported in full in Acts 15. It is clear that he tried to justify the change of tactics from a Judaic point of view. Then followed Paul and Barnabas. Like skilful debaters they allowed the facts to speak for themselves. In actual fact, the Gentiles were adhering to their Christian faith; this can only be the work of the Holy Spirit. Finally, James spoke and placed the problem in the right perspective: the problem was not whether the converted Gentiles should adopt Judaism as well, but only as to what they should eliminate from their behaviour as former pagans. He mentioned idolatry in any form as the chief factor to be excluded. Both Paul and Barnabas and James opted for universalism, for a turning out to the world outside the Judaeo-Christian enclaves of Palestine, for an updating of their methods, for a discarding of elements which hindered catholicity. Their viewpoint carried the day; the motion was passed; and a letter was written by the Apostles and seniors: 'It has seemed good to the Holy Spirit and to us . . .' The *Logos* could take wings, and it did. Westwards.

Looking back now on this first Council, one admits readily that it was an axis-point on which the future depended. A handful of Judaeo-Christians gathered in one room, rooted each one of them in a narrow parochial outlook, still clinging to elements which had nothing essential to do with the message they were supposed to bring, and condemning themselves mistakenly, if in good faith, to an attitude which could only mean the death of the entire movement, the stifling of possible catholicity, inclined to opt for conditions of thought and of work that would preclude them from expansion, would retain them in a historical ghetto, would incarnate the *Logos* in a form unacceptable to the majority of mankind.

Just as the historical Christ, while being the incarnation of God, sprang from specifically Jewish stock, and was a Jew, and had Jewish colouring in all He did and said, so the mystical Christ while springing

[56] Cf. *Gal.* 2:11.

from the divine action of Christ was, in its first incarnate form, of specifically Jewish colouring. The preaching of the Apostles and early Christians, their liturgical language, their attitude to the Scriptures, were all Jewish. The first Christians were Judaeo-Christians. The decision at Jerusalem prepared the Judaeo-Christian Church for the dispersion of the Jews after the fall of Jerusalem (A.D. 70) and the ruthless suppression of Judaism in Palestine by Hadrian (A.D. 135). Before the latter event, Christian communities had been established around the shores of the eastern Mediterranean basin.

Peter present at the first meeting with the others could not possibly foresee that twenty centuries later another group of men, claiming to be their direct descendants, numbering at least four hundred times the group of Apostles, seniors and elders around him, would gather in a larger room called after him, convoked by a man who was his successor and who bore the same name as Paul of Tarsus in whom Peter found many hard things, and to whose impassioned speech he was then listening. Above all he could not foresee the acute problem facing that larger group of men: to opt for conditions of thought and of work that would make them truly Catholic, to crawl voluntarily out of a historical and terminological ghetto to turn to the larger, ever-expanding world around them, to conform to the reality of things. Between the first Council and this latter one, had flowed not only twenty centuries: something else had happened. Something analogously identical with the development with which they were then painfully struggling. The Word of God had become incarnate in the physical being of Jesus the Nazarene, and it was His very Nazareneness, His Jewishness and all it connoted which created the problem dealt with by the first Council.

The faith of these first witnesses in its purity and without any adulteration was at issue because of their very nearness to the historical Jesus with His Jewishness. Over a period of twenty centuries the Word had become incarnate, analogously speaking, and the form of its historical incarnation was now the great hindrance. The faith of the men partaking in the twenty-first general council of the Church was being put to the test of its purity, because of their nearness to this latter-day incarnation of the Word, because the historical Jesus had receded into twenty centuries of involved history.

When St Paul described the incarnation of the Word of Jesus he used the term 'emptying out,' kenōsis. He remarked that, while being God, Christ did not hesitate to empty Himself out by taking the physical being of a real man.[57] It was the specifically Jewish nature of Jesus which had become the stumbling block for the Judaeo-Christian group. They opted finally for an emptying out of the specifically Jewish so as to fulfil the will of Him Who had set the example. Similarly, the issue facing the twenty-first council would be an issue of *kenōsis*, of emptying out. Peter required illumination from heaven to understand this. Paul was called by Christ to be an apostle for the Gentiles. But it required the courage of a Peter and a Paul to go against their own people; against their own inclinations, to oppose the elders and the seniors and even the Apostles who were not far-visioned. The man who today unites the name of Paul with the office of Peter requires also the same courage. The parallel between the two situations has been drawn even closer and in an almost bizarre way; the present Paul, the successor of Peter, finally chose in the agony of his doubt and ambivalent counsels, to go as pilgrim to Jerusalem, to seek light, to seek illumination from on high, to consult with other apostles. The illumination of Peter strengthened by the courage of Paul.

During the second and third centuries we find pockets of Christianity springing up throughout the Graeco-Roman world. Taking root there, Christianity assimilated what was assimilable in the Hellenistic civilization: it adopted a new terminology from Greek philosophy and adapted a few details from the forms of ancient mystery cults. The Graeco-Hellenistic way of thinking and the linguistic expression of this thought took possession of Christian circles. The Hellenistic dualism reposing in a perilous opposition of body and soul, the depreciation of the sensory realm, the tendency to over-speculation, were non-Judaic elements adopted as new garments for the *Logos*. And the pagan civilization Christianity had now entered was no closed system or sterile rationalism. It could boast of the primacy of contemplation in its outlook and this it passed on to the new religion. Above the reasoning faculty (or *logos*), Hellenistic thought acknowledged the existence of an intuitive and contemplative faculty (the *nous*), which was the organ of intellectual mysticism for the Platonists. The big scholars, Irenaeus, Clement of Alexandria, Origen, wrote and thought as Hellenistic citizens.

With the Edict of Milan (A.D. 313), the establishment of Christianity as the state religion (A.D. 380), and the interdiction of paganism throughout the empire (A.D. 392), Christianity emerged from the status of the pursued and persecuted. It had an organization based on a threefold

[57] *Philip*, 2:6-7.

ministry: bishop, presbyter, deacon. Loyalty to the Empire became easy. By A.D. 330, Constantine had shifted his court and capital to Constantinople in order to redirect the centrifugal forces, pagan, Christian, Eastern, Western, which were tearing apart the unity of his empire. Just over a hundred years after the change of capital, Leo, the bishop of Rome, went and stopped Attila, the Hun. Constantine's move had left a vacuum. The new force had to fill that vacuum. The Bishop of Rome now called himself by the old pagan Roman title of supreme pontiff, *pontifex maximus*. Occidentalization had set in. The course of ecclesial development and ecclesiastical organization was now set for well over fifteen hundred years.

From Roman civilization, the Christian Church acquired many things. The character of imperial Rome spelled law, meant authority, implied a sense of history and long memory based on a laborious tradition. Rome also connoted organization, juridical organization. In fact, it was this latter central characteristic which for ancient Rome had proved its greatest asset. From it flowed civic order, obedience, authority, domination.

Gradually, through the centuries, surviving the collapse of the Western and Eastern empires, the onslaught of the barbarian hordes, the establishment of new kingdoms and empires in northern and central Europe, the *ecclesia principalis* of Rome and its occupant became the magnet-point of all power, ecclesiastical and secular, in the world. Pope Gregory VII would claim a direct power over all kings and princes.

But the occidentalization was not yet complete. The Church headed by the Bishop of Rome was organizationally westernized and thoroughly dominant. Yet, conceptually and in her systematic reflection on herself, she had not adopted a definitely occidental mode of speech and thought. This was accomplished by the rise of the Schools of medieval philosophy and culminated in the consecration of Thomism as *the* system of thought in which the Church would express what she knew of revelation. Thomas Aquinas took the Aristotelian system and systematically Christianized it. His greatest problem was with the prevalent doctrines of Augustine whose influence stretched from the fourth century, until his time. The hierarchic view of the universe was fashioned. Everything from lifeless stones to archangels was conceived within a formulary that appeared clear, that possessed a cosmology in the Ptolemaic system, that corresponded most adequately to the westernized character of Church organization. The *Logos* of revelation was now imprisoned beneath the Roman dome. Even the Gothic spire flaring upwards to heaven was never anything else but a Nordic invention; it never caught on in the south and is out of place among the domed or low-roofed basilicas of imperial Rome. The *Logos* was now individualized in one type of civilization.

Officially and as the will of God, there had been established in the very vitals of Christianity a basic antinomy between universalism and individualism, between the untrammelled force of the *Logos* in its purity and the western conception of that revelation. This would imperil, would limit, would even work for the destruction of Christianity when it endeavoured to return to the Orient.

The *Logos* was now individualized in one form of civilization and its accents were of one linguistic type. The millennial process started at that first meeting in Jerusalem had come to a high water mark. It started with a gradual dejudaization of the primitive message, a process in which the prophets and the teachers of the Old Testament were transformed into pre-Christian Christians saved by their faith in Christ, into a class of non-Jewish individuals who had nothing to do with the living thing that was Judaism in the time of Jesus.

The God Who had spoken to Israel no longer spoke in the New Testament. Abraham, Isaac, Jacob, David, Isaiah, Ezra, Daniel, figures whose personalities and teachings as Jewish leaders had entered the very warp and woof of Jesus' religious mentality, were appropriated, transmuted, depicted as ultimately Christian, something analogous to their representation on the ceiling and walls of the Sistine Chapel in the Vatican, by Michelangelo. And the Jewish element, the living tradition into which the eternal Word of God entered by incarnation, was left to flow into the exterior darkness of unreligion, of ethical banality, and even today the major tendency of Catholic exegesis is towards a scientific interpretation of the New and Old Testaments in the light of ancient Near Eastern culture. Only in a minor way are both studied according to the light and mind of the Hebrews.

We must now turn to the question of Romanization for it went hand in hand with occidentalization and shares in the same dreadful defects. Here the second antinomy was established.

In the inter-testamentary period, due to foreign oppression, due also to the Hellenization of a part of Judaism, there sprang up the tradition of a great impending cataclysm. The Almighty Himself would come to exterminate His enemies, to purify the world by fire and reward His faithful ones. Eschatological thinking was linked with apocalyptic vision. The communities of Qumran and southern Judaea lived in this expectation. When Christianity fanned out over the Graeco-Roman world, it made its first impact on the ancient mind by fundamentally changing man's attitude to time. Instead of the unflagging cycles of seasons and years dominated by pagan deities, Christianity presented the overwhelming belief that time was rushing to an end, a definite, proximate end, the Kingdom was at hand, and the end of the world was near. No matter how we consider certain statements of Jesus and Paul, we receive this impression from their words. The early Christians believed them fully. The universe had been mortally wounded by the divine irruption. And Montanus could point dramatically to the plain of Pepuza (Phrygia) as the exact spot on which the Kingdom would descend from heaven and usher in the end of all things. Christians had been liberated from the coming threat of death. But they must live in the world as if they were not in it. The two great waves of persecution under Septimius Severus, Caracalla and Alexander Severus (202–257), and under Diocletian (303–304), were taken merely as signs of the coming disaster and promise of heavenly release.

The rather abrupt ending of the persecution, the advent of the Christian Emperors, the sudden achievement of social and national respectability, brought about a refinement of the first belief. The universe now was entirely Christian. It was weary and sick at heart, harbouring in its very nature the seeds of its own annihilation. A fission was introduced in the Christian ethos. On the one hand, Christians took their place in public life. The organization of the Church, for so long existing in quasi-underground circumstances, now acquired a public decorum and respect, and came to be recognized as the only valid spokesman for government and civic order. The roads of imperial Rome were pounded by missionary feet, the Church had moved from persecution to affluence, from poverty to riches, from oppression to power, from catacomb to throne. On the other hand, the ideas about the corruptibility and imminent cataclysmic end of the world remained.

The Christian reaction to this clash of the worldly and other-worldly was released in two currents; by flights from the world to the desert or by a pragmatic attitude of taking over the reins of government, of assuming a providentially ordered place at the centres of power. Monasticism covered the entire face of Egypt from Alexandria to Isna. The Church accepted collaboration with the civic authority and in time assumed that authority. The fission and the antinomy we have spoken about are present here in their beginnings. On the one hand the 'flight' mentality gave rise to the intense interest in virginity, in ascetism, in the martyr-saint, in the value of suffering, in the sanctity of filth. On the other hand, the official Church bowed to history, assumed the role thrust upon it by events. But it did this by effecting a deep change in its conception of itself. To the primordial idea of an other-worldly group of men travelling to a fast-approaching heaven on earth, there was now joined the pragmatic decision to assume a worldly stance, to become a permanent part of the world. The two elements remain in deep antinomy at the heart of the Roman Catholic concept of itself as a juridical body.

We can only appreciate the poignancy and puzzling contradiction of this antinomy in Catholicism if we remember that the Christian message in its essence announces *events*. God has interfered in human history by historical actions, the birth, the death, the resurrection of His Son. The God of Christians like the God of the Hebrews is a God of history. On to the plane of history has come the mystery of God's plan for humanity. Between these two poles, human history and divine mystery, lies the aching problem of Catholicism. For the moment, Catholicism has ringed this polarity by adopting one historical stance, by assimilating itself to one phase of historical culture and civilization. Today, historical events are stripping her of the most objectionable accretions of history. Yet, deep within her being lies the source of all her troubles and the cause of the explosive choice now confronting her.

Until 1870, the Pope considered himself as a temporal ruler by divine right. Before the Reformation, there were even moments when the Bishops of Rome claimed to have temporal jurisdiction over all mankind – kings, rulers and peoples. Allied to this was his title as Vicar of Christ, Successor of Peter, Patriarch of the West. As the latter, his eyes were fixed on heaven away from the world. The age-old attempt to harmonize these two can only produce a sharp antinomy which could issue in tragedy: the oppression carried out in the name of papal power, the strange alliance of Peter's power with intellectual, national and cultural stifling, for example the latter-day ruthlessness with which the Roman dicasteries violate the fundamental precepts of justice and charity – for the glory of God. Even the notions of primacy and infallibility, as they have been interpreted after the First Vatican Council, have not escaped contamination.

This antinomy lies at the heart of Roman Catholicism. It caused Julius II to gird himself for battle over temporal issues while Martin Luther in Germany was hammering out his theses. It gave rise to the

Cardinal Consalvi methods of Vatican diplomacy: to spread a network of Concordats all over the world and to assume the trappings of an accredited government. It has given birth to the conservative and, up to the present moment, the official Catholic view that a government, to be a really good government, must be Catholic and that the confessional state is the order willed by God. It gave rise to the strange contradiction between a papal document like the encyclical letter *Quantum Cura*[58] and the encyclical letter *Pacem in Terris*[59] in which the relations of Church and State are discussed. It is the fundamental reason why the Church never condemned slavery in its heyday, and why it shrinks from any public, official condemnation of racialist excesses against the Negroes in America or in South Africa. Above all, it installed in Rome, by slow process, a powerful Byzantine bureaucracy, the much-criticized Roman Curia, which would claim to speak for the Pope, would aid in the centralization of all Catholic forces for the glory of God, and exercise some of the forms of human suppression which all condemned in the recent Nazi and Fascist regimes, accompanied by condemnations without trial, the silencing of the condemned, the anonymity of witnesses, the suppression of news, a rigid censorship of books according to hoary norms, to mention but a few of the defects. And yet the Church must and does ceaselessly claim to be 'holy,' must claim to belong to another world, to be on the way to eternity. The active presence of these two basic antinomies in Christianity rendered the Church ill-adapted for suffering the two searing experiences of the East-West Schism and the Reformation. By the ninth century, Rome had absorbed the old system of local jurisdiction within the framework of a patriarchal outlook: in France, in Spain, in Germany, in England, Romanization of the liturgy had taken place. Roman laws and customs were introduced. Even after the Schism, Rome continued to extend its jurisdiction: it set up the Latin patriarchate of Constantinople after 1204 in the wake of the conquering Crusader armies; it did the same in Jerusalem earlier. The attitude of Rome and the Papacy could not but result in a complete rupture between Western Christianity and its Eastern counterpart. Orthodoxy, as a separate Christian body, was born.

Luther was excommunicated in 1520. The Council of Trent began in 1545 and ended in 1563. The total reaction of the Church in Rome was to reject the protest of the Reformers. It is true that on the grounds

[58] Issued by Pope Pius IX on the 8th of December, 1864.
[59] By John XXIII.

of moral house-cleaning, the Council of Trent must be accepted as having effected a great change. It was with regard to the substance and meaning of the Christian message that the Church failed to grasp the deep issues at stake. This seems to have been due to the two antinomies we mentioned earlier. The fossilized philosophical terminology and decadent Thomism of the day rendered churchmen incapable of understanding the purport of Luther and of Calvin as witnesses to the voice of Scripture and the Fathers. The jurisdictional pretensions and overbearing hegemony of the Bishop of Rome, his entanglement in European politics, his claim to temporal power, sprang from the Romanization of the message of Christ, and made it impossible for Rome to carry on the dialogue with the objectors.

The freezing of mutual positions following Trent was a pitiful consequence. We must, for instance, always speak of post-Tridentine Catholicism, because Trent implies a demarcation-line of absolutely definite proportions. Out of it came what is called today the modern Catholic mind. From the same time also date the myriad Christian sects that now pose the problem of Christian unity. During three centuries after Trent, the Roman Church fought a battle against the two main forces at its throat, the Germanic and the Gallic influence. The tradition-bound juridical minded Roman spirit could not abide the Germanic tendency to subjectivism, the restlessness which resists any congealing or incrustation of traditional elements, its creative power, its stimulating energy, its instinctive penetration to the essence and refusal to accept the merely accidental, finally its tendency to change and adapt. A clash between Romanism and Germanism was inevitable.

The clash with the Gallican spirit was also inevitable. The latter is characterized by an irrepressible, effervescent intellectual ferment, a dynamism toward analysis and synthesis, a marked preference for rational processes. In itself a precious gift, a refusal of rigid formulas, it is for ever relating concept to experience and modifying the former in the light of the latter. It clashes by its very nature with the frozen, occidentalized mentality of official Rome. It has spawned changes in biblical research, in liturgical and patristic studies, in political and sociological theories, that have at one time or another attracted the authoritarian attention of Rome.

Out of these struggles Roman Catholicism has emerged still whole and still extending its influence in the twentieth century. But her dress and appearance bespeak the long journey she has gone through.

She has many wrinkles on her countenance, and her dress seems old-fashioned. She seems to rely on the values of a bygone age, to be attached to a narrow point of view, to advocate a formalistic, abstract, intolerant way of thinking, and suffers at the same time from pretensions.

Her concept of herself seems to be composed of distinctions and definitions and syllogisms. Her method of thought seems to be wrapped up in the dry trappings of medieval scholasticism. Her path to God seems to be paved with canonical precepts and laws, bounded by the unbending parapets of dogmatic declarations. The validity of sacramental communion seems to be more important than the Presence. Ecclesiastical dignity is more significant than priestly office and function. And, withal, she carries on her shoulders several burdens which mar her stature and hinder her free movement: doctrinal positions hardened to absolutism unnecessarily, pools of anticlericalism among people who can only remember the once all-powerful clerical domination of their social, political, and intellectual life, one-sided outlooks on basic matters, the dominance of power-centres in the government of the Church.

As we leave these brief reflections on the Roman Catholic Church, we may ask ourselves what purpose there can be in calling an Ecumenical Council of Catholicism? Can an Ecumenical Council provide any answer to the problems facing humanity? The question has a certain urgency. Many of those who did not participate in the sessions of the Council and who read about them in newspapers were either aghast or were confirmed in their ideas about the irrelevancy of the Roman Catholic Church. Here were over 2,000 men, leaders of Catholicism, who came to Rome to discuss such seemingly pointless things as two sources of revelations and the prayer-book used by Catholic priests, who spent much energy, passion, ink, on what the Church has to say about television or about matters called sacramentals. They acted as if the problem was how to better the Church, how to preserve her intact. The problem, many think, is how to preserve man himself.

It is not that man is threatened because the Church is not getting across to man, but that man is threatened by an inner liquidation of his moral being, while outside the mushrooming clouds of nuclear dust or population explosion loom on the horizon. Why bother about the way in which we know that God was *incarnated* when the real problem is how to prevent God from being further *eliminated* from human considerations?

The irrelevancy of the problems which Catholicism considers

fundamental and over which it has consumed itself in two long, expensive sessions is a direct offshoot of the Church's attitude to humanity. This is an age of climactic choices: universal extinction or universal peace, prosperity or poverty, freedom or slavery due to intolerance, to ignorance, to conformity. The questions before the world reduce themselves, one by one, to that of human relations: the Negro in America, the Buddhist in South Vietnam, the peasant in Brazil, the Bantu in South Africa, the Protestants in Spain, the Jews in the Soviet Union, the Catholics in satellite countries. On this very question of human relations, the Council directorate has so far refused to say anything.

The difficulty is that we are no longer in the age of Trent or even in the eighteenth century. This is the twentieth century: the momentum today is arrow-swift, the inner dynamism of human development is pushing beyond all recognizable frontiers. As it now is, the Roman Catholic Church does not speak the language of the people. Such contact as it has is through its works. And whether it is the St Peter in Chains Noodle Plant in Hong Kong, or the Buluba Leprosarium in Uganda, the Franciscan Sisters' Assunta Hospital in Malaya, or the worker-priests in France's steel factories, the Church is really only intelligible to modern man when it engages in work that speaks the language of modern man and is proof of Catholicism's adherence to the law of love.

In other words, what has the Church to say to the actual world in which it lives? To its problems and its anguish? While this Ecumenical Council is swimming in theological problems, the world's problems are in a pre-theological state, and the language used by the conciliar mentality is unintelligible, because irrelevant, to the mind and language of modern man. There is detectable here a certain escapism in Catholicism and its leaders. At this moment, for instance, the whole stress of conciliar activity is on ecumenism, and specifically on ecumenical relations with Orthodoxy and Anglicanism. Supposing that tomorrow or next year, by a miracle of Christian love and forbearance, a reunion was effected and that the Bishop of Rome obtained the spiritual precedence and primacy of jurisdiction over the Patriarchs of Constantinople and Moscow, over the Archbishop of Canterbury, and over all others. What would have been effected – the salvation of the world? The betterment of the Church?

The problem would only have begun. For Orthodoxy and Anglicanism are as far removed from the reality of life and as hampered by historical accretions as the Roman Catholic Church. Both are frozen in the ghetto of 'traditional religious blocs.' Outside them there is developing that unity of nations of which John XXIII spoke, the drawing together of men based on principles of material welfare and scientific progress. Catholics, but only as individuals, exercise some influence on these events. Catholicism has little voice in the councils of the great, of those who decide on the unity of Europe, on rapprochement with the Soviet Empire, on the admission of China to the family of nations, on the hemispheric problems that afflict the United States. It has no voice because it has no solution to the problems. It is beset from within by tensions of its own making and hardened from without by attitudes it has adopted gratuitously.

This, then, is the Pyramid, its sharp apex, its upper cornerstones, the primitive solidity of its walls, the ruptured symmetry of its pointed frame, the weakening base. There also is the Plain on which it is based. No man would dare claim that the structure has anything to do with Christ's revelation. And time, the great witherer, is beating against its walls and playing on its inherent weaknesses. Yet the spirit is again stirring at the choices that lie before it, for the Ecumenical Council as such is the theatre of a great choice.

TWO

THE JOANNINE ERA

Future historians, in trying to assess the significance of the Joannine period for the Catholic Church and the world, may well be tempted to point to the 11th of October, 1962, the day that John inaugurated the Second Vatican Council. And this, not so much because the panoply of the occasion has burnt itself into the imagination of all, or because it is true to say that no other human organization in existence today could have been able to stage the scene, to assemble such a galaxy of human players, such a *décor* or setting for the actions and the words of one man and one man only. It is rather because never before has any one Roman Pope so gracefully and skilfully wielded the splendour of Vatican ceremonial and the primitive strength of his hoary lineage and tried to make the Roman Catholic Church relevant to the world in which it lives. That John did. He offered his guests no mere phrases of traditional greeting, but he skilfully outlined a programme of world interest to representatives of the world. This gives the lie to a recently projected image of him as the rough, peasant personage stumbling into the Papacy without any deep intellectual insight or understanding.

We must distinguish carefully between the 'scholastic' mind, the humanly trained faculties which close like traps on mental propositions and doctrinal formularies, and that intellectual quality of perception and understanding which can never be small, that eats through the outer rind in flaring intuition and judges the essence of men, situations, things. Humanly, the former impresses us because it encircles, compels respect. Humanly, the latter succeeds because it absorbs, attracts, warms, creates. This is what lies at the roots of the mystery of John and his achievement.

Cardinal Wyszynski, Primate of Poland, expressed this most aptly[1] when he wrote of John: 'He was endowed with an extraordinary sensitivity for human life ... and contemplated it with the eye of a historian, assembling each single phenomenon, impression and event, into a spacious, general synthesis ... He had a truly Christian mode of thought pervaded with a grace crowning the natural order ... He not only thought in this way; he *acted* thus. And from him there flowed a goodness and a wisdom.' The Polish prelate had had many difficult

[1] *L'Osservatore Romano*, November 17, 1963, p. 1.

things to discuss with John. Apparently he was impressed by three qualities in him: his understanding, his wisdom and his goodness.

John stated quietly that 'divine Providence is leading us to a new order in human relations.' He was not merely talking about Church matters. He had already mentioned 'the new political world' in his radio message of September 14. And, he continued, 'The salient point of this Council is . . . a step forward towards a deeper penetration and developing realization of the Faith which should be studied and expounded through modern research and modern scholarly disciplines . . . For the substance of the ancient doctrine is one thing. The way in which it is presented is another.'

The delicate juxtaposition of these two elements: the substance of the ancient doctrine and the new order in human relations, this was the Joannine contribution to his world. He had fixed his sight on two co-ordinates: one, that of contemporary human development, was a line streaking ahead with high velocity pushed by explosive elements, population expansion, material welfare, general education, international communications, international blocs, world tension; another, that of Christian and, particularly, Catholic evolution, was arrested in its flight, tangential in tendency, inclined to turn back on itself. One was heading for something that lay beyond and above mere internationalism such as the United Nations Organization represented, something supranational, a political version of the common mind already born and developing among the nations. It implied a new order in human relations, a lack of servant and master, a lack of historical or political monopolies, a pentecostal seizure of the human spirit by the communal instinct of the species. The other was in no way tending to meet this first co-ordinate. Rather it tended to self-defence, to outmoded methods and mentalities. John insisted that the two co-ordinates should meet at a point, criss-cross, and intermingle. For this, *aggiornamento*, updating, was essential.

To understand the Joannine period, therefore, we must know what the aims were of the Council, what the achievements were of the Council, and how all this dovetailed with his general government of the Church.

The Council was not an end but a means to an end in John's eyes. Ecumenism, was not an end but a means to an end. Reunion with the dissident Oriental Churches, with the Churches of the Reformation, was not an end. All were means. His final aim was to make the Church relevant to the world around it. A primary step, of course, was the reuniting of the various segments of Christianity; the scandal of Christians hating each other was a primary obstacle. Obstructing his way to his proximate goal were several things. In the world: indifference to Catholicity as to something irrelevant, and inner tensions between world blocs and the Church. In the universal Catholic Church: an ever-growing gap between official presentation and practice of the revealed truth and the developing mentality of the people. In the bureaucratic and administrative centres of the Church: an ingrained myopia for the real conditions of human life, a topsy-turvy subservience of the Church to ecclesiastical managers.

His approach to this triple problem was not analytic; he did not take it in easy stages or artificially separate each aspect of the problem. He chose one way of educating the bishops – the Council in Rome. And while the pedagogy of conciliar activity was having effect, he himself was stretching out feelers to Eastern Europe, to the lands of the Soviet Empire. At home, he was gently detaching the Church from involvement in Italian politics. In Western Europe he was co-ordinating his attitude with that of a group of 'Europeans' who refused to build another world bloc in addition to the two already existing: a unified Europe need not imply economic and military ties to either of the two existing blocs. It was the basic reason for the Gaullist refusal of England's entry into the Common Market. And it was this attitude that made the alliance between John and the German hierarchy ultimately frail. Ecumenically and doctrinally the Germans supported John; geopolitically and sociologically his policies went against their outlook. Over all his activities hung the concern for human relations: the starting-point for any discussion was the individual human being who by the very fact of his nature had certain inalienable rights which no law, human or divine, could overrule.

The preparatory period of the Council stretched from the day of its announcement (January 29, 1959) to the day of its inauguration, October 11, 1962. A vast machinery was set up for the coming event: preparatory commissions, offices, secretariats. As was to be expected, John had to work with the officialdom of the Vatican. So frustrating was this period, and so deliberately one-sided were the preparations that Mazzini, the editor of *L'Osservatore Romano*, could write a short article in September 1962 entitled 'The Trust of the Pope'; this was an inspired article and said quite plainly: let no one be dismayed but imitate the trust of John XXIII that all will go well *once* the Council starts.

There were a few consoling elements. John had appointed Cardinal Bea, a German Jesuit, as head of a new unheard-of thing, the *Secretariat for Promoting Christian Unity*. Its purpose was to prepare the ground for, firstly, the participation of observers from other Christian communions, and, secondly, to develop the principles of ecumenism in the Roman Catholic Church. To it he also confided the task of preparing a statement concerning the age-old injustice against the Jews. But a mere statement would not suffice; Bea set out to educate public opinion by writing, lecturing, personal contacts. So independent was this Secretariat of Bea's that on the eve of the Council, it was a common observation in Rome that the only conciliar group that had not suffered from Curial interference and dictation was Bea's group. Bea was to pay dearly for this achievement. Even though he would stand closer to John than any other Curial cardinal, even though by the force of his personality he would, in the space of two years, become a world figure, and even though he could with impunity attack an age-old thesis of Romanism (disputing the right of non-Catholics to their religion), he would finally come to grief and be broken at the summit of his achievement and because of his achievement.

John had not miscalculated when he counted on the collegial sense of the bishops. They refused to accept the nominees of the central bureaucracy at Rome for the conciliar commissions. They insisted on changes in the liturgical practices of the Church. They eschewed the Tridentine mentality when faced with the basic question: how do we know what Christ taught? They hailed the presence of non-Catholic observers at the Council. They openly supported John's proposal to liberate Jews from an age-old, untrue accusation. They applauded a fresh announcement of the principle of universal religious liberty. And yet, when all is said and done, the main achievement of the first session was a pedagogic one: a man who was bishop by divine right learned that he could contradict a man who was cardinal by human ordinance: non-Italian bishops learned that they agreed in rejecting the Italianate mentality prevalent in Roman offices. They found, in other words, that they were all members of a college, that they were endowed with a group quality called collegiality. And this was the chief concrete achievement of the first session.

On the negative side, things looked black enough. The obvious spirit of independence manifested by the bishops had alarmed the centralist government of the Roman Church, alarmed it on two chief scores: doctrinally, a majority of the bishops seemed bent on destroying the traditional position of authority enjoyed by the Roman Curia and disturbing theological tenets that had been canonized by Curial custom as quasi-articles of faith; politically, the internal Italian policy of John had frightened the Right-wing segments of the country. John's easy relations with Italian Socialists and Left-wing elements was taken as a tacit blessing of political *sinistrismo;* his reception of Adjubei, Khrushchev's son-in-law, and his winning of the Balzan Prize (with Khrushchev's express approbation), the cordial exchange of birthday greetings between the two men, were events which bordered on madness in the eyes of both Right-wing cardinal and politician.

Furthermore, his desire to produce a conciliar document stating that the Jews were neither deicides nor accursed had been unacceptable to Nasserism and Arab nationalism. Doctrinally, the theses in the document were hard enough to swallow for the Roman mentality. Politically, it spelt trouble: Italy, in the wake of its post-war 'economic miracle,' depended on the development of markets in the Maghreb and in the Near East. Italian foreign policy and investments were at stake. The Arab powers in question were not slow to point this out. And there was more than mere political affiliations between the Roman Curia and Italian Right-wing elements at stake; there was also the question of Vatican investments. So well organized was the opposition to this document, so well orchestrated the voices from the Secretariat of State, Vatican City, and obedient Apostolic Delegates in the Near East, that Bea was forced to withdraw the document from the first session and bide his time.

But the whole session ended on a positive note. Even a silent, watchful eye like that of Cardinal Montini of Milan, saw that it was necessary to speak clearly on the side of the majority and for conciliar progress. The spring of 1963 ended with the publication of *Pacem in Terris.* Conciliar Commissions had been reduced and tightened in organization. Some Curial members kept on reminding themselves that John was being eaten alive by an inexorable disease and referred to it as 'the hand of God.' The opposing elements (mainly non-Italians) saw only rosy skies: the second session would be a final victory for Christian love, for *giovannismo.*

When John closed the Council in December, 1962, he was already dying: he had barely six months to live. In one sense, he had achieved nothing, but in another sense, he had achieved everything. And to assess his achievement, it is not sufficient to restrict our examination to the

Council and the conciliar context.

First of all, a brief review of the intersessional period (from December 1962) to the death of John in the early days of June 1963. In spite of the clear crystallization of a conciliar voice during the first session, Montini was obliged to stand up on December 5, 1962, and tell the Council precisely why it was bogging down: it had been presented with a mass of excellent material; but this was too much, too varied in nature; the Council was drowning in paper, and must therefore choose a central theme which would serve as a norm to prune this material drastically but prudently. He was preceded by Cardinal Suenens of Belgium, who stated, quite frankly, that the Council must reveal the Church to the world, and it must face the problems which tortured humanity: racial hatred, war and peace, population explosion. On December 6, John published his six norms to guide the work during the intersessional period. The Council still had the same purpose as he had proposed in his opening address. New and shorter drafts were to be drawn up. A new commission under Cardinal Cicognani was to oversee and co-ordinate this work.

This work did go forward during the intersessional period. We can leave it to future historians and more detailed studies to point out exactly how the central purpose of John was frustrated on many points, how it progressed in many others. And we must concentrate on the main events of that period in order to aid us to a more accurate understanding of the condition of things when John died. In passing, one can note that the main interest of European churchmen concentrated on the new documents to be drawn up concerning the nature of the Church and the functions, rights and duties of the bishops of the Church. American Churchmen either did not show much active interest in the work or they concentrated on the ideas of religious liberty and the reform of the Liturgy.

The two most important events within the context of *giovanismo* were: the political evolution in Italy, and the success of Cardinal Bea in propagating the basic ideas underlying religious liberty and his proposed document on the Jews. For these two elements were of prime importance in conditioning the mind of both conservatives and progressives with regard to the second session and the successor of John XXIII.

First of all, the Italian elections. These took place on April 28, 1963. The actual Communist vote at that time attained 25.3 per cent of the total electorate. This was another gain in the rising parabola of Communist electorate fortunes: 19 per cent in 1946, 22.6 per cent in 1953, 22.7 per cent in 1958. In the 'communal' elections, the Communist vote had increased from 22.7 per cent in 1957 to 24 per cent in 1963. One must set down beside this the fact that the number of Communist militants had diminished by about 12 per cent by 1963; but this is a common phenomenon where Communist electoral gains are manifest.

Before the elections, the conservative and ecclesiastical authorities in Italy took great pains to warn against voting Communist. The Italian bishops at their regular conference stated that Catholics were obliged to vote with party unity in mind. This was a clear order to the faithful to vote for the Demochristian ticket. And *L'Osservatore Romano*, praising this 'masterful statement,' reminded the people that they must obey the precept under pain of sin. The Secretary of the Holy Office, Cardinal Ottaviani, took pains to reiterate bluntly that the excommunication threat for all those who vote for Communists is still in force: 'Those who profess, defend or propagate the materialist and anti-Christian doctrine of Communism' are punished by an immediate sanction that operates without further ado: they are excommunicated. Ottaviani also went out of his way to speak disparagingly of those who shake hands with the reddened hands of Communists and warned that the doctrine of the Church had not, and could not, change. The organization of Italian Catholic Action which stretches its tentacles into every town and village and parish, used pulpit and piazza to inculcate the same general message. Yet, on April 28, the Communist vote had definitely and dangerously increased. It was all to no purpose.

Apart from his management of the Council, no other one fact of John's pontificate incurred so much displeasure from the conservative circles of Italy as the result of the elections in April. John was blamed, of course, for the results. His reception of Adjubei, Khrushchev's son-in-law, his endeavour to obtain some abatement of tension with the governments of the satellite countries, his refusal to exercise any papal pressure on the electorate, his tacit blessing on the former Centre-Left government, these were things that rendered his name and policy positively odious to certain quarters. And when Ottaviani referred to those who shake hands with hands stained by blood, what could he have been referring to? There is a certain political myopia inherent in this. Even the official analysts of the Demochristian party conceded that the results of the April elections were prefigured in the 1960 elections, and that the Communist victory cannot, seriously, be attributed to the political and social conditions of Italy in the year preceding the election of April.

For John, however, the decrease in the Demochristian returns and the swing to the Left were but signs of the breaking-up of traditional patterns. And he saw this breaking-up as a necessary prelude to any healthy political development on the Italian political scene. Let it be said once and for all, here, that this political attitude of John was not dictated merely by a blind, a-conceptual *mystique* in virtue of which the Pontiff was willing to let things 'slide,' as it were. There are those who represent Roncalli as the Eyeless One in Gaza endeavouring to shake the twin columns of ecclesiastical control and political charlatanism – and perishing in the attempt. This is again the wishful projection of John as the bumbling, intuitive peasant-Pope to which we referred previously. It does not do honour to his intelligence, and it does not correspond to the truth.

This action of Roncalli must be seen within his realization that Italy was definitely committed to the West and, particularly, to the new Europe that was taking shape in his day as in ours. He realized that the Communist threat in Italy was bi-frontal: the short-range and long-range threat. In the short-range view of things, Communism could only hope to attain 50 per cent of the electorate (necessary for a place in government) through penetration and complicity with other parties of the Left. In the long-range view, the Communists would always suffer from problems of party-member recruitment while exercising a continually rising pressure politically, because of the divorce between the reality of the country's condition (poverty, chasmic differences between the 'haves' and the 'have-nots,' concentration of economic and commercial power in the hands of large combines) and the political institutions which govern the country. And this cameo of Italian political activity had to be seen within the larger framework of European unity: its ultimate political 'face' would not be 'Catholic' in the traditional sense, would be 'Socialist' with a Socialism that smacked of nothing anti-clerical or anti-religious, but which would take up stances as regards religion and the Church identical with the ones towards which America was now tending.

Papa Roncalli could not see why the Church should remain tied to a form of government and political outlook which could not possibly last out the next twenty years. This would leave it again with a historical accretion that would characterize it once more as provincial and particularized.

If we mention the success and the policy of Bea here as the second factor worthy of mention, it is not merely because this man has been identified with the establishment of a new organ of the Holy See, his Secretariat *for Promoting Christian Unity*. For some time, Bea's name has stood for a spirit and a way of thought, has seemed to be a miracle of human ingenuity and Christian grace. His achievements should be considered under three headings: ecumenism, religious liberty, the Jews. On these three counts, Bea has effected one of the most profound changes in Catholic thought. That his adversaries only too late understood the far-reaching consequences of his activity merely underscores the method which Bea uses: complete serenity, complete tranquillity, complete confidence in himself and God, and a masterful capacity to present change as organically associated with preceding ways of acting and thought.

Basic to Bea's thinking on the three headings mentioned above was his principle: every man has a right to live according to his own conscience, and secondly this right must be recognized in the concrete order, in the ordering of the institutions in which man lives and moves as a social, political and cultural being. He first outlined this in his talk to an international meeting in January 1963. On that occasion, after Christians (Catholics and Protestants) and non-Christians had spoken, he used the formula which both Papa Roncalli and Papa Montini have taken from him: *truth in charity*, or the *truth in love*. Briefly, this means: truth is one, but men seek it in different ways depending on their background, education and environment; the only reasonable way for any modern man to act when faced with this pluralism of ethical and moral thinking is to seek to know the truth held by the other person, but with love and respect and openness.

His January talk (called his *agape* talk, January 13, 1963) made a deep impression. And Bea followed it up by attending another conference of the same kind in New York in the spring (April 1, 1963). Here again, he announced the same principle.

The period between this New York talk and September 1963 marks the high-point of Bea's achievement. He was allowed by papal authority to propose the ground-principles of ecumenism, of religious Liberty, and of his statement on anti-Semitism. He conducted a lecture-tour of the United States which put his name, and therefore his doctrine, in the forefront of everyone's mind, Catholics and non-Catholics, bishops and priests. He was the authentic voice of *giovannismo*. He displaced Cicognani as the central cardinalitial figure before the eyes of the American public. And he was an assurance to all that the Church meant business.

Bea suffered from one almost congenital defect, and his work suffered consequently. It was his policy of strategic silence until the right moment in the right circumstances had arrived before he consented to act. And there is no doubt about it that, *if* at that time he had capitalized on the popularity which he had gained, *if* he had vociferously and ruthlessly utilized the forces put at his disposal, he would not have ended up at the end of the second session with complete defeat as his lot. In this he was badly served by some of his immediate aides, who have no idea that public opinion can be managed in curial fashion or that swift action is at times called for. Thus, the policy throughout this period was one of 'keeping quiet,' not saying anything that could irritate, no organizing or lobbying or assembling a consensus of opinion. No one was to write or speak on the subjects involved, or if they did, it was to be in such a way that the 'others' would not take umbrage.

The fallacy behind this is as old as Rienzi, the last of the Roman Tribunes. In view of the large field of human activity over which Bea extended his efforts, there was need for a certain ruthlessness, a definite type of victory consciousness, which was absolutely necessary for success. One can gain some idea of the huge potential at Bea's disposal by reflecting that, at any given moment, Bea would have had only to telephone or write to a gamut of personalities in the political, social, and religious fields, personalities of every known colouring, to obtain a favourable reception for anything he proposed. It is true that Bea was finally restrained by the policy and the command of Montini as Pope. Yet, this does not excuse the 'political' error into which he fell together with his advisers.

If the majority of the cardinals entering the conclave in June 1963 were for a 'progressive' and 'conciliar' candidate, and if the movement of progressive bishops was so strong in the Council at the beginning of the second session, it is certainly and solely to be laid at the door of this frail man of 83, to the force of his personality, to the genius of his central ideas. And now, in the autumn of his life, he has still to achieve in the concrete order the chief purposes for which he has struggled so skilfully for over three years. Not without reason was he addressed as *pater ecumenicus* at the New York meeting, not without reason was he the repository of Jewish hopes as expressed to him through official channels of Jewish organizations. He had and still has at his command an overwhelming potential. He has not used it skilfully. He has allowed a large part of it to be dissipated. The life of his Secretariat hangs in the balance.

We, of course, have to acknowledge the ancient forces of dislike, opposition and resistance which opposed and still oppose Bea. We must never underestimate the unscrupulous methods employed against him. And we must heartily congratulate him and admire the pragmatic way in which he analyzed the most complex ecclesiastical problems down to their human content. Bea, for instance, was one of the prime protagonists in the struggle to get the Council to achieve a conscious-ness and adopt a formulation of the principle of collegiality. Collegi-ality means that the government of the universal Church belongs to *both* pope and bishops: Peter *with* the eleven -- not merely to the pope 'served' by the bishops.

Collegiality by itself is a Church question. And the sources of Christian revelation or cultic methods of worship are Church matters; they do not bring world peace nor do they solve the problems of birth-control, nuclear disarmament, or human hunger. But Bea knew that the official Church would never turn to consider the world it lived in until it broke from the trammels of centralist control, and until it ceased to consider itself as a juridical body – until, that is to say, it ceased to practise narcissus-like contemplation, and looked out to the world, and healed the divisions with Protestants, Orthodox, Jews, and Muslims, with men of goodwill everywhere. For how could a juridical structure dispense love? And how could a house divided and riven by inner tensions smile at the world? And this was also the view of Papa Roncalli. This was the meeting-place of minds between the two.

We must admire also, but cannot approve, the accuracy of judge-ment manifested by the conservative forces: Bea must go. Bea was not merely a symbol; he was a dynamo of ideas, he was the centre of the movement which John blessed. And part of Papa Montini's huge tactical error in the running of the second session was to sacrifice Bea, his lore, his wisdom, his potential. We must proceed in the next chap-ter to consider how Montini did this, and why. For in the ultimate analysis, it is Papa Montini who must bear the responsibility for the course of events.

The proper context for any adequate judgement of John includes the world and the Council. Conciliarly, John had aroused the group in-stinct of the bishops. The majority were convinced that the Church would have to revise its attitude towards age-old tensions, the tension with the Protestant Churches, the tension with Orthodoxy, the tension with the Jews and Judaism, the tension with other religions and with modern man, religiously and civically considered.

He had, in addition, brought this new proposed 'look' of the Roman Church before the world. He had created good feeling and warmth both in Moscow and in the UN Headquarters in New York. For once, in Italy, the Pope was blessed by all the segments of the Centre and the Centre-Left, and correspondingly feared and disliked by those of the Right. His *Pacem in Terris* encyclical of spring 1963 took the world by surprise: it was the first time that a pope had spoken a modern language, called nuclear disarmament by its name, analyzed the internationalism of our day in lucid terms, called off the war with secularists, with Communists, with non-Christians, while maintaining Catholic truth as against the teachings of secularists, Communists, non-Christians, and the very first time that a pope had asserted the right of any man to hold his own religious convictions in harmony with his own conscience, no matter what the Catholic Church taught.

This is what Stefan Wyszynski meant when he spoke about the 'mystery of *Pacem in Terris* and of John XXIII.' It is difficult to express it in a few words. For we have assisted at an orbital flight of Catholic and Christian fortunes in this world of ours, an apogee period which will not soon take place again. It happens perhaps once in many centuries. The conversion of Constantine represented such a one – in cameo and in microcosm. But the differences between the two conjunctures are total. The Joannine period began with the inauguration of the Council on October 11, 1962; its end was marked by, but not directly connected with, the unheralded death of another man called John, the President of the United States of America, in November 1963.

Both men came from political worlds literally thousands of miles apart, and from social and cultural backgrounds as distinct and different as Sotto il Monte in northern Italy and the American-Irish wards of Boston. But the old man of 82 and the young man of 47, both at the head of the two major forces in the modern world, arose before the eyes of contemporaries, as twin flashes of a new constellation, in terms of human hope, in the skies of the twentieth century. Men looked up and gazed.

The conjuncture of which I here speak was not so much that Kennedy was the symbol of youth, of freshness, of forward gaze, and John the symbol of age-old wisdom leavened by love. Kennedy did incarnate an American dream, John pictured forth the gentleness and personality of all mankind's father, of patience unending, of deep wisdom, of availing love. And the physique of both men mirrored these images.

The slightly askew stance of Kennedy, his arms slightly curved, the youthful hair, always masking the height of his forehead, steep, square, unfurrowed; the full, not big, not small, satisfyingly alive eyes, with hooded upper lids, watchful, calculating, appraising, under definitive but almost delicate eyebrows; the chiselled smoothness of his cheeks; the long nose ever so slightly turned up in an Irish caprice; the full lips, the even teeth, the rounded chin; the pleasing amalgam between the lines of temple, ears, neck, running imperceptibly, each one of them, into an oval complex, at once complete, symmetrical, attractive, masculine, healthy, also provocative, mystifying, due in part to the quick succession of heartiness, craftiness, humour, horse-dealing, age, youth, foreboding, triumph, challenge, stubbornness, openness, things that were seen passing across his face as summer clouds drift over the fields; the clipped words, the trim, well-cared for, elegant, simply-clad figure; the whole an image, both naturally and by his own careful schooling in public relations, an image of an American wish, a walking expression of an American dream, of what is good, of what is desirable, of what is to be striven for.

John XXIII spoke with his voice, with his hands, with his eyes, and his whole physical presence radiated at once harmlessness and over-whelming force, at once the genuineness of love and the terrifying insistence of love. His solid four-square stance and ponderous move-ments were unshakeably receptive of all and receptively concerned with each individual. But it was not this complement of youth and old age, of morning freshness and years-old maturity, which generated a special epoch. It was based on these elements, but the cause lay deeper.

Both men acted as a swift catalytic on their surroundings and the context of men's minds. On the one hand, Kennedy by his very election and his careful behaviour dispelled for once and all the ancient fears that Catholicism was incompatible with the genuine American spirit. His attainment of high office immediately endowed the religion in which he was raised with the crown of acceptability, of respectability. No one could doubt his adherence to the American Constitution, yet no one could be blind to the fact that he went to Mass. More than that, during his short term of office, component elements in the America of today came into a state of precipitation, as much because of his advent to office as because of the policies associated with his name. And the

D

vital question of the American consensus was raised in the minds of rightwing elements and liberal circles, among the followers of the John Birch Society and the segregationists of the South as well as among the large Jewish community and the Negro population.

But these latter groups are only the vestigial traces of a crisis which has swept over American society and which has, as yet, to be resolved. Any form of the traditional American consensus, in any self-identified and operative form, is fast disappearing; and the rise of rather massive non-Protestant segments within the American framework has given rise to a pluralistic society which has sounded the knell of the former consensus: a pan-American Protestant ethos and way of life accepted as the dominant and national one, with permission for other groups – minority groups – to exist side by side with the Protestant mass merely because of constitutional rights, and a consequent profession of the American way of life as a Christian one. This consensus has ceased to be valid or operative.

There was too much against it from the start. Into its composition from the very beginning, America received two explosive elements: European Catholics and Jews. The Catholic, through a long history and an increasing numerical strength, challenged the primacy of Protestantism as the American way to God, and succeeded in integrating himself powerfully and effectively into the American way of thought. The Jew, coming from the Old World with its pogroms and its ghettos and persecutions, held as an ideal his banishment from public life, public institutions and constitutional institutions, anything bearing the imprint of the religion which had cost him so dear. This was based on no hatred of religion or of Christianity, but on the sound conviction that only the most delicate and scrupulously observed religious neutrality could save him finally from what he had suffered in the Old World.

Now, on the one hand, the Catholic can positively reject the idea that Christianity in America means primarily or necessarily Protestant Christianity. The Jew, on the other hand, can positively reject the idea that Christianity in America, Christianity of any kind, is something inherently American.

There is here, patently, a vacuum in the American outlook. And it is not enough to say that America is not a country, that it is a continent, that it is useless and inaccurate to speak of a 'national' outlook in any matter, and much less in religious matters. This is begging the central question, and leaving it without a solution. Into this vacuum, it is possible, Kennedy might have succeeded in pouring a new spirit. He held out that hope to those who believed in the basic concept of the New Frontier. He represented the one chance of such an eventuality to many.

John, by his summoning of a Council, performed an act of creative genius, for he created a forum in which the explosive elements of his Church could solemnly, legally, canonically, display the very vitals of the biting issues that were beating against the restrictive walls of a Church organization outworn, outmoded, outrun. He forced both liberal and conservative into the open, and thereby made his Church so modern, at least in tendency and import, that those who five years before would not have stopped to consider Catholicism, now paused and wondered. They were fascinated by the signs, involved in the issues, drawn to the huge, hunched-up, bald-headed, smiling face that shone out at them in newspapers, magazines and television. And they listened and watched.

Protestant, Orthodox, and other Christian groups listened: 'If you could read my heart, you would perhaps understand much more than words can say.'[2] Perhaps, after all, the Bishop of Rome was the Supreme Pastor? The Jews listened: 'I am Joseph your brother.'[3] Perhaps Christian charity did mean love, and perhaps the blood of the Innocent One would no longer be unjustly imputed to them?

The Orthodox and other Orientals listened: 'In Sofia and Istanbul and Athens I cannot remember any occasion on which we were divided on principle or had any disagreement on the plane of charity. We loved one another.'[4] Perhaps this Bishop of Rome would understand the heart and mind of Orthodoxy, would recognize the meaning of *sobornost*?

The Negroes listened: 'Racial discrimination can in no way be justified ... The very nature of the common good requires that all members of the political community be entitled to share in it.'[5] If this was the voice of the Church, Christianity had a meaning, and they had a strong defender. Non-Christian religious leaders listened: 'We wish to emphasize everything that unites, and to remove anything that unduly divides, believers in God.'[6]

Political thinkers and statesmen listened: 'It can happen that a draw-

[2] John to the non-Roman Catholic observer-delegates on October 12, 1962.
[3] John to a Jewish delegation, October 1960.
[4] John to the observer-delegates on October 12, 1962.
[5] *Pacem in Terris*.   [6] John at Easter, 1961.

ing nearer together or a meeting for the attainment of some practical end, which was formerly deemed inopportune, might now or in the future be considered opportune and useful.'[7] Was it time to end the prolonged deadlock of East and West on the basis of a moral principle? And a world seeking desperately for an equitable solution to international negotiation listened: 'At this historical moment, the present system of organization and the way its principle of authority operates on a world basis no longer correspond to the objective requirements of the universal common good ... The public authorities of the individual political communities are no longer capable of facing the task of finding an adequate solution because of a structural defect which hinders them.'[8] Was this the inherent difficulty in the working of the United Nations and this the reason why it had not been able to prevent a Korean stalemate, a Budapest massacre, Tibetan genocide?

And Khrushchev and Communist leaders listened: 'Neither can false philosophical teachings regarding the nature, origin and destiny of the universe and of man be identified with historical movements that have economic, social, cultural or political ends, not even when these movements have originated from those teachings and still draw inspiration from them.'[9] Perhaps here was the warm wind of a thaw blowing from the West? Here was one who understood the gap between original theorizing and the present pragmatic difficulties.

The world and Catholicism cannot easily recapture an atmosphere of such interest and respect and attentive cordiality as that created by the presence of Kennedy as President of the United States and the conciliar appeal of John XXIII. Not that Kennedy or his advisers always understood John. Especially in the matter of East-West relations, there was misunderstanding. As hard-headed politicians, the American administrators could not understand a man who would approach with love and understanding a dictator and an ideology whom they had been confronting for over fifteen years with nuclear bombs and armed might. But it was the Kennedy presence, the New Frontier, the renewed energy in the field of international politics, the graciousness and family dignity of the White House, and the wordless disappearance of the 'No Catholics need apply' spirit, on the one hand, and the sudden hearkening of the world at large to the voice of a man whose predecessors had shortly before been either unknown or a subject of derision and opposition. It was a moment of awakening for peoples, a second spring of human expectations.

[7] *Pacem in Terris.*   [8] *Ibid.*   [9] *Ibid.*

The Joannine period of modern Church history appeared as an exceptional act of Providence and a foredestined hour of grace. Only once in a thousand years does some human being, as the leader of over 500,000,000 other human beings, unite in his person the radiant harmony of ecclesiastical dignity and the hallmark of genius, originality and a creative touch. It was not that, instead of cursing the surrounding darkness as Satan's creation, he lighted a small candle of perseverance: for this would be the illumination of a martyr, a heroic missionary, an everyday Christian who lives his faith. It was that, Midas-like, every corner of the human spirit was touched and flared with the yearning of sons for the father's house, that he incarnated the genuine substance of the human salvation, resurrection and ascension effected by Jesus Christ, which over the centuries had been 'encased within an ever-hardening crust.' It was that the warm love of his spirit melted and broke through this hardness, this crust, revealed tenderly the substance of our inheritance in the saints of God, and 'exercises a peculiar fascination. Then we can see what was once the life-substance of us all, and what we have now lost, and a deep yearning awakens in us for the departed youth of our culture.'[10]

The murder of President Kennedy in November coincided, as we shall subsequently see, with the extinction of conciliarism as John had launched it. His death was in no way connected with it, causally. Yet John F. Kennedy's death was symbolically the end of an era.

Only time will tell us what the ultimate fate of Roncalli's ideas will be. In the meantime, one of the most telling tributes ever paid to John XXIII was made by the Lutheran theologian, Richard Baumann, of Tübingen. Speaking to the Divine Word News Service in Rome, Baumann recalled a saying of Martin Luther at Leipzig in 1519 during one of his disputes with Dr Eck. Luther asked Eck to pray with him that Christ would accord to the Supreme Pastor (the Pope) and to all bishops the grace to be good pastors for their flocks. And Luther and Eck made this prayer. Luther added: 'There is no doubt that the entire world will receive with open arms and with abundant tears the man who will desire to act in accordance with the words of this prayer.' Dr Baumann added: 'This man was John XXIII.'

[10] Both quotations are from Paul Tillich, *The Protestant Era*, translated by J. L. Adams, University of Chicago Press, Chicago, 1948, p. 194.

THREE

THE SUMMITS OF DARKNESS

1. De Eligendo Pontifice

After a little over one week of intense physical suffering, Angelo Roncalli, known to the world at large as John XXIII, died in a coma at the hour of 7.49 p.m. on Monday, June 3, 1963. On Friday, June 21, at 11.05 a.m. Giambattista Montini, then Cardinal Archbishop of Milan in northern Italy, was elected Pope by eighty cardinals. At 12.12, the crowd waiting in the piazza knew his name. At 12.25, Paul reached the central balcony, was hurrahed, huzzahed, *viva*-ed, and gave his blessing. As the crowds drifted home at 12.35, they bought newspapers which carried screaming headlines: 'Montini elected Pope.' The papers had gone to press two hours before. It was a foregone conclusion and accurate information. On Sunday, June 30, Montini was solemnly crowned in St Peter's square, and given the traditional titles – Bishop of Rome, Patriarch of the West, Vicar of Christ, Successor of St Peter, Head of the Universal Church. An era had ceased. No new era had, as yet, been born.

The author of *giovannismo* had ceased to breathe: his Fisherman's ring and his seals of office were broken, his body embalmed, clothed in a mitre and full pontificals, carried in solemn procession once around the piazza outside, finally consigned to three coffins, of cypress, lead and elm, and buried beneath the basilica in the crypt of the popes. Officially, ecclesiastically, John had disappeared. Khrushchev sent his condolences with the other powers. The U.S. Senate passed a vote of sympathy. Flags hung at half-mast in Rome and throughout the world because John was dead. But so powerful was the spirit he had let loose over the wide places of our globe and throughout the corridors of the Vatican that his successor would not be able to shake off the mesmeric spell of that creation, would take all of eighteen weeks to realize that what John had created, only John could maintain.

Whenever a pope died, when Roncalli died, there came into play an entire *mise-en-scène*, the projection of an image that corresponds, rightly, to the state of mind of the faithful and to the higher truths of

Catholicism, but which merely pulls purple veils over actual conditions. Christ was without a Representative on earth. The Chair of Peter was without an occupant. The ministries of the pope, the organizational centres of Church life a short time ago alive and feeding like bees on the mellow substance of the former pontificate, were now embalmed in the amber of functional immobility, would only be electrified and revivified by exposure to the ineffable presence of an *alter Christus*, a new pontiff. Vatican *L'Osservatore Romano* carried no papal title and signified its interregnum pathos with a front-page framed in black. Vatican coins carried the Keys without the portrait of the Bearer of the Keys. The Power of the Kingdom of Heaven hung in suspended transmission, awaiting its lawful incumbent. Authority was silent. All decisions were interim.

This was *sede vacante* – as shadow to substance, as idea to reality.

Behind the purple veils, there took place a process both natural and complicated. The power-centres were once again unleashed from the *roncallist* grasp. The vast machinery of the bureaucracy, whose regular tempo had been tempered by the will and direction of the dead man, now changed its tune: huge levers of influence were raised, the wheels of inner authority, minute and mighty, started to turn over in a fresh effort to effect a harmony of effort. Foreign hands touched the switches and ran over the smooth casing to detect flaws, to interpret the vibrations, to seek the mood of the whole. When the cardinals finally elected a successor, they would do so in the mental framework of the Jerusalem Council: 'It has seemed good to the Holy Spirit and to us . . .' In the meantime, like the board of directors of some global corporation, the protagonists of the election and those interested in the outcome, began the careful culling of candidates and concerns. For the Holy Spirit no longer speaks by direct inspiration and the gift of tongues. He ratifies a decision reached by men who observe a juridical procedure in their choice.

The juridical procedure was laid down in a document drawn up by Pius XII in 1945. It had one major purpose: to avoid revelation of the inner workings of pre-conclave and conclave activities. It was administered by an official, the Cardinal Camerlengo, 85-year-old Cardinal Aloisi Masella. To each freshly arrived cardinal he administered the welcome of an inexpressive hand and an oath: to observe the rules laid down in 1945, not to place his votes at the disposal of any secular power, to maintain all the temporal rights of the Holy See that were necessary for its independence, and, finally, to preserve the secret of the conclave – under pain of excommunication.

All in all, the juridical structure allowed the maximum space for manoeuvring within the ranks of the cardinal-electors, the minimum influence of the body of the faithful, and the full play of the time-encrusted factors which hitherto had moulded its deepest motives. Alone among the cardinals, Aloisi Masella had the face and the temperament of a twentieth century version of a masculine *La Gioconda:* regular classical features, straight nose, full eyes, an inscrutable expression on his mouth – not unsmiling, not smiling, courteous manner, the image of the leonardesque world, of the universal man, *l'uomo* of the Italian *Risorgimento* literature, in whom all the mysteries of the cosmos found a recipient but no reflection. As the pre-conclave days neared their end, more and more he gave in to the inveterate habit of clenching his mouth: he heard Ottaviani out, he bowed to Antoniutti's recommendations, he listened to Tisserant, he talked with Bea, he smiled at Spellman, and gazed at McIntyre, he encouraged Pizzardo, humoured the explosive Ruffini, grappled with Rugambwa, satisfied Bacci's Latin tastes, and assured all and sundry of the formal nature of his attitude: he was the servant of the servants of the Lord for a brief period.

What was ultimately decided in a formal vote during the conclave would be merely the formalization of the decision which he saw taking shape during the pre-conclave activities. Masella's dry, pudgy hand and worried smile full of mild acquiescence and hooded irony were part of a juridical process, part of the *décor* behind which the real processes evolved. And even though he felt that the numen of a vanished empire overshadowed the goings and comings, and even if the thin veneer of *pax romana* thrown over the entire proceedings sometimes wore thin to reveal the naked force of interest and tendencies, it is improbable that he or most of his associates posed the central question of those days in the language of modern man. For, in plain language, what the Church needed was a man who understood the heart and soul of the ordinary man, Christian or non-Christian, in the twentieth-century world. Ottaviani was a walking encyclopaedia of precept, of dogma, of theological principles. He and so many others at the conclave had never felt the answers to the questions that burned themselves into the daily lives of millions, had never approached the solution to problems that made men commit suicide, divorce their wives and husbands, take to drugs or to drink, and left them crying into their pillows over the scars that life had inflicted on them.

Pre-conclave and, therefore, conclave discussions were polarized around two names: Montini and Antoniutti, the former 65, the latter 64 years old, both northerners, both strong-willed, both diplomats, both symbols and spearheads of differing tendencies. The polarization was due to two opposing currents. One: the regular curial current with Ottaviani, Siri, Antoniutti as its doctrinal formulators and Cicognani, Ciriaci and Micara as its political and economic experts. The other: composed of those who circled around the personality and were gripped by the spirit of the one man who embodied *giovannismo* even after Roncalli's death, Cardinal Bea.

The issues at stake between the two currents really reduced themselves to quite simple terms. It was not a hamletic question: to have the Council or not to have the Council. The Council *had* to go on to at least a second session; for the conservatives, in order to repair the damage already done; for the progressives, in order to crown the work already begun. Nor was it a question of a foreign candidate versus an Italian one; from the beginning there was never serious question of a non-Italian pope; for the moment and as long as Europe remained split up into several different polities, a non-Italian pope would just about complete the estrangement of papacy and the Italian people as a whole. A non-Italian Secretary of State was a possibility but it depended on the new pontiff.

At the heart of all disputes lay the very *raison d'être* of Roncalli's policy, his 'opening-out,' his *aperturismo*, as the Italians called it: *aperturismo* in Italian politics, conciliar *aperturismo*, ecumenical *aperturismo*, his *aperturismo* in human relations with the Jews, with non-Christians, with the Soviet bloc, with non-Catholics. Reduced to their abiding principle, these all signified an abandonment of the Tridentine stance, a letting loose of the forces pent-up in Catholicism, a consorting with alien things, an admission of past wrong-doing, of misinformation, of exaggerated historical poses and dogmatic formulations. It was the question of Romanism, of occidentalization, of the thing that made Rome Rome. It even went further: it acknowledged that the Church had developed further and faster than its administrative and juridical centre at Rome had, that it contained seeds that had to blossom, and elements that could explode, that the blossoms and the explosion should be welcomed, encouraged, that the blossoms should be tended and the explosions controlled.

It is very hard for us to realize the frustration of the conservative mind during the inter-sessional period of January to June, 1963. John's blessing of the Left-wing in Italy, his contacts with the Soviet rulers, his issuing of *Pacem in Terris*, his encouragement of a proposal to found a Secretariat for non-Christian Religions, his open support of the progressives during the Council, his dependence on Bea, and the total effect of this policy throughout Catholicism; the reception of Küng in the United States, Bea's enormous success there, the spate of articles and books attacking the Holy Office, the Roman methods, and the Roman mentality, the flood of inter-group meetings and *rencontres*, the vociferous cries from Germany, Holland and France for liberty to think and liberty to publish, the ominous Communist election aims and the shaky government of Leone in Italy, the hardening of the economic and financial interests who saw danger at home to their holdings and danger abroad either in the Middle-East owing to Arab resentment or in Europe among their European colleagues, the whole experience amounted to a nightmare which sent a shudder running through a vast number of influential people.

The question gnawing at the heart and vitals of all the electors was quite simple: on which of the two major candidates, Montini or Antoniutti, would the choice of conservative or progressive fall? The candidate chosen would have to satisfy the Joannine-inspired, and he would also have to satisfy the conservatives. As in all such tussles, the solution ends up as a compromise. That side wins whose configuration of future events was most in conformity with the potential of the compromise candidate chosen. In the actual outcome, the chosen candidate of the progressives, Montini, would win with conservative votes – enough of them to make up the required 54, but the conservatives only did this because they knowingly and subtly counted on Montini's potential as pontiff: they knew his weakness, they knew their strength; they also knew the weakness of their opponents. They verified Richelieu's maxim about the successful politician: 'It is not enough to know the potential of your situation; you must also know how to actuate those elements which favour your policy and to negative those elements which militate against it.'

The personality and the work of Bea was a thorn in the side for the conservatives. Enriched by his experience as collaborator of Pius XII, as confidant of Pope John, as member of the Holy Office, Bea had literally turned the apple-cart upside down with his Secretariat for Unity: he had created an atmosphere of cordiality and amity with the dissident Christian Churches, he had whipped up a *mea culpa* consciousness about the urgency of the Jewish question, he was the *pater ecumenicus* for

Roman Catholics and Christians all over the world, he had stamped his image on the minds and hearts of the American public, he could call on the support of German, Dutch, French, Austrian and a goodly number of American, Australian, Canadian and missionary bishops. Doctrinally, he had deserted age-old positions, proclaimed that those who differ in faith (those, therefore, considered by Catholics to be in grave error) had as equal religious rights as Catholics, he had held the centre of the stage with such personalities as U Thant, Zafrulla Khan, with innumerable members of the academic, political and social worlds. He was the academic spearhead of *giovannismo*. If John had gone so far and so dangerously with the satellite governments and with Italian Socialists, it was on the basis of Bea's doctrine.

Quite a time before Roncalli's death, an effort had been made to denigrate Bea, in a gentle and subtle way: Bea was old, he was rapidly coming to the end of his physical forces, his doctrine was suspect at the Holy Office – so went the murmur of carefully spread rumours: a first article in one French paper; a supporting article in a Spanish one; an article by a Spanish Jesuit spelling out the dangers of ecumenism and *giovannismo*. And thus it went, until finally a large English daily came out with a definite statement that Bea was to retire. On the other hand, Antoniutti suited the requirements of the conservative mentality. He had the correct age – fifteen years of such a steady hand at the tiller would suffice to get over the present impasse. He had some experience of diplomacy, was sound in doctrine, had shown his mettle in the promotion of the Opus Dei, a Spanish-founded organization which enjoyed the special blessing of the Holy Office. He was resolutely opposed to Bea and to *giovannismo*.

Montini was the great problem. Made a cardinal by John, banished to Milan through inner Vatican politics, this man seemed to be ambivalent. By family and friends, he belonged to the upper middle Italian class whose interests lay with the conservative mentality. His mother had been president of the Catholic Women's Association of Brescia. His father, a lawyer, had been president of the Electoral Union of Italian Catholics and one-time parliamentary deputy for Don Sturzo's Popular Italian Party, the forerunner of the Demochristian party. Schooled for the priesthood at home (through ill-health he could not stay in the seminary), formed at the Ecclesiastical Academy for Vatican Diplomats, after preliminary but not very profound studies in canon law and philosophy in Rome, he worked in the Vatican Secretariat of State from 1923 until 1954.

In Rome, as pro-Secretary of State under Pius XII, he had what is normally called a brilliant career. He had a personal devotion to Pius. He made two visits, both brief ones, to the United States. He visited South America and Africa briefly under Roncalli's pontificate. He was noted for his effort to penetrate Sesto San Giovanni, known as the little Stalingrad of Italy, for his effort at social reform, for his charitable activities.

Yet no impressive results attended his efforts, and those who had been working in the social centres of Milan before he came there, spoke sparingly of his abilities: he was too juridical, too self-reliant, too tied to ecclesiastical privileges, above all too identified in character and outlook with the dominant industrial interest blocs. Personally, they found him too messianic, too intent on impressing his own personality, too demanding of reverence and awe from his entourage.

In spite of all this, he was the one whom John had singled out in his private diary as the cardinal he would like to see succeed him as pope. He was favoured by John: placed at the head of the list of new cardinals created in 1958, asked to collaborate in the writing of some of Roncalli's major speeches, given special rooms in the Vatican during the first session of the Council. On the other hand, he remained on the fence during the session. He was silent at the most dramatic moments. He never once betrayed his hand. He did not oppose – as he could have done – the suppression of the Catholic fortnightly *Adesso* which was banned by the Holy Office because it published criticisms of the hierarchy. Then again, he granted an *imprimatur* to what one might describe as a comic-book digest of the Bible. He was prominent in saving individual Jews during the Nazi occupation of Rome. Yet he autographed and prefaced an anti-Semitic work of Angelo Alberti. He was known as fearless when principles were at stake, yet he signed a letter in answer to a query from the Fascist government of Mussolini concerning the marriages of Jews and Aryans, and the contents of the letter are, to say the least, definitely compromising.

He seemed, in addition, to promise progressive steps, to create the atmosphere necessary for their implementation, and then not to take them. And his appeal for clemency to Franco in 1962 was an error: there had been no question of a death-sentence and the man convicted was lawfully and justly convicted.

In his pastoral letters, sermons and writings, Montini quoted freely from progressive French thinkers, Congar, de Lubac, Daniel-Rops, Dumont, Teilhard de Chardin, and German theologians like Küng and

Rahner. He translated Grandmaison's book, an author associated with suspect biblical studies. He wrote a preface to Maritain's *True Humanism* and made the Italian translation of Maritain's *Three Reformers*. Yet in spite of all this, he gave the impression that he never seemed to have absorbed it all, but that – like so many Italians – he had understood the exterior *form*, the style of thinking but not the thought-content or the swing of ideas. Actually Montini has a mind primarily attuned to scholastic outlooks and ecclesiastical standpoints.

The chief mark against him was the obvious support he enjoyed among the Bea-centred votes in the pre-conclave period. For the conservatives, at best, he was a calculated risk; at worst, he was vowed to bring Roncalli's work to fruition. For the progressives, at best, he was the only Italian on whom they could count to continue John's work; at worst, he might turn out to be a Pius XII if things went rather well, or a Pius IX if things really took a turn for the worse.

From June 13 onwards, Bea's offices on the Via Aurelia were the centre of pre-conclavist activity. To consult with him came the American cardinals and the German bishops, French churchmen and missionary Dutchmen and Austrians. The big question: was Montini bent on carrying on the work of John? The work of the Council? What was Montini's attitude to ecumenism? And to the Jewish question? And to internationalization of the Curia? Finally, what would be his attitude to the political policies of John both in Italy and abroad? Montini knew that Bea was aware of the answers to these questions, was perfectly cognizant of his attitudes. More than one cardinal decided, like Spellman of New York, to drop in at Milan and see Montini face-to-face. To Bea there came also curial cardinals, Tisserant among others; and papal officials paid their visits, the Princes Pacelli among them. There were a couple of visits by important representatives of the Press, diplomats of European countries bent on assessing the possibilities and expounding the point of view they had received from home.

By the time that Wednesday, June 19, had arrived, the criss-crossing lines of discussions and disputes, enlightening conversations, representations, and, finally, that delicate operation which the Italians feelingly describe as *sensibilizzazione* – a term drawn from the tactile order – had been duly followed and executed. The latter terms connote the 'feeling out' of dispositions, the 'rendering sensitive' to points of view. The surge in favour of Montani was so great that one Vatican *minutante* was heard shouting irately into a telephone to a less prudent colleague: '*Macché*, it may be true that Montini wins, but you must not say so until

Friday, *dio mio*!' And, significantly, it was reported that Bea, before entering the conclave on the afternoon of Wednesday, made appointments for the afternoon of Friday, June 21. The stage was set.

One European cardinal manifested his mind frankly on the issues of this conclave. 'Now that John is dead, this is what is needed: The Council must be called after a suitable period of preparation; next autumn is far too early. The period of preparation should be marked by four actions of the new pontiff. Firstly, he should streamline the Council structure both as regards personnel and its functional parts. At present, it is an invention of the Constantine era. Secondly, he must divert the reformed Council structure to the true problems of the age we live in: ecumenism; human relations with Jews, with non-Christians; for this a summit meeting of leaders should be called. Thirdly, he must weed out his own government right here in Rome. Until he does that, he cannot hope to effect anything. Fourthly, he must denude the Vatican of as many historical accretions as possible, detach it above all, from involvement in Italian politics.' Asked whether any of the favourite candidates were even capable of tackling this fourfold programme, he answered: 'Frankly, I don't know. Nobody does, you realize. What did we know about Roncalli before he took over? Nothing, except that he was extremely kind and liked to travel. But whoever is elected, we must not – as we are inclined to do always – blame God for all the mistakes he makes and conclude that God positively wished this man rather than that man to be pope. This is utter nonsense.'

To carry out a programme like the above, John's successor would have had to possess the doctrinal flexibility of Bea, the inspiration of John himself, the ruthlessness of Sixtus V, the *mystique* of Montini, the iron resolve of Pius IX, the stubbornness of Clement VII, and the cold resolve of a Richelieu. Above all, that person would need to have his hand on the pulse of Christians, be someone who had risen to the top but had not been conditioned by the very system itself.

At the other end of the city, the people most concerned about the dangers to traditional positions met and discussed the situation: Antoniutti was the prime candidate, Lercaro a secondary one. Something had to be done about the influence of Bea, it was decided. Monsignor Hamlet Tondini, the Secretary of Briefs to Princes, was to give the traditional discourse *De eligendo pontifice* (concerning the election of the pontiff) which was always preached to the cardinal-electors just before they entered the conclave and were shut off from the outside world. Tondini would be told the general lines of his discourse, for the issue must be clearly put before the electors. Actually, Tondini went far beyond the bounds of prescribed form and usage: the sermon is not supposed to be polemical. Tondini's was.

John had sweetness and love, intoned Tondini, but not a few of his enthusiastic applauders lacked a true grasp of spiritual values. Consequently, reasoned Tondini, by an apparent *non sequitur*, the successor of John 'must take care to re-establish the supernatural principles of Christian life.' On the other hand, he continued, while John sought the unity of all peoples, we must still be careful: there is much talk of a unity based on Marxist principles. John really intended to tell the separated brethren to return to the Church of Christ if they wanted to be saved.

Then turning directly to the solemn faces of the cardinals, where passivity, dumbfoundedness, distaste, conviction, satisfaction, could be variously read (Montini had his eyes closed and his lips pursed tightly together at this moment): 'You, Most Eminent Fathers, have the duty to choose one from among you who will have the task of deciding whether the problems, the studies already undertaken and, in particular, the state of mind, are at such a maturity that we can hope for the results which the healthiest part of humanity awaits.' This was of course a mistake of the first order, besides being a violation of protocol and usage. But it was in the style of the Roman mind: defiance, stubbornness, presumption.

By the end of the first day of the conclave and at the fourth ballot, Montini was only four votes short of election. By that time, the conservatives had despaired of getting their compromise candidate, Cardinal Lercaro of Bologna, to the pontificate. On the following morning, after some more *sensibilizzazione*, Montini received more than the required votes. Tisserant, Gonçalves Cerejeira, and Ottaviani approached Montini's throne and asked whether he had accepted the nomination. Yes, he had, although unworthy, yielded to the manifest will of God. By what name would he be called? Paul. It was a programme as well as a name. Not without official inspiration did *L'Osservatore Romano* describe how Papa Sarto (Pius X) greeted his election saying: 'May this chalice pass from me. Yet may the will of God be done.' It was Montini's recorded reaction.

2. The Summits of Darkness

We must now review the first eighteen weeks of Paul's pontificate – to be more precise, the period of time lying between June 21 and November 22. The chief components of such a review are: Paul's mind on taking over the reins of government from John, his serenity and confidence during the summer vacation period, the accompanying projection of a public image of himself, the intentions of the conservatives, and the configuration of things-to-come which he had forged before he returned to Rome from Castelgandolfo. We propose to take these up one by one.

We have referred to the dualism that is part of his character, the marriage of intellectual formulation and voluntaristic dynamism, the synchronized and smoothly conceived movement of schematization beneath the ever-deepening penumbra of a *mystique*. What changes, what reversals took place when he eased himself into the Chair of Peter? No doubt about it: Montini conceived himself as an *alter Joannes*, an extension in time and papal personality of his predecessor. His 'principal work,' as he termed it in his first radio message, would be the work of John, the Council. But – and this was the key concept of his mind – he would incarnate Joannine conciliarism and ecclesiology within the structure of his own make-up.

Paul has never delivered, in public or private, a profound critique of his predecessor. He did deliver himself of the heart of such a critique on September 6, when speaking of the coming Council session. He asserted that the Council had geared its activity of *reform* and *renewal* to a pastoral purpose. But, he remarked pointedly to his hearers, you must not think that, by describing this solemn gathering of bishops as one of reform and renewal, we imply 'an inadvertent but perilous inclination towards the pragmatism and activism of our time, at the cost of *interiority* and of *contemplation*. These should hold prime place in our religious evaluation. Their primacy remains absolute even if the exigencies of pastoral care ... claim a preferential amount of time given to the exercise of love of our neighbour.' Then he went on to give a twentieth-century expression to the interplay of the Alexandrian *nous* and *logos*. 'Speculative theology retains its dignity and its pre-excellence, even if compulsive reasons demand that sacred doctrine remain not purely speculative, but be considered and examined in the complete perspective of the Christian outlook.' With a figurative glance over the previous two months of personal synthesis, he went on lapidary-wise to enunciate: 'Today, mind and will, thought and work, truth and action, doctrine and apostolate, faith and love, teaching and ministry, have acquired complementary functions.'

Thought and work. Truth and action. Interiority and pragmatism. Contemplation and activism. *Mystique* and schematization. Never has Montini so clearly formulated the basic dualism of his character and the congenital requirements for any achievement of his own. In fact, the ambivalence of which many would accuse him, would be the superficial analysis of this dualism. In the short history of *giovannismo*, there was pragmatism and activism, love and action, work and will. But there was lacking the mental formulation, the necessary interiority. 'This is John with a brain and twenty years younger,' the *cognoscenti* had said at Paul's election. To put the criticism in another way: many a statesman and politician and many a churchman was puzzled by John when he said: 'Yes, yes, love Nikita, love them all.' This was all right in the abstract, but in politics you must know where you are going. And where was the old man going? More than once, intelligence agencies of Western governments probed Roman circles to find out exactly where John was going. And more than once, Vatican official and curial members complained that John did not know where love stopped and dogma began. Roncalli had described himself as a 'pragmatic man and well-balanced.'

Of himself, without any prodding, Montini clarified this point in his own regard. He would act as the continuation of another man's creation. But he would do it as a Roman of the Romans, as Roman Pontiff, heir to a long tradition.[1] For thus he was elevated to a rarified climate amid the summits that were dark with past greatness, with abiding permanence, with assured futures. Dark, too, because in the last analysis, he was the only one to judge, dark therefore to ordinary mortals. The summits of darkness. 'This authority renders us Master and Pastor, with complete fullness, of the Roman Church and of the

[1] *L'Oss. Rom.*, July 4, 1963.

Universal Church.'[2] Summits of authority, of primacy, of infallibility, of dignity, of understanding, of direction, of inspiration. Summits from which he could hear the 'deep voices of the modern world aspiring to peace and justice.' Summits clad in the darkness of 'Peter's shadow beneath which we take position for protection.'[3]

Standing in the background were the key figures of his inspiration; Pius XI 'who was pre-eminent for the indomitable strength of his soul'; Pius XII 'who glorified the Church with brilliant monuments of wisdom'; John XXIII 'who conquered the minds of all men ... by his sincere and active love ... and was distinguished by the supernal light which shone like a burning flame in him.'[4] Strength, wisdom, love, these three qualities shone like sanctuary lamps on the terraces of Paul's memory. He was on no pilgrimage of self-knowledge now. He contemplated the future, not fearfully, not proclaiming fresh hope, but as one continuing the work. No harrowing review. No criss-crossing doubts. Revelations and illuminations from the gone and the dead, the intertwining images of his days in Warsaw, the enthusiasm of the Bantus in De Wildt,[5] the coldness of the snow he had kissed on alighting from the train in Milan in January 1954, the ebullience of the Americans at Notre Dame in 1960, his last letter from John, the *evvivas* at his coronation, the salutations of literally an entire world. All the memories and experiences were synthetized unfalteringly and all the voices were orchestrated immaculately, into the framework of a pontificate he saw as the corrected continuation and crowning of *giovannismo*.

It is a false assessment, therefore, of Montini's mind to speak of self-effacement, to think that he wished merely to continue John's work. Paul re-assumed all the gyrating elements of the passing moment under the umbrella of his *mystique*. The Joannine spirit among his cardinals and bishops, the acclamations of the world, the huge expectations of Catholic, Orthodox, Protestant, Jew, non-Christian, of political and social circles, the pressures of intellectuals, these became in his hands fine threads spun into a strong shining web that clothed his spirit, encompassed all his fears, melted every tension.

It is important, I say, to realize this. Before many months Paul would be transformed, his actions apparently contradictory, his words

[2] *L'Oss. Rom.*, July 1–2, 1963.
[3] *Ibid.*
[4] Radiomessage, *L'Oss. Rom.*, July 23, 1963.
[5] Near Pretoria, South Africa; Montini had visited there in 1962.

semantically at least different. Now, he was acting as the adjusted continuation of another man's personality. Then he would be delivered mercilessly to a search for his own truth. His purpose now was imbued with the distillation of the very recent past. Then he would set out to hunt for harmony in the painful chaos of reality and for his own answers to the eternal riddles that had proved his undoing. Now, he reincarnated John and his spirit. Then he would endeavour to hew out his own image by cutting to the bone. And the Romanism inherent in him would blossom out to fullness, would even dominate his penetration to the heart of the ecumenical problem. But more about this point, when we treat of his post-sessional development.

Paul's air of serenity and confidence during the summer months of 1963, was due to his summation of events up to that point and the framework in which he projected his proximate conciliar and ecclesial activity. Over and above the petty details of Council sessions and speeches and particular schemata, he saw the chief issues as ecumenism (or relations with other Christian bodies), the Jewish question (about which he had a theological problem), the complicated area of human relations, and the nature of the Church (this last included the allied problems of the Roman Curia and the function of bishops, the Italian and world political scene, and the tension with the East).

In his review, these subjects were marshalled carefully and their inwards analyzed. Significantly, his marshalling began with the Church and ended up with the bigger, world-wide problems. He grouped ecumenism and the Church together as related subjects. Here, according to Paul, the issues were clear: the Curia would have to be internationalized, the blot of injustice and impersonal treatment would have to be removed especially from the Holy Office; the bishops would have to participate in the government of the universal Church – it was their divine right. A de-Italianized Curia, efficiently-run ministries, a supranational outlook, would be the results. And, most importantly, this was the feeling of the Council. This was the voice of the Church.

Then ecumenism. With this emphasis on the bishops' role in the Church, a return to the formula *Peter with the Eleven*, the way would be clear to speak with the dissident Christian bodies. For them, particularly for the Orthodox, *sobornost*, the Khomiakovian concept of collegial Church government, was of paramount importance. At this point, Bea's schema on Ecumenism found its place. To judge the temper of the Council, Bea's propositions, contained in three chapters and proposing the principles of a relationship with Christians belonging to Churches other than Rome, would be an apt paradigm of references for the *rapprochement* between Orthodoxy and Rome. The only difficulty was that so far, as Bea complained, only juridical connections with Orthodoxy or the Protestants could be conceived of: none of the Roman ministries, the Congregation for the Oriental Churches, in particular, was acceptable to the Orthodox.

The Jews. Here again, Paul approached the question from the Church point of view. For him it was not, as in reality it is, primarily a question of human relations based on a so-called traditional dogmatic standpoint. It was a theologico-political question. Bea had his document ready: it absolved the Jews as a people from the accusation of deicide; it rejected as unscriptural the notion of a divine curse pursuing the Jews through history; it asserted the human rights of Jews and condemned their persecution and sufferings. Then, again, the Jews were not Christians, but how could one consider them as non-Christians in the way that Buddhists or Shintoists were? Were they not an integral part of divine revelation and of Pauline theology? Even to term them monotheists and group them, with Islam, as the People of the Book was inadequate. Bea's propositions had aroused rabid passions among traditional theologians.

Politically, too, the thing was fraught with possibilities; Nasserism was built on anti-Semitism as a keystone. And many Christians lived in Arab lands where Nasser's full-toothed smile grinned down on all and sundry from photographs and billboards. The Arab opposition to Bea's document had been so bad back in November 1962 that it had to be put in cold storage. An important article on the problem of deicide was published under the name of a Jesuit professor of Gregorian University.[6] A bulky anti-Semitic tract called *Complotto contro la Chiesa* was printed in 4,000 copies (costing over 6 millions of Italian lire), and distributed to all the bishops of the Council. And rumours in Rome linked the name of Vatican officials with those of industrial names in the north of Italy in its production. At heart, the makers of Italian foreign policy were set against any such decree as Bea envisaged, because it would disturb Italian economico-cultural penetration in

---

[6] Originally intended for *Civiltà Cattolica*, the article was withdrawn at the instances of Cicognani, Secretary of State. Father L. Hertling, S.J., of the Gregorian University, Rome, published the article in *Stimmen der Zeit* 171, 1, pp. 16–25, under his name. The article makes some valid points, but sins rather egregiously in the reasoning manifest at the end of the discussion: the sufferings of Jews are somehow taken as the proof of God's mercy.

Arab countries. The whole situation was extremely delicate for Paul. Still Bea had granted a Press interview to the *Jewish Chronicle* in August, 1962, and stated unequivocally: the Council authorities intend to condemn anti-Semitism officially and radically, and this was the wish of the Holy Father.[7]

Thus, Paul was led to have severe doubts about the advisability of proposing the Jewish document or its viability if proposed, because of his starting-point: he started from the narrow ecclesiastical point of view, and this led him in turn to the theological difficulties (which he knew were false difficulties) and to the political considerations. And, yet, he always came back to a nagging difficulty: Bea and John had promised the document, the Jews expected it, there was deep anti-Semitism among Catholics and Bea said that nothing short of a formal decree on the lines he proposed, would suffice under the circumstances. Here again, the blurred outlines of the entire schema as conceived by John would have to be worked over and clarified.

Italian politics. Paul had definite ideas on the subject. He did not go so far as to agree with Cavour's principle, 'a free Church in a free State.' The Church had a mission in Italy. What must go was the external panoply, the lay officials, the association with the black aristocracy of Rome and of Lombardy, some of the more ridiculous manifestations of pomp – ostrich plumes, gaitered and silk-hosed gentlemen-in-waiting, perhaps even such an historical *residuum absurdum* as the *sedia gestatoria*. Political role? Yes and no. The influence of the Vatican and its followers was salutary and necessary to maintain the unity of any sort of Christian political front. Besides, the economy of the Vatican was tied to a certain economic structure of Italy. The economic unity of Europe, when assumed within the international framework of political institutions of a unified Europe, would certainly affect the Vatican. But that day was not exactly near . . .

It was natural that his approach here sprang from a Church point of view. What was faulty was that it was in essence the traditional point of view in a modified form. It would be as impossible for Paul to give up all ideas of influence on the Italian political field as it would have been for Pius IX to withdraw completely from the idea of the existence of a Vatican State in 1870. Yet that is what Pius IX should have done. But Paul adopted political *giovannismo*, political *sinistrismo* to this extent: the Vatican would support a government for the simple reason that there was no question of a Rightist government. What John had

[7] *The Jewish Chronicle*, August 10, 1962.

proposed on political principle, Paul adopted from political expediency.

Satellite countries. Here, again, Paul proceeded in his orderly fashion. The behaviour of John had been loving, but the effects were bad. Paul was worried about the drift to Communism among Italian workers. He thought about it as a political, and not an ideological, drift. But it was a worry. A middle course was necessary. Balzan prizes on Khrushchev's recommendation, birthday greetings from the same person, were all right in their way. But they did not warrant the admission of Adjubei, Khrushchev's son-in-law, to a private audience. Actually, Adjubei would make another attempt to see the Pope in October: his request would not even be answered. And Monsignor Capovilla, Secretary of John XXIII, would have to be restrained in his remarks about Communism. And what John had taught in his ency-clical, *Pacem in Terris*, concerning collaboration and contact with the Left would have to be interpreted correctly. With these adjustments, the entire policy of John regarding the satellite countries and the USSR could be adopted.

The world at large as such did not figure in the summation of Paul. The problems of population explosion, of nuclear disarmament, birth-control, peace, the expansion of Communism, were to be treated summarily in a document known in conciliar circles as Schema 17. But these subjects were not Church subjects as such. The problem of human relations: racialism in South Africa and in America, the vast masses of Asia and Africa, were classified in his mind as aftermath subjects. But the non-Christian religions of Asia held his attention. Some method of penetration, even on a purely human level, was necessary. He tended to look at the Church in the world, rather than the world around the Church. Thus one aching problem was that of the priesthood. And here again the myopia of the Roman interfered to some degree. The problems arose mainly in Italy and in traditionally Catholic areas like Puerto Rico and South America. Not only was Paul's gaze primarily fixed on the shifting sands of Italian conditions, he seemed to see the rest of the world as kaleidoscoped in the Italian socio-religious *Proble-matik*.

In Italy, as elsewhere, the priesthood had fallen on evil days. Priests were pitifully reduced in numbers, were ill-clothed, ill-fed, ill-educated, ill-regarded, ill-provided for economically, ill-fitted for preaching an intelligible Gospel, caught in a social and religious posture that makes them repugnant to cultured Italians, negligible to the ordinary man, hampered by the historical burden that has congealed into a myth of former political dominance still yearned for, which holds them incommunicado from any living contact with masses and renders them unfit for the task of reconverting people to the Gospel of truth. Then Communism. Shades of Milan's little Stalingrad and the sneers of workers at his outstretched hands. The Church, under Roncalli, had tended to remain aloof from politics. Now, many cardinals and advisers saw this as a mistake: the clamorous weapon of Italian Catholic Action (ACI) and the powerful pincers of pulpit and purse-strings were no longer playing their role. Leone's government could not last. And what then? For mission countries such as Africa, Paul would favour a married clergy. He told African bishops to propose this at the Council. And he even inclined at one stage to the revival of married deacons, clerics who, without being priests, could perform some of the functions of a priest.

It is important to note Paul's starting-point in the consideration of each of these problems. Actually, one is forced to say that, in fact, his information was global but his point of view was ecclesiastical and, at most, ecclesial. He would quote more than once the saying of Terence's: *Homo sum: humani nihil a me alienum puto* (I am a human being, I consider nothing human as alien to me). Yet, in virtue of his very *mystique*, he could not but regard everything in one way. It is difficult to sum this up in a short formula. But the essence of it can be grasped by contrast with the heart of *giovannismo*. The latter was basically human, primarily Christian, formally Roman Catholic. Paul's *mystique* was basically juridical, primarily Roman Catholic, formally Romanist. Understanding the difference between the two was going to be difficult even for Paul's friends, mainly because for a long time, he would use Joannine language, perform Joannine actions, yet at the back of it all, the texture of his deep purpose was different.

The point is worth emphasizing before we pass on. An analysis of his address at a general audience in St Peter's on Wednesday, January 15, 1964, will reveal what we mean. Realize that, at this moment, Paul had returned from the Holy Places, that by now he had deserted *the very heart of giovannismo*, that he had adopted openly another stance (all matters to be explained in the appropriate chapter). We wish to communicate to you, he said, a very strange and marvellous happening during our voyage to the Holy Places. There, in a strange land, 'instead of being foreigners and unknown – just think, after such a long time and so many transformations in that land – we were perfectly known. And not only as a Pope of Rome, but precisely as the Successor of

Simon, son of Jona, the fisherman of Betsaïda, the Brother of Andrew, called Peter by the Messiah Jesus, head of that religious society which is called the Church. You would have said that only a short time ago Peter had left that place and that he was awaited in his country to be fêted on account of the fame he had acquired and, still more, on account of the many reasons which bound him to those blessed places. And to crown the wonderment: the welcome he received not only from his brothers in faith, but also from the separate brethren, and from Muslims and Jews.'

It is difficult to get an intelligible meaning out of these words of Paul, unless we choose one of two assumptions: either he indulged in poetic licence and by hyperbole took the cheers of the Arabs in Jerusalem and Bethlehem as acts of faith in the Church, saw the super-stitious stroking of his limousine by the Bedouins at the Jordan as modern examples of the woman with the issue of blood who touched the hem of Jesus' garment so that power would go out and cure her, and took the courteous reception by the Israelis at Megiddo as sym-bolical concessions to the primacy of Christianity over Judaism; or, he had some deeper meaning, really conceived his tumultuous welcome as meaning that Arabs and Jews saw in him Peter, but haloed in the glory that only Peter's successors knew.

It may seem far-fetched, but it is more in consonance with the *mystique* of Paul VI to assume that what was purely a civic welcome in Israel and what was certainly a politico-religious reaction in Jordan calculated to raise the stock of precariously balanced Hussein and satisfy the self-esteem of Muslims, was assumed by Paul into a higher outlook, transmuted and sublimated in accord with his approach to the world around him. This was in January 1964. The traumatic experience of the Council was past. The pilgrimage had begun. The Joannine era had been dead since November. Paul, the real Paul, was now acting as himself.

The establishment of a public image in the international sphere was one of his earlier achievements. In late June, he received Baudouin and Fabiola of the Belgians, and the day afterwards, President Goulart of Brazil. A mere catalogue of his principal interviews in July fills an entire paragraph; it also shows how he strove and succeeded in impress-ing his image, at home and abroad. On July 1, he received the repre-sentatives of the ninety-three Extraordinary Missions, governmental and international bodies who had attended his coronation. The follow-ing day he conferred with President Kennedy. The President, besides presenting his congratulations in person and allowing himself to be photographed seated with the Pope, had some things to discuss with Paul: South Vietnam and the position of the Church, the Vatican's policy and actions *vis-à-vis* the satellite countries, the racialist question in the States in which Kennedy did not want any embarrassing statements by the Church. Loquacious tongues around the Vatican maintained also that the President requested a replacement for the Apostolic Delegate, Archbishop Egidio Vagnozzi – who had, true enough, irritated the most influential American churchmen and laity. We do know that the President had been urged to make this request. Vagnozzi was called to see Paul at the end of the month.

From July 2 onwards, Paul granted audiences to Orthodox students from Greece, to pilgrims from Czechoslovakia, Philadelphia, to Italian and foreign journalists, a group of 'European' exponents of the Common Market, students from South Vietnam, Italian Catholic Actionists, Nigerian pilgrims, pan-African students. He received U Thant, President Segni of Italy, President Cyril Adoula of the Congo, Nigerian Minister of urban planning P. O. Nwoga, Sir Wilberforce Nadkopel the hereditary sovereign of Busoga in Uganda, the Minister of Foreign Affairs of the South Korean Republic, among others. Paul's own newspaper published the congratulations of non-Roman Catholic Church leaders: Archbishop Georges, Exarch of Paris, Archbishop Michael Ramsey of Canterbury, the Metropolitan Elie Karam (of Lebanon) and Damaskinos (of Greece), the chief rabbinical authorities of Tel Aviv, Israel. It also published a list of over eighty governments, including Surinam as well as the USSR and Gabon and Nasser's Egypt, who congratulated Paul VI on his accession. He would continue to impress this image in the succeeding months: in August he wrote a letter to the people of Vietnam exhorting them to be calm, sent messages of congratulations to the American and British governments and to U Thant on the conclusion of the test-ban treaty of Moscow. In September he would be photographed standing with Buddhist priests from Vietnam.

Over the mass of details, organizational problems, ecclesiastical complications, political motives, doctrinal values, religious trends, Paul poured the warm aura of his assumption that as Pope, as Vicar of Christ, as successor of John XXIII, he would be able to correct the blurred edges of operations, would fuse the amorphous mass of Joannine impulses into an organic stream of development. We must keep this in mind. It is Paul's interiority and contemplation at work.

And it was this cloying flaw, this 'mole of nature,' that finally brought the first phase of his evolution to an abrupt stop. Paul's outlook was not ecclesial but ecclesiastical, not evangelical but juridical. His charity was intellectual, not visceral. He endeavoured to continue on the work of John by consecrating the very structure which, at this point in the evolution, should have been reviewed, re-examined, dismembered, re-assembled. It is hard to force the intellect thus to dissect his performance coldly and analytically. For he had brilliance. From the day of election he projected himself in a flow of images that shaded off imperceptibly, one into the other, as graded harmonies in the overture of a magnificent opera. Activity and motion, yes, and intensity and impressive will-power and initiative into the bargain. No shrill notes, no sudden abruptnesses, no uneven pauses. An ever-growing serenity, according as he felt the machinery responding to his very touch.

It is not probable that Paul at this stage conceived of the future as one carrying an explosion of any sort. Precisely, he thought, because of the corrections to *giovannismo* which he had effected, an explosion would be avoided. None of his advisers conveyed to him this dangerous potential. Afterwards, the fact would be repeated to him over and over again in a thousand and one ways like a note twanged on the strings of a bull-fiddle, paining his nerves by the force of its monstrous repetitiousness.

As the days of July and August wore on, Paul VI indulged in the activity characteristic of him: quickly announced, scintillating actions, obviously the fruit of careful meditation and reflection, clearly calculated as to effect. We may list these actions in inventory fashion. In actual fact, during those months they sprang from his continuously developing synthesis – thought and work, knowledge and will in harmonious action, reaction, counteraction.

He left the Vatican on what one papal secretary described as a whim – to visit ailing prelates. He proclaimed the continuation of the Vatican Council and named September 29 as the opening day. He sent encouraging messages to the beleaguered Jesuit scholars at the Biblical Institute, Rome: 'Have confidence; during our pontificate, there will be no persecutions, no admonitions, no suppressions.' He consulted long with Bea, dismissed the attacks on the latter's orthodoxy with a wave of the hand: Bea was to go ahead with his plans for ecumenism, for ecumenical contacts with the other Christian Churches, for a document resolving the age-old Christian anti-Semitic bias, for a statement on basic human and religious rights. Even the illegal drawing up of a decree on May 25, 1963 by Pizzardo and Staffa (respectively, prefect and secretary of the Congregation of Seminaries and University Studies) without a plenary session of the cardinals and without approval of the Pope (John was in his second-last coma on May 25) did not ruffle Paul.[8] Apart from scolding the people concerned, he complained about the Jesuit General: 'Why did he not come and tell me all about it?'[9]

But Paul had tired of the tyranny of Roman dicasteries, in particular of the Holy Office which John XXIII had once described as 'my God-given crown of thorns.' But it was not the Holy Office as such. It was the solidly ensconced, dyed-in-the-wool, bred-in-the-bone, medieval-minded, closely knit phalanx of the curial directorate. He had complaints from his bishops; he read the spate of newspaper and magazine articles about it. He despised the tactics it employed in the first session. It must be reformed, not merely the Holy Office, but the entire Roman administration. Here again, Paul the Roman, the curial trained administrator intervened, leavening his original proposition to an impossible strain: he would reform it himself, and he would openly proclaim such a reform. This was one major address which he must get off before the Council convened, so that the bishops returning to Rome would have a pledge of security, an encouragement to take up their divine right to govern the Church.

To obviate the stalling, the prevarications, the blocking, the filibustering evident in the first session, he decided that the governing structure of the Council had better be reorganized. More than that, he

---

[8] This was drawn up on official paper, signed by Cardinal Pizzardo, prefect of the Congregation, and by Monshignor Dino Staffa, Secretary. It spoke in the plural, in the name of the Congregation, and decreed that henceforth no Catholic Institute, College or University could confer an honorary degree (ecclesiastical or lay) without express permission of the Congregation. It was a decree, there can be no doubt about it. The official 'nos' (we) is used, making it a document of the Congregation as such. 'There are many experts of the Council who speak stupidities,' said Staffa. 'If we give honorary degrees to him (Hans Küng), it would seem that we approve his ideas.' Cardinal Spellman objected to the peremptory tone of the accompanying letter sent with the decree to his New York chancery, but an exchange of letters brought no change in the Congregation. Later on, the Congregation sent out an instruction that the decree did not apply in the United States. It still applies all over the remainder of the world.

[9] The occasion was the conferring of honorary degrees on Gronchi and Segni. Although Loyola University authorities and the Congregation of Seminaries and Universities have denied it, there is no doubt that originally Bea's name was slated by the authorities for an honorary degree, but the General of the Jesuits ruled it out because of the Congregation's objections.

would clearly show where his sympathies lay and on whom he counted. Paul's plans included chiefly the appointment of a board of four to be called Moderators: Suenens of Belgium, Doepfner of Munich, Lercaro of Bologna, Agagianian of the Curia. He preferred a small manageable committee instead of the ten-man presidency board that had managed the first session of the Council.

But having taken this radical step, he proceeded to impose conditions which made the functioning power of the four-man board extremely difficult. Suenens, Doepfner, and Lercaro could be depended on to share identical views. And Agagianian was conservative but not aggressively so. Now Paul proposed and decided that the Council would plunge immediately into the consideration of the nature of the Church and the rights and duties of bishops in the government of the Church. This was merely to provide the board of four with a situation they could not manage: Suenens would, very early, disagree violently with Doepfner, Lercaro would disagree with both of them. There was never any monolithic unity among the four Moderators.

Over the summer, Paul received two items of news which inclined him positively to encourage Bea in his presentation of a statement on the Jewish question. There was first of all the increasing wave of public opinion about Rolf Hochhuth's play *The Deputy*.[10] Montini himself as Cardinal Archbishop of Milan had written a letter to *The Tablet* in London to decry the play as unjust and inaccurate.[11] The *Times* of London commented on this letter saying that it was obvious Cardinal Montini had not understood the play. In fact the majority of those who have contributed to the already vast literature on the subject of the play do not seem to have understood it. Hochhuth's thesis is quite simple: Pius XII did help the Jews, but his position as Pope required him to do more than that; he should have come out publicly against the grisly solution which the Nazi mind devised to get rid of over 6,000,000 Jews.

To get around the difficulty, Papa Montini now urged the Jewish statement by Bea. Such a statement, whatever the past, would quiet all doubts on the part of Jews and Gentile about the Vatican's attitude today. Besides, Paul now had in his hands a perfect answer to the fundamental political objection urged against Bea's document on the Jews by Cicognani, by Mansourati of Bea's own secretariat, and by the

[10] Published in German as *Der Stellvertreter*, Rowohlt, Hamburg, 1963, with foreword by Erwin Piscator.
[11] *Tablet*, July, 1963. Reprinted by *Commonweal*, February 28, 1964.

conservative group: a *felix culpa* of Gustave Weigel at the end of June[12] had provoked the Arab League spokesman in America, Saadat Hassan, to issue an official statement asserting that 'it is very unlikely that such a statement (on the Jewish question) by the Ecumenical Council could cause any misunderstanding between the Muslims and Christians of the Arab world . . . as Arabs we cannot be anti-Semitic . . . A clear and forthright statement by the Ecumenical Council on anti-Semitism would be welcomed by the Arab States.'[13] Nasser forbade the broadcast of this statement over the Voice of the Arabs, his Cairo station. Nevertheless it provided Paul with an answer to the critics.

But this was not the only point on which Paul agreed with Bea. The masses of non-Christians in the East were on his mind. And the only feasible solution for a lack of contact was that he should finally meet the leaders of these masses in a religious summit. To prepare for this he envisaged the setting up of a special Secretariat for non-Christian Religions. The only exception to the rule would be Judaism and the Jews: Paul had integrated them into his Christian theology. Besides, the new Secretariat would not be established in time for the second session. As president for this secretariat, Paul thought of either Suenens of Belgium or König of Vienna. Of the two, Suenens wanted the presidency personally; König had no intention of leaving Vienna to reside in Rome. And besides, König had definite reservations about Paul's chances of success.

It was in the area of ecumenism that Paul conceded most to Bea and the spirit of Bea. A pasquinade dating from that time ran: 'Papa Giambattista by name, Papa Giam*beat*ista by action.' For *beatista*, or supporter of Bea's policy and outlook, was already one of the phenomena of conciliar Rome. In early August, a message arrived from Father Joseph Gauthier, a priest who runs a housing co-operative in Nazareth, Israel. In it, Gauthier made two points: there was need in the Council to stress the poverty of Christ and of the Church, and would His Holiness consider coming to the Holy Land on pilgrimage? Paul charged his close friend, Cardinal Lercaro of Bologna, to study the letter; Lercaro had spoken on this very theme (the poverty of the

[12] When speaking to newsmen, he stated that the statement condemning anti-Semitism was prepared for the Council in 1962, but that it was not presented out of concern lest the Arab states view such action as taking sides with Israel. He went on to opine that the document would never come up for discussion. Father Weigel, who has since died rather suddenly, mourned by both Christian and Jew, may have been a prophet without realizing it.

[13] The statement was quoted widely in newspapers at the time.

Church) during the first session of the Council. *L'Osservatore Romano*, on August 11, carried a notice mentioning the prayers of hundreds of Orthodox Churches for unity among Christians. It also bore photographs, one featuring the Orthodox Metropolitan of Nadox with the Catholic Archbishop during the celebration of the feast of the Annunciation in 1963, the other showing the Archbishop of the Orthodox Church presenting the Gospel to the Greek Royal Family in Athens cathedral during the centenary commemoration of the dynasty.

He read the correspondence between John and the Patriarch of Constantinople, Athenagoras; the latter had written to John in August 1962 and requested that they meet and 'weep over their lost unity and start together the long road back to fraternal love and harmony.' Now messages were filtering through which clearly indicated that Athenagoras had the same thing in mind for Paul.

His contacts with Athenagoras had blossomed into a concrete resolution: he must meet with the Patriarch. Athenagoras had suggested two things: they take the Gospel as the basis of their contact, so that no juridical or ecclesiastical element might interfere with their personal contact, and secondly, that they meet on neutral ground. Now the letter from Nazareth started Paul on a train of thought which ended in his resolution to go as pilgrim to the Holy Land. It is to be noted that, at that time, there was no question of going to Israel. By August 18, Paul had made up his mind. He visited the Greek abbey of Santa Maria at Grottaferrata, and his ecumenical decision was transparently visible in his words: 'We are all a little deaf and dumb. May the Lord open our understanding and loosen our tongues! May He render us capable of hearing the voices of history, of chosen spirits. May He help us always to hearken to His voice, the echoing Gospel, which should always be our law, our strength, because it is the Word of God.' Paul knew the history of the painful schism with Constantinople, recognized in Athenagoras a chosen spirit, hoped that he, Paul, would be a chosen vessel, like the Apostle of the Gentiles.

Paul sent a long letter to Athenagoras outlining his ideas for their meeting: it would have to take place after the second session of the Council was concluded in December; his view was that their contact should be evangelical, that just as Peter in the Gospels is given a special place of mention and honour, so he, as Peter's successor, should receive the same; all told, the Holy Places of the East where Christianity emerged would be the best place for their meeting; he hoped that at the end of the second session, the bishops would have put into his hand a

E

paradigm of ecumenical references, a blue-print of ecumenical relations, so that his meeting with Athenagoras would be the first in a chain-reaction of meetings, contacts, discussions, mutual knowledge and mutual love. And Bea up in Germany, speaking at the *Hochschulwochen* celebration in Salzburg and *au courant* with the new development, said in public: 'The untiring work of John XXIII for the union of Christians has proceeded to the point of dealing with the long-awaited question.'

3. The Summits

Before the election of Paul VI, the post of Secretary of State was discussed extensively. It was generally expected that Cardinal Cicognani would retire and that the new Pope would appoint a new man to the post. The curial candidate was Cardinal Antoniutti, close collaborator of the central power bloc and dedicated defender of the traditionalist outlook, with its high-pitched overtones of triumph and glory and unique righteousness, of Rome. But Paul did not want Antoniutti coming into his office every day and gently but insistently forcing his hand away from the work he wished to do. In early August, he cut the Gordian knot: Antoniutti was given the presidency of the Congregation for Religious Orders. This would satisfy the career requirements of Antoniutti – for a time. As to Cicognani, Paul decided to let him stay.

As head of the Congregation for Religious Orders, Antoniutti began a careful probe into the names and number of the Council theologians and experts drawn from the Religious Orders, mainly from the Jesuits and Dominicans. And later on in the autumn he would send a letter to the heads of these Orders admonishing them to restrain the more prominent members. Later still, Antoniutti approached Paul about Bea, presented a long requisitory against the German Cardinal, reminded His Holiness that he, Antoniutti, should be a member of the Holy Office, and in general made trouble. Paul's answer was to name Antoniutti to the Holy Office – with Bea!

It is doubted in Rome that the curial onslaught on Paul in November would have been as bad as it was, if Paul had not taken the definitive but maddeningly dangerous step of making his famous 'curial' speech of September 21, in which he served notice on them. But this was Paul's dilemma when the moment of confrontation came. He had yielded to the traditional careerist demands of the bureaucrats. In turn the bureaucrats turned on him and used the positions they held under him to undermine his effort.

One of the last moves made by the conservatives concerned a document on Communism which was to take the form of a letter to the Italian people. At this early stage and in its original form, the message was a travesty of the concrete situation. It would finally be published during the Council, and we will mention it in its place. It was conceived within the shaky framework of the Leone government; this could only last a short time into the autumn. To obviate the possibility of any deeper collaboration with the political Left, they planned a very overt attack on Leftism in any sense. The president of the Italian Bishops' Conference, Cardinal Siri, with two others, undertook to prepare a text. It would be produced in good time.

The conservative circles in the Vatican and in Rome regarded Paul VI from the very beginning with narrowed eyes. Even before his election and during the pre-conclave period they had earmarked two major objectives: the election of a candidate who would arrest the onward development of *giovannismo* and the appointment of someone they could trust as Secretary of State. Even if they were defeated in the election, the post of Secretary of State was considered of key importance: only someone really dedicated to their principles could choke off the foolish dallying with a supposed *détente* with Eastern European states. Already, they had instructed the Catholic bookshops of Rome (who depended for their licences on the Roman Vicariate) to withdraw from sale the works of Xavier Rynne, Robert B. Kaiser, Henri de Lubac and Teilhard de Chardin. And they hoped to prevent any further public consecration of 'dangerous individuals' like the Germans Hans Küng of Tübingen, through the conferring of honorary degrees by Catholic Universities, when they issued the May 25 decree of which I have spoken before. Bea had been the particular object of this decree: Loyola University, Chicago, a Jesuit institution, had wished to confer honorary degrees on President Antonio Segni, Giovanni Gronchi – creator of political *aperturismo*, confidant of John XXIII, and former President of Italy – and on Bea.

The Jesuit General, Father Janssens, had asked the Congregation, privately, whether it would be wise to submit these three names to them for permission to grant the degrees according to the prescriptions of the May 25 decree. Affirmative for the two statesmen, came the answer, negative for the cardinal. Between Janssens and Bea relations had never been cordial or friendly. So Bea did not get the honorary degree. The real purpose, however, was to prevent Bea from receiving still another tribute on the American scene.

After Paul's election, and before the high-water mark of his speech on September 21 (when he proposed reform and internationalization of the Roman ministries), the plans of the Curia were general in nature. We must never think of these men as lit by the flame of bad will or cowed by circumstances, and seeking some tiny mode of egress, some narrow, straitened crack through which they might crawl out from under the thumb of extinction. Never for a moment did they or do they doubt the permanence of the system they run or the type they embody. They were and are the Establishment. 'Popes may come, Popes may go,' but We, the Church in their definition, go on for ever.

One channel of influence used extensively was *L'Osservatore Romano*, official organ of the Vatican. Enough has been written elsewhere to demonstrate the type of language which is used in the paper, and we need not dwell on it here. The Pope used to be described with such hyperbolic phrases as 'The Holiness of Our Lord,' his discourses as 'radiant messages,' 'illuminated discourses,' 'distinguished allocutions' or similar things, in which he manifests 'immutable solicitude' or the 'firmness of Peter's charity' or the 'supernal inspiration of the Petrine Chair' or the 'admirable insistences of the divine heart,' to 'deeply-moved faithful ears' of 'tremulous sons and daughters' in the 'celestial vault' or 'sacral and substantial hall' of St Peter's Basilica. Even now *L'Osservatore Romano* indulges in such artificial language that it does not bear reading even in Italian: 'With his arms lifted, the patient smile, the transparent and firm look in his eyes, fervour overflowing from his whole person, the Pope moves along on the *sedia gestatoria*, the very image of that which his spirit is invoking and preparing for the Church and for the world.'[14] Here we are at grips with the triumphalism and vaunting glorification attacked during the pontificate of John, a kind of hieratic apotheosis of Paul as a pharaonic incarnation perched on the lofty top of the sacred pyramid.

But in more serious ways, in carefully-written articles, an endeavour was made to present one point of view as officially blessed: e.g., an attack on Oscar Cullmann,[15] Cardinal Bacci writing on Latin as 'the bond of Christian unity and particularly adapted to expound with precision, clarity and conciseness the concepts of doctrine and the norms of discipline,'[16] the exaltation of Italian Catholic Action Societies

---

[14] By Charles Boyer, S.J., a well-known conservative theologian, *L'Oss. Rom.*, July 6, 1963.
[15] *L'Oss. Rom.*, September 26, p. 1.
[16] *L'Oss. Rom.*, December 12.

as 'belonging to the constitutional lines of the Church,'[17] or R. Mazzini, the editor, entitling a leading article 'You, Romans!' or attacking Marxism in a way which implicates the Centre-Left tendency in Italy,[18] or proclaiming the necessity of authoritarian statements and dogmatic affirmations from the Council – if it is to be a real Council[19] – or projecting an untrue image of the Pope, untrue because not corresponding to reality, as having a 'universal paternity,'[20] and stating that 'the teaching authority of the Pope is inserted more than ever in the life of the world.'[21]

During the summer recess, it had been decided also that the theme of the Council of Trent would be orchestrated symphonically to correspond with the progress of the discussions of the second session. The reason is clear: the Tridentine stance into which the Church had fallen meant the consecration of Romanism and the juridical idea of the Church. In September there was held a convention on 'The Council of Trent and the Tridentine Reform,' whose avowed purpose was to correlate the Council of Trent with the Second Vatican Council. The commemoration took place at Trent. Apart from Cardinal Bacci's impassioned appeal for Latin as the cement binding all peoples in one harmonious culture, the main emphasis was upon the doctrinal standpoints and the ecclesiastical mentality of the Council of Trent. One whole day of the second session, December 3, was also devoted to the same purpose.

Later, on December 11, Paul received Cardinal Urbani, his representative at Trent for the centenary celebrations, and spoke of Tridentine values as constituting a 'strong bulwark and defence of the Christian and Catholic mentality,' and remarked that the present Vatican Council was working 'to dispel the confusion of ideas and multiple errors of our time.' On December 11, Cardinal Castaldo inaugurated a book exhibition on the subject of the Council of Trent. Most significantly, Paul in his apostolic letter of November 4, 1963, on seminary development, took a position as regards Trent and seminary development which could only be characterized as retrograde. There was no penetration of the developments that had taken place in the world, no account was taken of modern difficulties which did not exist at the time of Trent, and the words and decrees of Trent were quoted

---

[17] The phrase is Paul's. Cf. its use in *L'Oss. Rom.*, December 15.
[18] Cf. *L'Oss. Rom.*, August 1, for example.   [19] *L'Oss. Rom.*, November 16.
[20] Caption of a photograph of Paul with Buddhist priests in *L'Oss. Rom.*, September 19.   [21] *L'Oss. Rom.*, August 31.

as if their validity were just as efficacious as in the sixteenth century. Although this letter came before the sudden descent in Paul's development, it came as a partial triumph of conservative ideas and purposes.

This insistence on the Tridentine spirit had a real purpose difficult to convey to the ordinary layman or non-Catholic: each bishop at the Council and each theologian had been reared in seminaries organized according to Tridentine principles. If such principles could be aligned in their minds with the conservative trend in conciliar discussions, it would be a definite advantage. It was a question of the very warp and woof of what made priests out of each of the Council members. It had its desired effect on a certain number.

Apart from a multifarious activity, balancing the currents and cross-currents, preparations, groupings, crystallization of positions and weaknesses, among his employees and servitors, Paul was clarifying some final points towards the second week in September, 1963. He did not suspect or foresee what lay ahead, nor did he for one moment realize that a wave of opposition and recalcitrancy, of wearying insistence and intransigent attitudes, would arise and assault him, leaving him as a bare stalk stripped by the winds of conflict. In assessing Paul's development at this point, we must make a preliminary summation of it as a total thing. His vision of the entire undertaking on a global scale must be ascertained. Once that is done, it is easy to see how particular details, minute operations, single actions, merge into a coherent outlook.

Paul has adopted *giovannismo* in a readjusted form. That this readjusted form provided him with a global vision, a world outlook, there can be no doubt. Nevertheless, the value of any world vision depends on the degree of correspondence between the basic suppositions of the vision and the concrete conditions obtaining outside the human spirit and in world reality. It is along these lines that our summation must proceed. The world vision of Paul VI at this time, his *mystique*, concerned the position of the Roman Pontiff. By his schooling in theology, by his association with the Vatican for thirty-four years, by some particular bent of his character, Paul's spirit bathed and swam in the effulgence of a Romanism, new, purified, modernized.

Once upon a time, the Roman Pontiff had been the centre of the world, for the world then was Christendom and Christendom was the world, known to its limited borders, evangelized in all spoken tongues. He was the centre in a very definite sense: as a high mountain is when set overlooking, overshadowing and projecting the rolling expanses of fertile valleys. He was the centre of a hierarchic structure: all others were lower in grade, in dignity, in privilege, in authority. Or, it could be conceived, he was the link between God and man, the universal father of mankind, the interpreter of God's revelation, the Walker of the Summits, a Christian fulfilment of the biblical Moses, communing in the darkness and unseen fire of Sinai and bringing down the Tablets to the people. And his name for ever was Peter. 'You also have come to Rome,' he told a group of pilgrims,[22] 'to see Peter, the Prince of the Apostles, the foundation of the Church, its visible head, the Vicar of Christ in the latest and least person of his successor.' But there is a distinct grading, all are 'distinct members of the same mystical body,' he told his hearers in October. 'Therefore we have a special salute, full of reverence and esteem for the bishops present, for the priests, for the religious men and women who are at this audience. Then we salute the lay people, those who make up with honour and fidelity Christian families.'[23]

In his first radio message he etched the entire pyramidal structure in broad lines: 'The purple-clothed cardinals ... the venerable brother bishops of the East and West ... our esteem for the Roman Curia especially in its preparation and conduct of the Vatican Council ... religious men throughout the world ... the children of this Roman diocese ... the clergy and the faithful of the Milan diocese ... the oppressed Churches of the East ... the preachers of the Gospel every-where ... the members of Catholic Action societies everywhere ... the sick, the poor, the exiled ... youth.' And on all he acts as an *alter Christus:* 'From the Pope to you comes a certain influence of the presence of Christ of whom he is the visible representative.'[24] Rai-mondo Mazzini, editor of *L'Osservatore Romano*, commented on Paul's Romanism in an officially inspired article, adding bluntly: 'The people of the City (Rome) are the true custodians of the sacred character of Rome ... the fulcrum of the entire Christian story. This is the privilege of the *primogeniture of the Romans*.'[25]

Then, however, had come the fission; schisms, heresies, frag-mentation of the unity of Christendom. To increase the diversity and multiply the restless detail of the world, new continents had unfolded from the mists of the Atlantic and from beyond the sands and steppes of the East. And to render this entire world even more opaque to the light of the Papacy and its teaching, there had intervened an intellectual revolution, an industrial revolution, a social revolution, an ideological

[22] *L'Oss. Rom.*, November 21.   [23] *L'Oss. Rom.*, October 17.
[24] *L'Oss. Rom.*, September 18.   [25] *L'Oss. Rom.*, November 20.

revolution, humanism, science, nationalism, Marxism.

In the course of time, a man rose to the dignity of Pope. His name was Roncalli and he called himself John. And fittingly so: for he preached love and he was a forerunner. The fire of his love pierced the opaqueness, awakened everywhere amid the diversity of a changed world a yearning for the homestead of the human spirit, an instinctual reverence for the truth that had made man noble once upon a time. He was a precursor. He had sown where another would reap: he had preached the coming unity of the human race.

Because of his very character and the way in which he acted, the only possible unity – around the mountain – became impossible of realization. Love is one thing. Rationalization of that love, its canalization into operable and operating human structures is another. He had been a creator. Another would have to tend his creation and bring it to fullness. It would again be a repetition in time of the Pauline thrust out into the exterior darkness of the world, a rushing conquest by a new rationalization of old truths, a transposition of the substance of the ancient doctrine into a framework of references easily understood by the world and adapted to the world's needs.

Roncalli's abstention from Italian politics was refined into an abstention from interference with ancient political formulas: the black aristocracy of Italy, unbending adhesion to one outmoded form of political thought – the traditional Right, the maintenance of an offended attitude for having been evicted from temporal power. Instead, an injection of Vatican interests in the real sinews of power – the managers of the socio-economic life of Italy. Instead, the adoption of the Centre-Left movement, the leavening of it, the defence of it. Instead, clear and oft-affirmed rejection of any desire to return to pre-1870 power, and a constant harping on the present equilibrium of State and Church, of Quirinal and Vatican, of President and Pope, as the twin columns of Italian civilization and national being.

Roncalli's stance as regards the modern world and its developing contours would have to be rid of some of its awkwardness, its lack of crystallized principles. It left his successor too much off guard, too amorphous in conceptualization. There was certainly forming on the horizon of human events a unity of the human family; Roncalli had seen it, just as the other great figures of his time, De Gaulle, Adenauer, Kennedy. The huge unleavened populations adhering to non-Christian religions were attaining a self-consciousness that called for formal relations with them. There was also a trend to a gathering-in of all the non-Roman Catholic Christians in a brand of ecumenism that could no longer be ignored. There was, finally, a sudden sharpening of the weakest links in human relations, Jews with Christians, Negroes with white men, Europeans with Americans, Africans with former colonial nations, Muslim with Hindu, Chinese Marxist with Russian Marxist, Marxist with Socialist, Soviet with the 'West,' Asiatic with Occidental. This was a network of strains and polarized forces, an ugly, bizarre, irregular alignment of human spirits running according to no geographical or ethnic principle, and dividing humanity even as it inevitably toiled on towards unity through internationalism and international activity and communication.

There was, most disturbing phenomenon of all, an evident dislocation within the closed circles of Roman Catholicism: for a long time, in spite of the fatal advents of the Reform and Enlightenment, the rise of nationalism, and the temporal hewing-down to size of the Vatican in 1870, the development of Catholicism outside the immediate borders of the Vatican had coincided with the doctrinal and administrative development of the Vatican itself: they formed two concentric circles, the former contained in and pinned to the latter. Now, however, the circle of development in the Church as a whole had been unpinned, had widened out, while the circle of the administrative Church was congealed in historical attitudes: the gradual civilization of the masses in place of the former civilization of the *élite*, the rise of mass education and mass media of communication, the advent of a religiously pluralistic society, the formation of new thought structures due to scientific advances and social evolution, all these had percolated through the circle of the faithful, swollen its delimited size to almost breaking-point, to explosion-point. John had seen the coming explosion, and this was one of his motives in demanding *aggiornamento*.

For the developing unity of the human family with its sharpened difficulties, and for the potential explosion within the borders of Catholicism, Paul refined *giovannismo*. Unity of Europe: here alignment with the general lines of Italian foreign policy was necessary; he would be guided by the development of the Rome-London axis as a parallel to and control of the Paris-Bonn axis; political Communism in the East was subsumed under the accepted Italian concept of the *Drang nach Westen* of Slavism. Unity of the world: for the moment, the Church belonged to the West, Europe in particular; until the static American policy towards the mainland colossus of Communist China had melted into something more fluid, until the already mobile lines of

American policy towards the Soviet bloc had meshed into something more viable than negative test-ban treaties, trade and cultural exchanges, and a 'hot-line' relationship between Moscow and Washington, until, finally, the desperate, last-minute attempt of American policy to contain Fidelist Communism and prevent it from seeping through the rickety political and social structure of South and Central America, the Church would have to remain as it was, Europe-centred, Western-minded, dependent on the traditional network of Vatican diplomats, apostolic delegations, concordats, accredited representatives.

But he would push the image of the Pope, of Peter, the venerable depository of the values that made Western civilization what it was. And out beyond the fringes of this civilization, he would project the image of a figurehead of peace, of skilful diplomatic representation, of someone who, standing apart from all particular sides and factions, would juridically and ideologically provide a focal point for the centripetal forces slowly forcing the race of man to concrete expression of their specific unity as men.

The proximate step and the first big move towards effecting this would be through conciliarism,* through the Council, for through it he could implement the concepts of internationalization, harmony between groups differing in race, colour, religion, politics. This is why, within the ambit of conciliarism and its offshoot, ecumenism, Paul included his aims of peacemaking with Jews, with non-Christian religions. And with this interwoven vision of his world, he proceeded to erect the structure of his principles of activity, the schematization in concrete plans of what he wished to obtain. And thus, at the beginning of September, 1963, and before he returned from his summer residence at Castelgandolfo, Paul had made his first choice. His objectives in the second session had been definitively chosen, and his tactics to obtain those objectives had been clearly defined.

Conciliarly speaking, Paul wanted one thing and one thing only: a theoretic and a practical conclusion to the question of episcopal collegiality. A theoretic statement from the Council bishops on the dogmatic validity of such collegiality: 'We are one of the bishops. Peter was one of the Apostles, united by the Lord in a common charge.' A practical conclusion: by conciliar vote and by his own consent

---

* The author uses this word in a modern and unaccustomed sense, meaning generally 'conciliar awareness,' 'consciousness of collegiality on the part of the bishops,' not as implying any opposition to the Pope as such. Historically, the word refers to the movement subordinating the Pope to a Council, in the 14th and 15th centuries. See author's comment on page 225.

and acceptance, the bishops must be representatively associated with him in such universal government. His tactics: an utterly frank public stand on the theoretic and practical aspects, by serving notice gently but firmly on the ranks of Vatican bureaucratic administration and by inviting the bishops to consent to such an association with their head. His pedagogy: the Council floor and its day-to-day discussions, his private talks with Council members, the dissemination of the project through private circulation and canvassing.

Ecumenically speaking, Paul limited himself, again, to one thing with a theoretic and a practical aspect: theoretically, he wished the Council to put into his hands a useful document, terms of reference for his ecumenical activities, a brief of pastoral principles and positive dispositions, with which he could travel to a summit with Athenagoras of Istanbul, with Ramsey of Canterbury, with Alexis of Moscow, with the Orthodox Church of America. In this regard, Paul considered Chapters 4 and 5 of Bea's schema on Ecumenism as godsends: Chapter 5 delineated the Church's stand on Religious Liberty and proclaimed freedom of conscience and the inalienable rights of every man even if supposed to be in error. Chapter 4, dealing with the Jewish problem, was a particular application of Chapter 5, for in it the Church quite literally undid an age-old accusation and acknowledged Judaism as an ethic of perennial value, a belief of divine origin and a way of life that should command respect. Chapters 1–3 of Bea's schema were other applications to other forms of Christianity. Between them, Chapters 1–4 applied the principles of Chapter 5. His main tactic: protect Bea so that the latter could be free to manage all the rest. His pedagogy: again, the Council discussions and a private strengthening of the resolve of American bishops.

Ecclesiastically speaking, Paul had multiple objectives: a definition of the Church which would de-emphasize the juridical aspect, the pyramidal concept; the active participation of lay auditors, men and women, in the Council; a relaxation of clerical celibacy in certain disaster areas of the Catholic Church such as Italy, South America, Puerto Rico or in certain new fields of Catholic effort, such as the newly-born African nations; the re-establishment of an order of married deacons to supply the need for priests in certain countries; conciliar approaches to the great non-Christian religions with a view to dispelling misunderstandings about the missionary effort of the Church and the establishment of concrete means of mutual knowledge and understanding: for this purpose he even toyed, at this date, with a personal papal visit to Africa; last but not least, a clear unequivocal stand by the Council on the Jewish question and some illumination of the relationship between Synagogue and Church, not only in order to cut absolutely at the root of anti-Semitism, but to destroy for ever an infamous historical tension: 'We must not only wipe away those imaginary bloodstains of a deicide, we must contemplate and observe closely our intimate relationship with the children of Abraham.' He would decide, after adoption and promulgation of the Jewish document by the Council, and depending on the decision of the bishops, whether Jewish questions could finally, perhaps, be handled by a new Secretariat for non-Christian Religions which he was to create. At that stage, no final decision had been made on this latter point.

Besides these objectives and tactics, Paul had worked out in his own mind certain principles of action and earmarked certain things to be avoided. Within the Council, there must be no acrid polemics: any discussion was ruled out on the burning subjects that had provoked near-revolt during the first session a year before. Thus, the questions of divine revelation, of tradition, of biblical exegesis, of Roman curial abuses, were not to be touched upon. Pamphlets destined for the Council Fathers must not emanate either from the *Pensionato Romano* where Monsignor Spadafora lived and worked, from the Biblical Institute, or from anywhere else. He would visit both the Lateran and the Gregorian Universities. There would be no discussion on the ticklish question of the relations between the Church and the modern State. Outside the Council's circle, but certainly not peripheral to the Council's discussions and interests, he had formulated a few guide-lines of conduct: a diplomatic offensive directed at the governments and the peoples of the emergent African nations, especially those of Muslim persuasion; a probing of the delicate situation in the Near and Middle East relying on the decline of Nasserism as a positive threat to the existing *status quo;* the continuation of negotiations with governments in Soviet satellite countries and even with the central USSR Government; and, finally, abstention from any interference in the shakily developing Italian internal political situation, more in the subconscious fear that political *combinazioni* might have pejorative repercussions in the conciliar sphere, than from any native desire to keep out of politics. For Paul is a man fascinated by politics and the art of the politician.

Thus harmoniously arranged and synthetized in theory and in practice, Paul's objectives seemed definitely if not easily attainable. The Council would get off the ground. Ecumenism would attain just proportions. A definite contribution would be made to world peace. The promise of the near future was good, and the skies seemed clear and full of affirmations. The lake near his summer palace mirrored the cloudless Italian sky on its faultless surface, and merged in the calm, reflected blue were the hills and trees of the quiet banks; the light peculiar to the Italian sky enhanced the whole with gleams of future promise. It was a physical representation of his spiritual state in those final summer days: he had merged the stark outlines of his concrete objectives during the coming session into the solvent, embracing unity of a mystical outlook and belief; and over the whole there flowed the winsomely serene light of his inner illumination.

FOUR

THE VALLEY OF DECISION

The period we are about to cover lies, properly speaking, between November 8 and November 23, 1963. And a strictly and merely chronological account would adhere to this division of the matter. I have, however, deliberately ranged the material belonging to the period from September 12 to November 8 with the account of what happened up to November 23, for a good reason: only by catching a glimpse of Paul's first flight and the plotted arc of his achievement will we realize the extent of the *débâcle* that overtook him after November 8. More importantly, only thus can we understand the motivation of his decision and its far-reaching consequences for conciliarism, for ecumenism, for Christianity, and for the world of our day.

We can also appreciate more deeply John XXIII, his faith, his courage, his intelligence. Single actions of his which may have smacked of the melodramatic or Italian emotionalism in this light acquire the acrid taste of bitter human experience. The words he penned, for example, in the spring of 1963 to the most prominent adversary of his in the Curia: 'Venerable brother: We are in continuous pain and suffering at the constant way in which you have organized your life and office to maintain a continued opposition to Our deepest wishes; and We only pray that God, Our common Father, may either shed light in your heart or take Us away from the pain of conflict with you,' would never be written by Montini, but the sentiments would be his, the pains, the frustration and resentment.

Much of our story from this point on consists of descriptive matter. It will help to remember that we are here describing the substructure which Paul erected as the logical filling-in of the structurization he planned for the second session. We will find that, until the turgid period of November 8 to 23, Paul's behaviour was consistently marked by decision, by swift, calculated actions which betray his seeming mastery of the situation, and by his use of surprise.

We are now going to deal with matters which at first sight may seem to be purely ecclesiastical, 'churchy' – to use a less reverential expression. This is true as regards the actual details. Yet, it is hoped that the human and Christian significance of the entire mosaic will stand out in clear profile. If we remember Paul's world outlook, the hierarchy of his values, his ultimate purpose as described in the previous chapter, each little fragment of the mosaic will fall into a definite place and form with the others a pattern which is undoubtedly of primary importance and interest to history. For they are the stuff of history. Here history was made.

1. September 12 to September 29

We first have to note the orchestrated way in which Paul suddenly, as it were, and with deft words, unveiled the totality of his plans. True enough, and characteristically, we are dealing with his *words*. Yet, for him who occupies the summit, words are commands, and commands, *ex hypothesi*, are virtual actions. They are words of authority, of dignity, of primacy. Words from the summit.

Paul focused his attention on six objectives. On each one he let loose a verbal barrage. Each one was a formulation of how he intended to run the Council. And each effort was shot through with the essential lines of his *mystique*. On September 12, he addressed a letter to Cardinal Tisserant, Dean of the College of Cardinals: Paul was speaking as head of the Vatican to the hierarchic Church. On September 14, he addressed a Letter and an Exhortation to the bishops of the world: Paul was speaking then as Pope to the leaders of the universal Church. On September 21, he addressed the entire officials of the Roman Curia: Paul was speaking as Bishop of Rome to his administrative right-arm. On September 22, he spoke to journalists, as the head of a large organization laying down the type of public relations he desired to have with the world at large. On September 26, he spoke to an assembly of pilgrims in St Peter's: his voice then was that of the universal Pastor to his flock. On September 29, he made his opening speech to the Council Fathers: he was then Peter, one of the original Eleven, speaking to the historical successors of the Eleven.

To the hierarchic Church, he spoke in precise terms as one member of the organization speaking to another: the reasons for continuing the Council were pragmatic – reverence for John XXIII who had begun it all, and the need to finish off the whole thing; the purposes of the session:[1] the setting up of a new secretariat to take away the *sollicitudines* (preoccupations) that were being thrust upon him in regard to

[1] The spiritual progress of the Church, the unity of Christians, the peace and progress of all men.

non-Christian religions. Paul was thinking primarily of the Jewish problem with its relationship to Islam, and of Buddhism and its relationship to Catholic missions abroad.[2] No longer was he stressing *aggiornamento;* the word had acquired a bad taste. The emphasis was on Church progress, which, along with the unity of Christians (ecumenism), was the all-important aim.

To the bishops of the world, Paul spoke authoritatively; let the bishops meet on September 29 for the new session; let them also introduce special prayers and penances for the success of the Council and its aims; the aims were, he said bluntly, the unity of Christians and the unity of all men.

To the Curia, Paul presented a twentieth century version of Paolo Sarpi's cry, *'Agnosco stylum Romanae Curiae.'*[3] In effect, said Paul smoothly, you have been accused of many things,[4] but to prove that there is nothing in all this, you can do only one thing: co-operate with me and with the bishops of the Council in reforming the Roman offices[5] and delegating bishops of the universal church to govern the universal Church with me.[6] Paul was here revealing one concrete plan he had for the session, of which we shall have more to say shortly.

To the faithful, Paul spoke as Peter in authority: Christ used three images to describe his Church figuratively: a rock (Peter), the keys (papal power), the net (the jurisdiction used by Peter); you are here in

---

[2] Actually the idea of such a secretariat was first launched by R. Wiltgen, S.V.D., director of the Divine Word News Service during the Council. He got Bishop Anthony Thijssen, head of the Larantuka diocese, Indonesia, to give a news conference on April 6, 1963, in which the Bishop suggested the idea. This was followed up by a statement of Cardinal Tien, of China (in exile), in which the cardinal said that he would give such an idea his full support. Cardinal König of Vienna also encouraged the idea, though he did not wish to leave his diocese of Vienna.

[3] 'I recognize the style (the knife *or* the style) of the Roman Curia.' At that time Pope Paul V had placed the Most Serene Republic of Venice under interdict. Paolo Sarpi, a theological consultor for the Doge of Venice, was attacked by hirelings of the Curia with stilettos (*stylum*) and left for dead on the evening of October 5, 1607. During his convalescence he reportedly used the above phrase. *Stylum* is used in its ambivalent sense of writing-stylo (or pen) and knife.

[4] Amongst other things, Paul said: 'You are said to be a bureaucratic hotbed of hidden ambitions and sordid antagonisms, pretensions, antipathetic, legalistic, and formalistic.'

[5] Paul spelled the reform out with the words 'to simplify,' 'to decentralize,' 'to cede to bishops the exercise of their rights,' 'to become supranational in its composition,' 'to acquire a more accurate ecumenical education.'

[6] Actually, bishops have the *right* to govern the universal Church with the Pope as their head. Rome has repeatedly curtailed the exercise of this right to the point of obfuscating its existence.

Peter's tomb; I am Peter's successor. This speech was so much to the liking of the editorial board of *L'Osservatore Romano* that a long editorial by R. Mazzini, the editor, claimed, among other things, that 'the Holy Spirit animates and moulds the successor of Peter (Paul VI) each day.' What is important is the deliberate way in which Paul insisted on his prerogatives. This became a rising note of insistence with him as the weeks passed.

To the journalists, Paul manifested his fears, his confidence, his desires: journalists are apt to pick up a phrase or word and read something into it. Yet account must be taken of the awesome power of the communications media in our modern world. The majority of the journalists listening were Catholic and Italian. The Pope knew, therefore, that they would live up to their solid traditions of objectivity and completeness of coverage.

To the assembled bishops of the Council, on September 29, Paul outlined a résumé of all that he had endeavoured to convey in his preceding messages. He insisted on identifying his own role: three times[7] he directed the attention of the entire assembly to himself as he affirmed the dignity of his office. He extolled the figure of John as amiable and priestly and praised Roncalli's uncanny creative power: 'He made a speech here at the opening of the first session of the Council which appeared as a downright inspiration not only to the Church but to the entire society of men.' Finally he spelled out the concrete objectives of the discussions: to define the nature of the Church (this, with a view to appealing more strongly to the dissident Christian Churches), to define the role of bishops in the government of the universal Church, to build a bridge with the world outside the Church. In addition, Paul addressed the bishops pointedly: 'You are apostles, you have your origin in the college of the apostles, and you are their true heirs.' This was a clear indication of what his thoughts were. His only concrete reference to the outside world was to the physical difficulties encountered by certain bishops in the satellite countries in attending the Council.

Paul's estimate of what the Council was to do, therefore, hinged on

[7] 'Thus you are welcomed by the servant of the servants of God, although loaded with the sovereign keys which Jesus Christ gave to Peter. Thus he thanks you for the signs of obedience and fidelity which you have given him. . . .' 'We testify that there is in our soul no plan of human domination or mere zeal for our own power. . . .' 'You know that on the twenty-first day of June the College of empurpled Fathers . . . chose us for the Roman episcopal see and thus for the sovereign pontificate over the universal Church.'

his own position as Peter's successor; he emphasized this far more than a Roncalli would ever have done, more in the style of Pius XII and Pius IX. He wished that the bishops should exercise their rights as bishops and govern the Church with him instead of leaving the business to the Roman Curia. He wished to create para-religious bonds with non-Christian religions. Finally, and chiefly, he wished to create suitable conditions for his ecumenical encounter with Orthodoxy.

Things were moving slowly in this regard. Athenagoras of Constantinople had not yet been able to answer Paul's letter in full. At the Pan-Orthodox Conference held on the island of Rhodes in the last days of September, two questions were tossed back and forth: would or should observers be sent to the second session of the Council? and would or should a delegation be sent to Rome to explore the possibilities of union? To the second question the general answer was affirmative, due mainly to the efforts of the Russian Archbishop Nikodim of Minsk. The Greek delegation abstained; 43 out of 55 bishops voted against. At a meeting of the Holy Synod, 10 of the 12 members voted against sending any representatives. In the final communiqué it was merely stated that it was left to each Church to decide for itself whether to send observers or not; it was also recommended that a *theological* dialogue with Rome be opened.

News of the relationship between Athenagoras and Paul, on the one hand, and of the slight break-through on the Orthodox front, on the other, aroused fears, animosities and apprehensions at the headquarters of the World Council of Churches. The possibilities were clear: if Rome and Constantinople or Moscow drew closer to each other, the Catholicism of those belonging to the World Council of Churches might disappear. This would mean that the various acephalous independent churches would be let loose like bobbing corks and lack an element that would entitle them to claim to belong to the *Catholica* or Church in the sense that non-Roman Catholic ecumenism and ecumenists had always claimed. Visser't Hooft, the secretary general of the World Council of Churches, and his immediate aides, were seriously perturbed about the possible fragmentation of the groups that had been merged in his organization. Later on, during the Council session, this subject was to introduce a certain amount of cleavage among the non-Catholic observers at the Council: some wished to refuse all participation (even by their presence) at the celebration commemorating the Council of Trent; others would decide to be present. On the other hand, Archbishop Ramsey of Canterbury, when asked about the apparent policy of Rome in drawing near to Constantinople and Moscow to the detriment of the other associated Churches, would defend the Roman position. Paul VI felt confident, however, that Athenagoras would overcome the opposition in his own Synod, and that ultimately he and Athenagoras would arrange a meeting.

Within the Vatican, Paul was arranging matters so that the session could launch into its work without any unnecessary delays. The usual notices about the secrecy of the Council were issued by the Secretariat of the Council and published in L'Osservatore Romano.[8] A small notice appearing in the L'Osservatore[9] granted the permission of the Congregation of Rites for all bishops, titular and residential, to wear a ceremonial article of clothing called the *mozzetta* even in the presence of the Pope. It was a small point, yet it underscored by its symbolism the desire of Paul to appear in the midst of the bishops as a bishop among episcopal colleagues.

Success attended the work of Cardinal Bea, which consisted chiefly in working over the text of his schema on Ecumenism, in maintaining contact with non-Catholic Churches, and in preparing the way for the introduction of his two documents on the Jewish question and religious liberty. Although Bea was not sure that any of the Greek Churches would send observer-delegates, he had, by the end of September and before opening day on September 29, a substantial roster of names.[10] In more than one private discussion with Paul, Bea had come up against difficulties as regards the documents on the Jews and on religious liberty. Paul had also voiced to Bea the oft-repeated objections of the Holy Office and of Cardinal Ottaviani that any member of Bea's Secretariat – and this included Bea himself – should speak *in the name of the Secretariat* on the theme of the Church or the role of bishops in governing the Church. The Curial officials felt that a speech from Bea or one of his chief aides like De Smedt of Belgium, might tilt the scales unfavourably. They were also aware of the very strong influence that the mere name of Bea had on the majority of the American bishops. His authority with the group of Council Fathers known as the Central European bloc was too painfully obvious to merit comment. 'It would be fair and just for the cardinal to let the Council make up its

[8] L'Oss. Rom., September 23 and 27.   [9] L'Oss. Rom., September 16–17.
[10] Officially, there were 21 different religious groups represented by delegations, counting over 56 persons. In addition there were over 10 'guests' of the Secretariat, such people as Oscar Cullmann, Roger Schutz and Max Thurian (these last two of Taizé community in France). L'Oss. Rom. of October 19 printed the full official list.

mind,' they argued. Personal prestige in an Ecumenical Council of the Catholic Church was ruled out for everyone except His Holiness the Pope.

The pressure on Paul, chiefly from Cicognani, Ottaviani and An-tóniutti, was so great in this respect, and Bea's resistance – tranquil, subtle, hard to break down – so reasonable, that Paul was obliged to accept a fatal compromise, the first of a series of procrastinations, accepted by Bea in good faith and blessed by Paul in his reliance on his own authority: if neither Bea nor any member of his Secretariat spoke *in the name of the Secretariat* on the delicate subjects in question, then Ottaviani would guarantee that he would not speak publicly in opposition to Bea's documents on Ecumenism, the Jewish question, and religious liberty, *in the name of the Holy Office.*

The conservatives were duly worried about the tenor of Paul's speech to the members of the Curia on September 21. More than anything else, they were worried about the possible outcome of the principle enunciated on that occasion by Papa Montini: 'If the Council manifests the desire to see some representatives of their own number associated with the head of the Church in the study and the responsi-bility of the universal government of the Church, the Curia will certainly not be the one to offer any opposition . . . The *Curia Romana* is, of course, specifically administrative, consultative, and executive in nature.'

The general plan they adopted at this stage was not concerned with specific points in detail, but laid down certain guide-lines: they would endeavour to avoid all public controversy by pamphlet or speeches, and would press for the same behaviour on the part of their opponents. Paul VI went along with this proposal in so far as he refused adamantly to allow the Council to take up burning issues on which agreement could not be reached. In addition, the conservatives decided that a policy of prudent procrastination, a mixture of carefully handled filibustering, procedural obstacles, a constant diversion of the attention of the Council Fathers to the question of the Liturgy schema,[11] the leavening of conciliar spirits by harping on the theme of the Council of Trent, would carry them over into December when nothing conclusive would have been decided and no irreparable harm done to their cause and their expectations. They also knew that the most vociferous speakers were, not Americans, Germans, Frenchmen, or

---

[11] Left over from the first session and still undergoing amendments and emen-dations.

Dutchmen, but Italians and Spaniards. The latter could be depended on to collaborate. And thus it was hoped to create sufficient pressure to hold up any definitive voting on the question of bishops' rights to participate in the government of the universal Church. Even if the schema on Ecumenism were broached, it could not, under the circumstances, come to any conciliar action.

The chapter on religious liberty, as everyone knew, was lost in the bowels of a sub-commission of the Theological Commission of which Ottaviani was the head. And it would take some strong boring power to extract, print, distribute it to the Fathers and get any kind of discussion going – much less bring it to a definitive vote. As for Bea's document on the Jews, the plans were similar. First, this document was not even printed. Secondly, there were many potent reasons of state against its introduction in the Council. This document should be kept in the unprinted stage: if printed, it became at least a conciliar document.

The conservatives did not expect much trouble from the Jesuits in Rome. When the rectorship of the Gregorian University fell vacant, the Congregation of Seminaries and University Studies refused to accept any of the three candidates proposed by the General of the Jesuits: the latter wished to have a Father Dezza, but he was *persona non grata* with the Holy Office. In addition, the Holy Father, it was known, wanted to visit the Lateran and Gregorian Universities. Father Dezza would have co-operated most willingly with the proposal of a papal visit. Consequently, the Congregation, contrary to the usual procedure, proposed to the Jesuit General Janssens that a Father Dhanis be appointed to the post of rector. The latter was well-known as a self-professed conservative, had an exact, scholastic mind, devoid of any self-criticism, was very 'obedient' to the Curial authorities and could not understand and assimilate anything which was not expressed in scholastic terms. Instead of standing on his rights, the General of the Jesuits accepted Father Dhanis's nomination. Later, on November 1, Dhanis would be nominated also to the Holy Office. He was a reliable man.

It was thought useful, however, for two pamphlets to be prepared, one outlining the danger which the Central European bloc represented for the freedom and purity of the Council, the other expressing, without heat or controversy, the traditional position on the Jewish question. Both will be mentioned in the proper place. The latter was obviously the work of an authentic, if single-track-minded, theologian.

Both Pope Paul and Bea had decided on a very different pattern for the flow of events in the Council from September 30 onwards. First of all, in their estimate, the documents on the Church and on the rights of bishops would encounter no trouble in rallying the majority of the bishops. Here, Paul agreed to a special plan. Bea copied out the pertinent parts of Paul's speech to the Curia[12] which, when put together with a short preamble and conclusion, formed an impressive document. It would express three points: the Holy Father had asked the bishops whether they wished to join him in the government of the Church; the bishops would be very happy and eager to do this; the bishops asked His Holiness to indicate to them the type of men he desired, the length of time they should be at his disposal, and the type of problems they would be called upon to deal with. On Bea devolved the task of talking about this proposal to some of the more influential Council members, of getting a few thousand copies of the document multigraphed for distribution at the appropriate time, and of eventually finding a suitable non-European cardinal to propose it on the Council floor. It was to be proposed in the form of a wish or *votum* to the Holy Father. And the vote on it would be by acclamation.

If such an eventuality came to pass, the situation would roughly be as follows: the bishops of the universal Church would be in direct association with the Bishop of Rome, the apostles with Peter. But – Bea and Paul hoped – the Council would have predisposed minds for such an eventuality by adopting definite standpoints on the divine right of bishops to participate with the Pope in the government of the Church. It was on this hope or presumption that the whole plan foundered.

Towards the two documents on religious liberty and the Jewish question, a different attitude was deliberately adopted. If all went well, the texts on the Church and the rights of bishops would be passed and approved, and, in the bargain, a definite link between the Roman bishop and the bishops at large would be forged. After this, the obvious step was for the newly self-conscious entity, the Church, to turn around and tackle the basis of both ecumenism and relations with the world outside, whether Christian or non-Christian. It would seem better, they thought, for the Council to adopt the chapter on religious liberty as a document standing on its own legs and the Church's frank answer to its attitude towards *all* religions. The document on the Jews would be an implementation of this attitude on one issue only. Because

---

[12] Those parts which spoke about the need of reform, of internationalization, of the participation, according to their own wish, by the bishops in the universal government of the Church.

of its very nature, because of the history of the Church on the matter, because of the existing wave of anti-Semitism, and because of the expectations and hopes of Judaism all over the world, it would be better to set this document up on its own and let it stand as an isolated testimony to the Church's desire to make up for past wrongs and its teaching applied to a particular problem which was a world problem. After this, the schema on Ecumenism could be started, discussed, and voted upon. Paul needed this document, he thought, for further progress. His approach to Athenagoras must not be juridical, but pastoral and evangelical, and must be the expression of conciliar will.

The mood of the returning Council members when entering St Peter's on September 29, corresponded exactly to the pattern which Papa Montini skilfully outlined in his inaugural speech. The objectives seemed clear, the Pope was determined, the bishops appeared to be united on the issues at stake. All seemed well. On the Italian political scene, however, things were taking a turn for the worse. The Communist Press came out on September 29 attacking the tottering Leone government. Simultaneously, voices of the extreme Right were raised attacking any further collaboration with the Left or Centre-Left. It was a bad sign. It contained elements which would definitely and ultimately shape the course of conciliar events.

2. September 30 to November 8

The conciliar drama that now began to unfold falls into two very distinct periods: the first occupied almost the entire month of October up to and including October 30, the second lasted from that point until November 8. The first period consisted in a play of force and counter-force, conciliar force against curial counter-force: despite diversion and delay and resort to procedural tactics, the welling tide of majority opinion pushed aside the desperate opposition, and broke out into the freedom of a crushing vote on October 30. This was the high-point of achievement, the ultimate expression of conciliarism, the proof of its objective existence, the voice of the bishops. The second period was a lull, a dangerous pause such as good men, who are not looking for blood but only for their rights, unwittingly allow. In those days from October 30 to November 8, the mustered forces were allowed to relax, to become directed into various nondescript channels. The counter-force, on the contrary, bottled up, cornered, and made more compact in danger and resolute by the finality of the situation, proceeded to react with all the previous strength of the established order.

Let us see briefly and in schematic outline what the business of the Council was during the first phase. On September 30, discussions began on the document entitled *The Church*. By October 16 the first two chapters had been debated. Chapter 3 was concluded on October 25. Cloture was imposed on Chapter 4 by October 31. If one thumbs through the official communiqués and public commentaries on this period of conciliar discussion, it seems impossible at first sight to find a consistent thread running through it all. Detailed discussions, the concentration of energies on what seemed, and still seems, to have been minor points of no great consequence,[13] were the order of the day.

Central to all considerations was the big question: what does one

---

[13] 'Minor' interest in the sense that they rather obfuscated the basic issues that should have been hammered out.

mean when one speaks of the 'Church'? To understand the significa-
tion of the question, it was necessary to realize that in using the term
'Church,' the questioner has in mind not a scholastic definition conditioned, in the usual Aristototelian-Thomastic fashion, by substance and
accident; some kind of aprioristic somersault in the mental clouds of a
metaphysic which inevitably tosses the victim into an abyss of juridical
and ritualistic definitions. The question refers to the actual historical
nature of the group founded by Christ, which has lasted since His time.
It focuses on bishop, laity, Pope, patriarch, rites, priesthood – as they
are *de facto* and not *de jure*. This was the importance of the question for
the second session and for Paul's entire plan of ecumenical development.

'The stumbling block which prevents co-operation between the
Churches is the question of the Church, its authority, its government,'
wrote Professor Zernov.[14] 'You must have noticed,' wrote Alexis
Stepanovitch Khomiakov, the great Russian lay theologian, to his
friend, the Anglican O. W. Palmer, 'that the divergencies between the
Oriental Church and all the western Confessions, both Roman and
those who split away from Rome and became Protestant, do not
concern so much points of dogmatic belief or some part of the Credo,
but something completely different which has never as yet been
clearly defined and made explicit. The entire difference consists in
opposing ways in which the very essence of the Church is either
understood or defined.'[15] One could multiply such quotations from
various Christian sources, Roman Catholic, Anglican, Russian and
Greek Orthodox, in order to show the primordial importance of the
question. Now, if Paul and his Church were ever to present themselves
to any other Christian group, the first question they must be able to
answer clearly, unequivocally, would be: 'Who are you? and what is
the nature of the Christian body which you represent?'

At the heart of the matter, differences between the Orthodox and
Roman Catholic are not dogmatic but have to do with historical forms
and accretions which both Churches, especially the Roman Catholic,
have acquired through the ages. While Rome could subscribe to
Georgiadis's definition of the Orthodox Church as 'the pattern of the
koinōnia of the Apostles, a fellowship of Churches knit together in the
common faith and love of Our Lord Jesus Christ,'[16] Roman Catholic

[14] *The Church of the Eastern Christians*, New York, 1961, p. 52.
[15] Cf. R. Baron, *Un théologien laïc orthodoxe russe au XIXe siècle: A. St Khomiakof*,
Coll. Or. Christ. Anal., 127. Rome 1940, pp. 91–92.
[16] H. Georgiadis, *An Orthodox looks at the Re-union Problem*, in *Eastern Churches
Quarterly*, 1950, vol. 8, p. 422.

theologians would define their Church as 'the pattern of unity ... of St Peter, Prince of the Apostles and spokesman of the Apostolic band.'[17] In due proportion, the same remarks are valid with regard to the Anglican Communion.

During this first part of the session, the discussions centred on this problem. The two poles of thought most apparent were, of course, the conservative and the progressive. For the conservative, the Church was a juridical body headed by the Pope, served by bishops and priests, held together and cemented by the authority and power centred in the branching ramified musculature and ever-lengthening sinews of the Pope's right arm – the Roman Curia. And the people, the laity, belonging to this body, were ministered to, baptized, shriven, nourished, anointed and dispatched to eternity through a series of formulas and rituals to be observed unquestioningly and a body of teachings to be absorbed in childlike faith. For the progressive, this was too juridical, too unreal, too *un*-Christian. The Church was primarily the faithful, Pope, priest, layman. The government of the Church was confided to bishops, one of whom had been exalted to the position of the Vicar of Christ. But he remained one bishop among many, one of the Eleven Apostles, and the bishops had the privilege and the duty from God to govern the Church as a whole, not merely a small part of it called their diocese, together with the central Bishop of Rome.

Around these two concepts the discussion ebbed and flowed. And all other elements which entered the debate, the position of the Virgin Mary in the Church, the question of married priests or deacons, the people of God, the 'name' of the Church, the priesthood of the faithful, the sacramentality of bishops, the powers and rights of episcopal conferences, the presence of women in the Church, the relations of the bishops to the Bishop of Rome and/or to the *Curia Romana*, all these and similar questions were either the garrulous aberrations of confused minds or skilfully deployed red herrings intended to prolong the discussions and to create a mental vacuum in the minds of the uncommitted by posing too many particular questions to which answers were not forthcoming.

The question was of fundamental importance: on it hung the fate of Paul's ecumenical plans, and on their fate hung the outcome of his success in constituting the 'third force' he dreamt of, and on the emergence of such a 'third force' in Paul's mind depended the role – effective or weak – of Christianity in the world of the twentieth

[17] *Ibid.*, p. 420.

century. Paul saw this just as John had seen it before him.

Meanwhile, even in the staid columns of *L'Osservatore Romano*, strange things were appearing. An ambiguous article that made many people think, appeared under the name of Gianfranco Nolli. In discussing the parable of the wedding feast (Oct. 12), the author discovered that four groups of people received invitations to the wedding: the *egoists* or *indifferent, political adversaries* (of the king who organized the wedding feast), the *presumptuous*, and finally *volunteers* or the *generous*. The entire article was obviously a commentary on the current conciliar situation, but the identity of the groups was far from clear. It caused more than one lively exchange in the conciliar bars.

By the middle of October, a curious phenomenon was apparent in the Council: the majority of speakers and the most eloquent all seemed to belong to the conservative side, yet both conservatives and progressives knew that the majority of the Council members were progressive. This was made apparent by two events: the determination of the position of the Virgin Mary in the concept of the Church and the status and function of the bishop, as such, in the Church. Conservatives wanted to have a separate chapter on the Virgin Mary, progressives wished, prudently and wisely, to include any mention of Mary in the description of the Church itself, for she belonged to an integral Catholic exposition of its nature. Conservatives held that the bishops did not constitute any kind of *collegium* with the pope, were not the colleagues of the pope, were but administrators of their own dioceses. Theologically, each bishop had a divine right over his diocese. He had no divine right over the universal Church.

Several tactics of the progressives at this point failed miserably. They suffered chiefly from lack of leadership. They no longer found Bea fertile with suggestions, a spearhead of the movement, a collaborator in speech-writing, ready to suggest a word to the Moderators or higher up, to the figure on the fourth floor of the Vatican palace. Bea, in fact, had been admonished by Paul to abstain from any Council leadership. He did meet with Alter of Cincinnati on October 13 and discuss the problems of his documents on religious liberty and ecumenism. But this was, as it were, *en passant*. At one stage Cardinal Ritter of St Louis was asked by Bea, in a telephone conversation, to make a keynote speech on Monday, October 14, and to point out that long before the present pyramidal system of Pope and Curia ruled the Church, the latter had been governed by a system of patriarchs. But the points in the speech were badly articulated, perhaps Ritter did not understand exactly what was wanted, and it fell flat.

Then Monsignor Bettazzi, the young co-adjutor bishop of Bologna, made a speech on October 11 in which he asserted that the *transalpini* (the non-Italian bishops) could not claim to be the foremost champions of the idea of episcopal collegiality. Several Italian churchmen, he said, had championed the idea. It was therefore something quite natural to the Italian mind. The speech was displeasing to Paul, it is not clear why, and Lercaro, Cardinal of Bologna and Bettazzi's superior, was told to admonish Bettazzi. The other progressives, Americans and Europeans, were delighted by the speech but did not follow it up. Nobody, for instance, went to Paul and commended Bettazzi's effort.

Very soon, it became clear that in order to get the Council discussions out of the morass in which they had sunk, some extraordinary procedural device would have to be adopted. With the assent of Paul and at the instigation of the four Moderators, it was decided to hold two special votes, one on including Mary in the document on the Church and one on episcopal collegiality.

The vote on Mary was an example of what could be done by psychological warfare. The issue was presented by the conservatives as one between fidelity and devotion to the Madonna or a 'Protestant' attitude, as one Council Father observed on the floor. Special permission was granted to Father Balič, a well-known defender and promoter of Mariology, to have his pamphlet printed by the Vatican press and distributed not only outside the basilica but inside to the Fathers. Not one voice was raised, officially, in protest against this tactic. Yet later on when the progressives attempted the same tactic, towering figures like Cardinal Tisserant and Archbishop Pericle Felici, the partisan Secretary of the Council, would raise indignant voices and use physical force to stop it.

The Moderators, however, proceeded serenely. It was arranged to have a formal debate: König of Vienna gave a speech for the progressive point of view, Santos of Manila gave a speech for the conservative side. This was on October 24. The voting was very close on October 29: 1,114 votes for the progressive point of view and 1,074 votes for the conservative point of view.

On the second issue (episcopal collegiality), the process was more complicated. Already by October 12, the shape of things to come was visible to the conservatives: a majority of the bishops were progressive in outlook. Archbishop Vagnozzi, Apostolic Delegate to the United States, on the eve of his return to America, made a special point of con-

tacting American bishops at the Council and telling them in no uncertain terms that the Council was being run by German and French
churchmen and was therefore in danger of foundering. Cardinal Siri, as
president of the Italian Episcopal Conference, made it his business to
spread the word that the Italian bishops should be on their guard.
Rumours had it, at this time, that Vagnozzi was due to be removed
from his position as Apostolic Delegate.

The pressures on the conservatives were so great that, due to the
representations of the four Moderators, Archbishop Felici, Secretary
of the Council, announced to the Fathers on October 15 that a vote
would be taken on four specific points[18] on the following Thursday,
the 17th of the month. Then, after the session Felici betook himself to
Cicognani's office and proceeded to work out a point of view whereby
the entire process of such a vote would be declared inconsistent with
the procedural rulings of the Council. Cicognani agreed. Conversations between Cicognani and the Moderators and Felici produced no
solution of the impasse. On the 17th, instead of a vote, Felici saw Paul.
Cardinal Ottaviani during his weekly visit also raised his voice in
defence of Felici's point of view. The impasse grew thicker.

Tempers were now rising in the Council. There was no vote on the
17th, as promised. On the 18th, the Moderators met with Paul, but
still the difficulties were not ironed out. Various pressure groups on the
progressive side were trying to get Cardinal Meyer of Chicago to speak
on the subject, but to all and sundry his answer was the same: only with
a mandate from Paul would he or could he do this. But Paul would not
give such a mandate. He was assailed from within and from without.
Outside, in the Italian political arena, the governmental situation was
getting desperate. The Communist Party issued a document on October 22 which spoke of the 'contradictions of the old majority of the
Centre-Left' and appealed to the Socialists to resist 'the presumed effort
of the Demochristians to impose a policy of renouncement on the
Socialists, renouncement of all renewal.' And it invited the Socialists
not to yield 'to these tactics but, on the contrary, to re-enforce the
unitary action of the working classes.' The issues were clear. Leone's
government was on its way out; the Communists wished to wean
away Socialist support from the Demochristians.

The Italian Episcopal Conference, under the iron hand of Siri, had
already prepared a statement to be issued by the Italian Bishops *from the
Council*, in which Communism, all forms of Marxism, and collabora-

---

[18] The number was later increased to five. See footnote 19, p.163.

F

tion with any form of Marxism or Socialism would be excoriated. Paul was wrestling with the subtle, immovable Siri, in an effort to tone down the document, to render it more palatable. And the going was not easy. Already, political personalities of the Right were beginning to look uneasily over their shoulder: money was getting scarce, credit was drying up, a certain *malaise* was growing in the industrial classes. Paul's own friends were worried about the outcome of the governmental crisis.

To complicate things, strong, private voices urged Paul to invite the bishops of Communist China to the Council, including those who had, apparently, violated Vatican rules and collaborated with the government of Peking. Paul had no intention of exposing himself to a mounting wave of violence, no matter how influential the forces were which urged the matter. On October 22, he voiced his decision and sorrow: 'There is a shadow which we must note with paternal trepidation and deep pain,' Paul said to the students of Propaganda College, 'the thought of that great country, China, whose sons are not associated with us this day.' It is to be hoped, said Paul, that in spite of the present condition of 'the Church in China, a firm hope takes root in our soul that the seed sown in tears cannot but germinate in time.'

Paul received Dr Chou Kang Sie, Ambassador for Taipei: no, the Holy See had no intention of yielding to pressures exerted on it to invite the Chinese bishops of the mainland to the Council. Formosa was satisfied for the moment. But the uncertainty remained, as Paul knew from Paris that plans were already being formed at the Quai d'Orsay for the formal recognition of Peking. Sooner or later the vexatious problem of relations with Communist China would have to be squarely faced.

To add to his difficulties, President Segni saw the Pope on the 23rd and, after a talk with Paul, received Leone at the Quirinal: the stage was set for the resignation of the government. The bishops would issue a modified form of their letter on Communism, on the one hand; on the other, the organization of Catholic Action (ACI) would be at the disposal of the Demochristians for the coming governmental tussle. The Socialist Congress (35th) took decisions which, Nenni declared, would be put into operation in the next fifteen days. Lombardi, a Socialist leader, spoke of the emergence of a 'completely new society in Italy . . . Our neocapitalism is now capable of assuring several important achievements.' Clearly a political crisis was brewing.

It was against this background that Paul had to unravel the knotty problem of the Council and the desire of the majority to have the vote promised for the 17th. He met finally with the Moderators, Felici, and the Council Presidency. The decision: hold the vote on the 30th. This was bad enough from the conservative point of view. The voting was catastrophic on each of the five points submitted for consideration.[19]

A clear superb majority of voices were in favour of each of the five points voted on. This vote was known as an 'orientative' vote. The appellation was unfortunate. The term 'orientative' meant that the vote indicated the orientation or inclination of the Council, but Cardinal Suenens, as Moderator, pointed out that the votes had *decided* the matters involved in so far as the preliminary voting on any conciliar issue was decisive.[20]

The conservatives were struck with a certain feeling that a high-point had been passed and that nothing but strong action would now save their cause. Bea, conferring with Paul, pointed out that now was the time to prepare for the acceptance by the Council of the document which Bea had earlier drawn up in the form of a *votum* of the Council, asking Paul to associate certain bishops with him in the government of the Church.

On October 31, the Italian Bishops made public their letter on Marxism to the Italian people. A carefully worded commentary was prepared under Paul's guidance for broadcast on Vatican Radio; it stressed merely the general principles of social and political behaviour according to Catholic ethics and theology. But it was never broadcast. Another commentary quite 'politically' slanted, which reflected the political views of Siri and Ottaviani and the conservative group, was brought to the offices of Vatican Radio during a slack period, handed

[19] That episcopal consecration constitutes the peak of the sacrament of orders (2,123 for, 34 against); that every legitimately consecrated bishop in communion with the Church is a member of the episcopal body (2,049 for, 104 against); that the body of bishops succeeds the college of the apostles in union with the Roman Pontiff (1,808 for, 336 against); that the power, full and supreme, over the universal Church, belongs to this body of bishops in union with the Pope (1,717 for, 408 against); that it is opportune to restore the diaconate as a permanent and distinct rank of the sacred ministry (1,588 for, 525 against).

[20] The system of voting generally followed these lines: first, a document was presented to the assembly for general discussion, after which a vote of acceptability or non-acceptability (for detailed discussion later) was taken. If positive, then detailed discussion started on the document. When cloture on discussion was imposed, the document went back into Commission where the emendments recommended in the general assembly were made. The document then came back for further examination and discussion. This process could be repeated until it was felt that all exigencies had been satisfied. A general vote of approval was then taken.

to an underling, and broadcast over the air to the Italians and the world before anyone realized the neatness of the trick. No matter how thoroughly Paul sifted the matter, he never obtained satisfaction either on this point or on the use which *Il Tempo* (organ of the Right) and other channels of communication made of the Letter.

Besides, as Paul pointed out to Siri, certain elements in the original draft which he himself had found distasteful or downright imprudent and which he ordered removed, had appeared in the final version. To all this, Siri argued that his conscience did not allow him to comply with vague suggestions of the Pontiff especially when he knew that some of them ran counter to the express interests of the Holy See and the rights and position of the Sovereign Pontiff. *L'Osservatore Romano* did come out with a commentary on the Letter on Nov. 2 in an effort to right the error. And papers which willingly received intimations from Paul or Bea, like *L'Avvenire d'Italia* of Bologna,[21] castigated the slanted interpretation of *Il Tempo* of Rome and the Vatican Radio broadcast.

The success of the vote on the five questions represented a high-water mark. There were other encouraging signs mixed with certain portents of danger. Paul's efforts to obtain a meeting with Athenagoras were finally getting somewhere. He had decided to meet Athenagoras in the Holy Places of Jerusalem. Lercaro wrote a letter to Father Gauthier of Nazareth encouraging him but saying nothing about the projected visit.

Archbishop Slipyi had caused some little fracas by his proposal to create (or re-establish, as he argued) a patriarchate in Kiev to be occupied by a Ukrainian Uniat churchman. This did not sit well with the Moscow Patriarchate nor with the Soviet government. On the other hand, the Czech government released Archbishop Josef Beran from his internment, together with the Bishops of Brno and Spiš and two other titular bishops, on October 3. This was a sign of good-will. In the second week of October, Monsignor Agostino Casaroli, Under Secretary of the Secretariat of State for Special Ecclesiastical Affairs, consulted with Bishop Endre Hamvas of Csanád, chief of the Hungarian delegation to the Council. Hamvas told Casaroli that Cardinal Mindszenty agreed to self-exile in Rome provided the Hungarian government set free those members of the Hungarian hierarchy it still held in prison, permitted the Vatican to fill vacant sees with its own nominees, and helped restore church buildings and churches which had been either damaged or fallen

[21] Cf. issue of Nov. 1, 1963.

into disrepair. The negotiations were not to meet with success, however; the reaction to the Letter of the Italian Bishops was not favourable. One wonders if the Italian bishops and politicians had reflected on the lot of the suffering Church in Hungary and elsewhere before launching a document which, in the final analysis, produced no positive results.

Bea's particular interests seemed to be in the doldrums. There was a feeling of apprehension at the Secretariat for Christian Unity. It was not so much that Felici had failed to deliver typewriters to them for the use of the observer-delegates or that plans for more ample quarters were left in abeyance. The all-important documents on religious liberty and on the Jewish question were in hot water. The weekly meetings of the Theological Commission (which had technical possession of the documents for the moment) were travesties of free discussion : Ottaviani dominated all, either he had just spoken to the Holy Father on the point at issue, or the matter proposed for discussion was not for airing at present. How could the text on religious liberty be extracted from his grasp and printed?

On the Jewish question, more trouble. The attitude of the Secretariat seemed to be ambivalent to many, to waver between uncertainty, backsliding, and inefficient public relations. Archbishop Seper (Zagreb, Yugoslavia) had pleaded on October 3 that the Jews be mentioned in the schema on the Church. The reactions to this were disturbing. It was clear at this stage that the Secretariat, from Bea and Willebrands down, was doubtful whether the Jewish chapter would be introduced. Paul's interest was primarily with the ecumenical side of Bea's operations.

Paul was not sure if the document could be presented: he shared some of the fears voiced by Cicognani in the Secretariat of State. Still Bea kept stressing the past commitments of the Holy See, commitments repeatedly given to public and private representatives of Judaism. On the other hand, Paul was rather disturbed by the growing popularity and interest being shown *The Deputy*, Hochhuth's play. The play had resulted in riots in Basel, was causing a lot of criticism for the Holy See abroad and, in particular, for Pius XII. An inquiry directed to the Archivists of the Secretariat of State, as we noted before, merely brought back the reply that it would be better not to publish any White Paper on Pius XII and the Jews – for the moment.

Perhaps, after all, it would be better to let the Jewish document go through and override the objections coming from certain quarters? On the 14th of October Bea started to plan for an introduction of both documents (religious liberty, Jewish question) toward the end of the month. His plans were drawn up in agreement with Paul: the document on the Jewish question would be printed and distributed. On that day, Bea would make a major speech on the floor of the Council, and with permission of the Moderators, the speech would be translated into the major European and Oriental languages and broadcast over Vatican Radio and distributed over the wire-services and the Press offices.

The big question, settled at this time between Bea and the Pope, was the position of the Jewish document. Should it stand on its own feet, or be delayed until the Secretariat for non-Christian Religions had been established, or be included in the schema on Ecumenism? Finally, as a result of various pressures, Paul told Bea that it was to be included in the schema on Ecumenism. Bea decided to call it Chapter 4 of the schema, and to place the document on religious liberty at the end as Chapter 5. Paul spoke on October 31 with Monsignor Brini, the Internuncio in Egypt. With him he had two related subjects to discuss: the effect of a possible promulgation of the Jewish document and the political aspects of his proposed visit to the Holy Places in Jerusalem.

On Thursday, October 31, Paul visited the Lateran University and made another of his surprise speeches. He praised the 'venerable masters' and 'most worthy colleagues' of the old Apollinare Institute (the forerunner of the Lateran University), of course, but he had a very clear message to convey: if the University devoted itself to charitable collaboration with the 'other great institutes of Rome, to a loyal emulation, to a mutual reverence and friendly concord, but never[22] to any jealous competition or fastidious polemics, then the Lateran University will have a positive mission to accomplish ...' Paul was thus cutting at the jugular vein of the conservative brain whence had come the invective and academic polemics directed against the Biblical Institute, by Piolanti (the rector) and his associates like Romeo and Spadafora. The Lateran University speech earned Paul more resentment in the Curia than perhaps any other action.

Thus, by the beginning of November several interlocking lines of development were beginning to fall into a definite pattern. The principle of collegiality had been adopted by the Council by a clear majority. Bea's all-important documents were on the way to success. Paul had come down definitely on one side, as far as words went, and

[22] Actually Paul repeated the word 'never' three times. *L'Osservatore Romano* only gave two.

for the moment, he had put no serious obstacles in the way of concrete action.

At a meeting of the Curial directorate after the 30th of October and before the 3rd of November, the situation was reviewed and considered so unfavourable that extreme tactics were decided upon. The situation was, indeed, unfavourable. The principle of collegiality had been affirmed, resoundingly, on October 30. Deeper than that, the principle of conciliarity had been implicitly, but none the less definitely, asserted by the same vote. Theoretically this was bad enough. There was worse. They had in front of them a copy of a document being circulated among select Council Fathers: the *Votum* for the apostolic college or 'Senate' drafted by Bea and circulated by him with Paul's blessing. This was the handwriting on the wall. Bea also had had a series of talks with certain influential Council Fathers on the subject.

Again, on the debit side, was the known decision of Paul to distribute, discuss and promulgate at least Chapters 4 and 5 of Bea's schema on Ecumenism; Chapter 4 dealt with the Jewish question, and Chapter 5 with religious liberty, as we have said. Doctrinally and practically, both were utterly unacceptable to the conservative mind. Yet both were sure to command a large majority if put to a vote in the Council. In addition, the comings and goings of certain *periti* in Rome were noted: they had obviously been told to prepare the ground, to prepare a favourable reception for Chapters 4 and 5.

There were voices heard in the Council, moreover, that frightened the conservative forces and urged them quickly and logically to precipitate action at this stage. Kémérer of Argentina (on October 16) and Kobayashi of Japan (on the 17th) had both warmly advocated the establishment of a married diaconate. Had not Kobayashi himself asserted (October 17) that 'the formulation of the dogma of papal infallibility was not always correctly understood . . . The head cannot exist or act without the body, and the Pope is the head, the bishops are the body.' The Anglican Bishop of Ripon, John Moorman, asserted that 'if we ever have a final unity of Christianity, the head will manifestly be the Bishop of Rome . . . but historically and exegetically a certain amplification had been operated on the words of the Lord to Peter.' Archbishop T. D. Roberts, S.J., proclaimed openly the necessity for 'a holy inquisition of the Most Holy Inquisition.'

Voices were raised seemingly attacking the privileged place of clerics in the hierarchy. 'A formula must be inserted into the schema,' said Cardinal Gracias of Bombay on October 23, 'according to which lay people would find some canonical protection against priests and bishops, and bishops and priests against the lay folk.' 'This schema,' said Bishop Mark McGrath of Panama, on the 24th, 'presents an image of the Church in which the entire life of the believer seems to consist of submission to the hierarchy, in a sort of clerical pyramid, with the lay person at the lowest stage, like a small choir-boy at the service of all.' 'The paternalistic system of the past,' asserted Archbishop Denis Hurley of Durban, on the same day, 'cannot continue now that the laity is much better educated, more critical, more acquainted with the problems confronting the Church . . .'

On the 25th, Emile Inglessis, one of the thirteen lay-auditors allowed to sit but not to speak at the Council, declared in a Press interview: 'Yes, we all know that the Church is opposed to birth control. But that is not enough. The Church must come forward with a solution.' And Bishop Claude Rolland of Madagascar said proudly: 'Everybody knows that the Church in Madagascar cannot under any circumstances be called clerical.' And describing the reform of the breviary (the prayer-book used by Catholic priests), Bishop Bekkers of 's-Hertogen-bosch, Holland, said brusquely on October 28: 'The principle guiding us has been that the breviary must be a real prayer and not a set of iron-clad formalities.'

Lastly, although Paul's projected trip to Jordan was not yet known, there were rumours which had reached their ears that the Pope was thinking of a meeting with at least Athenagoras of Istanbul, if not with other leaders of dissident Christian Churches. The Council was sure to give Paul his desired ecumenical document in the shape of Chapters 1-3 of Bea's schema on Ecumenism.

It was clear that only the strongest measures could reverse the trend. The programme worked out was a masterpiece of bold action and excellent timing, the two absolute requisites for success in Roman power-circles. It implied, of course, the basic requisite: control over the main fulcra of power, and these they had under their control.

Their plan was based primarily on the sure knowledge they had, that in a few days (actually on the 5th of November) Prime Minister Leone of Italy would go to the Quirinal Palace and hand in the resignation of his government to President Antonio Segni. A political *sinistrismo* would again arise to bedevil the national situation and threaten the viability of parliamentary life.

It was based, secondly, on the knowledge of the inherent weaknesses of the American group of bishops: their total incapacity for 'politicking,' their respect for ecclesiastical dignity, for any grade above that of simple priest, their individuality and congenital dislike for following one leader, their implicit almost naïve reliance on Cardinal Cicognani (who had consecrated a goodly number of them as bishop) and on his judgement. Now if disarray and disunity could be cast into their ranks, the one biggest group in favour of the chapters on religious liberty and the Jewish problem would be rendered negligible in the coming struggle.

The main line of action decided upon, in view of these considerations, was as follows. The first, the most important target, was Paul himself. He must be made to see that any sanctioned ecclesiastical *sinistrismo* would inevitably have, as a counterpart, *sinistrismo* in the political field, a further drift leftwards. He must also be made to realize the doctrinal dangers inherent in the positions of Bea. Bea, therefore, must be criticized, criticized à *l'outrance*, even to the point of doctrinal assassination. With Paul, then, the dangers of the tendency towards collegiality among the bishops and the doctrinal views of Bea had to be stressed. Both had to be criticized in the light of the political situation in Italy.

To bring all these elements to a suitable state of ferment, it was decided that violence would be done, conciliarly speaking. The principle of conciliarity would be contradicted on the floor of the Council. The Secretary of the Holy Office, Cardinal Ottaviani, would assert the procedural illegality, the doctrinal unsuitability and theological weakness of the vote on October 30. He would do this by clearly setting the Holy Office up as outside and superior to the Council deliberations. This was, in effect, the assertion of the pride of place and privilege typical of the core of the *Curia Romana*. Reaction would be inevitable. Papal reaction, in particular, was inevitable, and the suitable occasion would arise for an ultimate confrontation with Paul. Such a confrontation was planned.

The probabilities seemed very good of choking off the rising flood of conciliarism and collegiality, to make it ebb back to the ocean of might-have-been errors and plagues of the Church, so that the old, solid, familiar positions would appear again in their pristine strength. Paul was suspicious of Siri, of the following he had at his command among the Italian episcopate, of his position as dauphin of the Italian cardinals, wary, ultimately, of his influence over and connections with the bloc of right-wing elements on the political and financial scenes.

They had an example of what Siri could effect in personal interview with Paul: Siri had emerged unscathed and stronger from his audience

with Paul when called to account for the distasteful manoeuvres
connected with the composition and the publication of the Italian
Bishops' letter to the Italian people on Communism. Apart from argu-
ments drawn from the politico-financial side of things, they could also
use some works of French and German theologians on the power of
the bishops; the spectre of Gallicanism could be pointedly raised.

More complicated manoeuvres were necessary to ensure that
Chapters 4 and 5 of Bea's schema on Ecumenism would not reach a
conciliar vote and promulgation. They knew that Paul had decided for
very specific reasons to circulate both chapters and to urge voting and
promulgation. They also knew the position of favour attained by John
Courtney Murray, his friendship with Pavan, his collaboration with
Bea's Secretariat, his usefulness to De Smedt, the iron force of his logic,
the breadth of his knowledge, the significance he had for Paul as the
voice of American progressiveness. Given a text containing Murray's
ideas, 'speechified' by De Smedt, advocated by Bea, and blessed by
Paul, there was no possibility of frustrating its passage through the
Council before December 4.

As to Chapter 4, on the Jews, things had already gone too far: Bea
had successfully obtained Paul's agreement to its principles, and this
was bad enough. But he had also in his hands the statement of Saadat
Hassan, made in the previous July, expressing Arab agreement to a
religious document on the Jewish question. He had also contacted a
large number of Oriental prelates from Arab countries and converted
them to a favourable viewpoint. He had, moreover, created over the
last three years a welling tide of expectation and desire both in world
Jewish circles and in the pluralistic society of America and Germany,
and now he was going to have to meet that expectation and satisfy that
desire. Had not Paul himself felt so strongly with regard to Chapter 4
that he had rather tersely answered the insinuating remarks of Nasser in
the course of his correspondence with Paul?

In view of these things, the main tactic as regards Chapters 4 and 5
was summed up in the Latin adage *divide et impera*, divide and conquer.
In spite of dilatory tactics, these men foresaw that the two chapters
would be printed, circulated, and proposed to the Council; Archbishop Felici, with various stratagems at his disposal as Secretary to the
Council, could only avoid this eventuality for a limited space of time.
The first Fabian tactic would be to induce a split vote on the question of
the acceptability of the schema on Ecumenism as a whole. In return for
a 'no trouble' agreement on Chapters 4 and 5 (when they came up for

their vote of acceptability), an arrangement would be worked out with Paul and Bea through Cicognani whereby only Chapters 1–3 of ecumenism would be voted upon first; a subsequent separate vote would be promised on Chapters 4 and 5. After this, the suppositious vote on the latter chapters would have to be blocked by increasing the potential threat of Arab anger at Chapter 4 (on the Jewish problem) and the doctrinal dangers of Chapter 5 (on religious liberty). Arab irritation would have to be increased and the danger of reprisals against Christians in Arab countries underlined. It was considered a boon that Council Fathers from Arab lands had been contacted by their respective governments, through their diplomatic missions in Rome, and warned that only a strong stand on the Council floor against the Jewish chapter would make possible their peaceful and welcome return to their dioceses. At least one member of Bea's Secretariat could be counted upon actively to organize the latter move and to keep a careful eye on the general situation. Lastly, the possibilities of spoiling the collaboration between Bea and certain Jewish organizations in America were explored. For nearly three years, these organizations had cooperated faithfully and skilfully with the cardinal with a view to drawing up a suitable document on the Jewish question. Could some division be created between some of the major organizations involved?

The key figure in practically all these tactics (except the last-named) was that of Cardinal Cicognani. They could rely on his control over a considerable segment of the American hierarchy. They could exploit his personal opposition to Bea. The power of his office as Secretary of State would be of paramount force in dealing with the Jewish chapter. His Italianate mentality would ultimately be the saving factor in an otherwise bleak situation.

These plans were geared to a rather strict time-table. Starting on November the 8th with Ottaviani's challenging speech, the pressure would have to be kept up unceasingly for about two to four weeks so that the whole of November would pass without any further progress in the dangerous trends already manifest in the Council. Siri had another interview with Paul about matters of the recent past, and as the resignation of the Leone government would only take place on November 5, it was decided to wait until after that date. A suitable opportunity would present itself and the occasion must be grasped immediately.

After a recess of a couple of days, the Council again met on November 5, and the document dealing with bishops and dioceses came up for discussion. This would be the time to press home criticisms of the Curia.

Already, a document had been passed around among Council members containing suggestions for the reform of the Curia. It was drawn up by theologians and bishops of Chile.[23]

In the discussions that followed, however, the progressive groups gave way to their inclination to concentrate on matters which in the larger view of things were rather insignificant. And there was the spectacle of Cardinal Meyer insisting on preparing a speech on episcopal conferences, when he should have been concentrating on the concrete interests of the moment. He did not realize that all the talk about episcopal conferences and the like would be all so much useless beating of the air unless the central point at issue was made, viz. unless the necessary conditions for such exercise of authority were firmly laid.

On the other hand, a goodly number of people were concentrating all their fury and attention on the suppression, or, at least, the evisceration, of the Holy Office. Again, this was short-sighted. And so, instead of hearing bishop after bishop proposing a close follow-up to the straw vote of October 30, we beheld these good men frittering away the unity achieved and deserting the position of strength acquired.

It was here that an inherent defect in Paul VI's character became clear. He could issue orders. He could plan. He could execute plans. He could behave diplomatically. He could make a good speech when he set himself to it. But he failed to give inspiring leadership. There was lacking that small quality of personal magnetism. He could inspire reverence due to office and personality. But he could not light up the candle of personal and group relationship. The Letter he wrote on the development of Seminaries which he read on the occasion of the fourth centenary of the Council of Trent (on November 4), was calculated to exercise an alienating influence on the assemblage of conciliar spirits around him. In effect, the speech was strictly 'normal,' full of sonorous phrases, quotations from the Fathers, reiterations of the excellence of all that a meeting of Churchmen four hundred years ago decided was good for their age, made no attempt to bring things up to date, took

[23] The substance of this document was as follows: Procedures should be public and those interested should have complete and free access to the documents on which accusations are based. If the accused is willing to retract or has retracted, the condemnation should not be made public unless the accused has caused grave scandal. The interested person or persons should be told of the decisions, all of them, and likewise his superiors (ecclesiastical) should be acquainted with the matters in hand. A proper juridical form must be set up for all processes, and this and all other activities of the Holy Office should be placed under the surveillance of a group of bishops and cardinals. The precise terrain under the jurisdiction of the Holy Office should be determined.

no account of the vastly changed conditions in Italy and other tradi-tionally Catholic countries, and left the reader, as it left those who heard it, completely baffled.

It was in effect, the first rallying point offered to the Curial party. Here was an outlook in perfect tune with theirs. Here was the same unreserved acceptance of the *status quo*. Paul did not seem to have in mind the woeful state of Italian seminaries, the declining numbers of priests in other countries. It was a lengthy exercise in turgid prose, unimaginative thought, and ecclesiastical traditionalism. It was such phenomena as this that made and makes for the Hamletic impression that many have formed of Paul. Others have endeavoured to explain the speech by pointing out that he asked the wrong people to write it, and that he did this because he had hinged his whole policy on prin-ciples which allowed for the presence and power of curial elements. Now, if you do this, you must necessarily throw some bones of satisfaction and contentment to the negative elements which you have decided to retain.

Towards the middle of the first week in November, therefore, the number of *generous* ones, to continue Nolli's image referred to pre-viously, diminished, the *political adversaries* grew stronger, the *egoists* merely abstained, the *presumptuous* ones grew more presumptuous. Perhaps, Nolli had more in his head than the Gospel images.

3. *November 8 to November 23*

The essential acts of the entire drama with which we are here concerned were enacted between Friday, November 8, and Tuesday, November 12. Beyond the 12th and up to November 23, the final touches and logical consequences were worked out. We shall have to examine these in detail and note their fateful dependence on the essential drama. However, it is between the 8th and the 12th that Paul's perspective was radically changed: he found himself no longer able to think, speak, act, on the summits of darkness, for the unbending, commanding finger of aching problems pointed mercilessly downwards to the long, sloping valley of coming decision.

Yet the texture of developments between those two dates was not a simple one: the patterns were interwoven, the colours merged at unexpected points, the entire warp and woof were to be spun out of the womb of pragmatism. For this reason, a mere exposition of the facts rather takes one's breath away. To outside observers there appeared only the underside of the woven fabric with its confusing criss-cross of skeins and threads, its resisting obstructing knots, its apparent blind-alley stretches, its interrupted symmetry. Only Paul and those at the power-centres of the inner drama, those who wove the whole-cloth of his decision, understand the entire development.

First as to the external framework of those days. By November 8, discussion was completed on Chapter 1 of the schema on the Bishops. By the 14th, Chapter 3 was completed and Chapter 4 started. By the 18th, cloture had been imposed on all further discussion on the schema, and the debate on Ecumenism had started. The document on the Jewish question was distributed to the Council members on the 8th. The document on religious liberty, now Chapter 5 of Bea's schema on Ecumenism, was distributed on the 19th.

Leading up to the fateful day of the 8th were several events which only jangled Paul's nerves and tightened his reflexes. First his audience with Siri: this was not only disappointing, it was positively foreboding. Siri had offered, in a diplomatic way, (i.e. threatened) to resign his post as president of the Italian Episcopate. Paul did not want to fall into this trap, for a trap it was. Siri knew and Paul knew that such a step would involve Paul directly in trouble within the confines of his own household.

There was some consolation to be derived from the public statements of Pinchas E. Lapide, former Israeli Consul in Milan, who came out in defence of Pius XII against the implications of Hochhuth's play, *The Deputy*. But then he received a visit from Maurice Fischer, Israeli Ambassador to the Quirinal, on November 2, who wanted to know what the chances were on the document dealing with the Jewish question, and whether it would come up for discussion and a vote. The questions were fair, but they bothered Paul: he wished to get the document through, but there was considerable doubt in his mind as to its feasibility.

Then he still had had unpleasant memories from his correspondence with the pocket dictator of the Nile, which ended about November 5. Nasser had written to him expressing the hope that nothing would be done at the Council which would upset the delicate balance between the Christian and Islamic communities in Egypt and the Arab world. Paul had answered tersely that His Excellency could be sure that nothing was ever done or would be done at the great council – a purely spiritual gathering and with no political colouring – that should disturb the delicate relationship in question. Of course, this depended on good-will and comprehension. The veiled threat in the Egyptian's remarks bothered Paul.

On the 5th, he received Segni who bore on his shoulders the problem of picking a new candidate for premier of a government still to be formed. Segni wanted to do more than merely chat and present his compliments; he wanted to explain the difficulties of the situation to His Holiness and to sound him out as to how he felt about a new government. There was a group of Demochristian politicians under Scelba who wished to avoid all connection with the Socialists. And they seemed to have the support of ecclesiastical elements high up in the Vatican. How did Paul feel about it? And would Paul lend his support to a Centre-Left government, even if Siri and the extreme Right-wing cardinals and churchmen objected? Could Paul depend on the support of certain industrial and financial blocs?

On the 7th, Felici, Secretary of the Council, came to see him, in particular about Chapters 4 and 5 of Bea's schema on Ecumenism.

Felici wanted to complain about undue pressure brought to bear on the Council by Bea's 'politicking.' What the Council wished and did not wish to consider was the Council's own business. Besides he, Felici, had heard talk about a document going the rounds obtaining the signatures of the Council members, an effort to railroad the Reverend Fathers of the Council into an obstreperous, irresponsible *votum* of devotion to the Holy Father. Then there was the question of procedure. Felici was afraid that, just as in the case of the Virgin Mary and collegiality, the Moderators, Bea and the 'others,' would again obtain permission to hold an 'orientative vote.' This was against the procedural rules and violated the freedom of the Council, Felici maintained stoutly.

Finally at this time, Paul was slowly making up his mind about his visit to the Holy Places. When exactly was it to be? Was his decision not to go to the Holy Places in Israel a wise one? Would the Greek Patriarch of Jerusalem, Benediktos, agree to the visit of himself and Athenagoras of Constantinople without demur? And what about the Armenian Patriarch?

Within the Council, too, a tension was mounting ever since the overwhelming vote of October 30. The progressives took it as a sign of their success: 'We are working up to a climax,' remarked one German cardinal, 'before the end of the month, we will have seen the establishment of a really pastoral government of the Church through the common will of Christ's bishops, with the Bishop of Rome at their head.'

On November 5, Cardinal Liénart of France demanded a complete revision of the chapters under discussion in order to bring out the true relations of Pope and bishops. Cardinal McIntyre of San Francisco countered that such suggestions endangered the unity and the divinely ordered hierarchy of the Church. Bishop Gargitter, Italian, followed this up by deriding the proposed internationalization of the Roman Curia. 'No one really wants this,' he alleged. On November 7, Cardinal König of Vienna again emphasized the principle of collegiality and called for the immediate establishment of an international body of bishops to govern the Church with the Pope. The same ideas were proposed by His Beatitude Maximos IV Saigh, Melchite patriarch of Antioch. 'Let His Holiness invite the bishops of the world to enter the Roman offices and ministries,' he said, 'we cannot be satisfied with the small and timid reform proposed by the text as it now stands.' Monsignor Pablo Correa of Colombia put his finger on the inherent defect of the text: 'It speaks as if there were question of conferring privileges on the bishops; but the plain truth is that the bishops have these things already as of divine right.'

These and other voices were building up to a crescendo. The conservatives saw the storm coming. By Friday, November 8, they witnessed the first delineation of the near future: Bea's document on the Jews was distributed. In a sense it was a miracle that it got out: Felici, Secretary of the Council, did his best to stop distribution. Then Bea's Secretariat released to newsmen an official communiqué giving the substance of the document.[24] Some minor official or office boy was bundled into a taxi and sent the rounds of Rome to all the Arab country embassies and legations, bearing a letter of introduction to the Ambassador or Consul in question together with a copy of the communiqué. To the Egyptian Embassy, a copy of the communiqué was sent some days beforehand, and great pains were taken to explain its purely religious nature. By one of those ironies of fate, it was Friday, the Muslim holy day, but the Egyptians were open and working. Cairo was informed immediately. It took the other diplomatic missions two days to realize what had happened. But those attending the Council barely realized what was going to happen. For this was the day of reckoning, the occasion to act.

On November 8, Ottaviani delivered himself of a courageous, testy, challenging, deliberately nettling talk on the Holy Office and on the uselessness of the 'orientative vote' of October 30. The immediate

[24] The communiqué was what is called by the Italians a *pasticcia*, obviously thrown together with a lot of good-will, timidity, and a defensive mentality, excessively negative, and exaggeratedly trying to exculpate itself, and lacking in serenity and confidence. It said rather what the document on the Jews was *not*, rather than what it was. This is probably due in part to the fact that it was composed in a hurry and was not the fruit of careful meditation. But it must be said that the innate fear of asserting the truth in which one believes also played a part. In effect, the communiqué said, this document declares that the Jewish people are not deicides, are not accursed by God. It admonishes Catholic preachers and catechists to avoid teaching the Catholic religion in such a way as to arouse contempt or opposition for Jews, but oddly this is a purely religious document and the Holy See has no intention of entering any political struggle; the Council has no wish to give or lend its weight to any one faction in any political arena in the world; the authorities of the Secretariat were not influenced by any Jewish organization, group, organism, or anything else; there is no wish to stamp Zionism with any sort of approval; the intent of the Holy See is purely pastoral; the wish of Catholics should be not to indulge in any form of anti-Semitism. The communiqué does not contain one passage or even sentence that rings out with the authentic tone of positive declaration and the consciousness of the historic step being contemplated by the Church. Having reported all this, one must conclude with the remark of a Rabbi in San Francisco: 'This is a great day, yes, but not *the* day.'

occasion was a speech by Cardinal Frings. The latter's speech was an exercise in courage, and in miscalculation. Ottaviani demanded an apology afterwards, but Frings demurred, because he had heard indirectly that Paul had liked the effort. Ottaviani was in bad humour. He met Suenens some days beforehand, in the square outside, and told him bluntly that he went far too often to see the Pope who had something more important to do. Suenens's answer and reaction are not on record. The Pope received Karl Rahner, an Austrian Jesuit, in the company of Bishop Hermann Schäufele of Freiburg the day before, and praised Rahner's theological works. This praise had a barb to it: during the first session Ottaviani had endeavoured to get John XXIII to remove Rahner as Council theologian and have him sent back to Innsbruck, Austria. John had refused. Rahner was still on the blacklist. Paul also received the four Moderators who, in addition to other procedural problems, had complaints to make about the behaviour of Ottaviani during the morning's session: Ottaviani had implied that his theological commission and the Holy Office were superior to the Council, and he had derided the value of the 'orientative vote.' This had to stop.

That evening Ottaviani, Antoniutti and Siri were called in to see the Pope. Paul wanted to make certain points clear: he insisted that the chapter on religious liberty be extracted from the bowels of the subcommission of the Theological Commission over which Cardinal Ottaviani presided with affable authoritarianism and iron assurance. The Pope wanted it to be printed and distributed to the Fathers of the Council, discussed and voted upon. He wanted to know why the Secretary of the Holy Office had contradicted the majority of the Council and challenged the collegial decision of the bishops on the delicate and all-important question of episcopal collegiality.

The reaction of the three cardinals to this was a careful, calculated one. In accordance with their earlier tactical decision, all immediate and direct resistance to his demands for the two chapters on religious liberty and the Jews was avoided. To the criticism of Ottaviani's stand on the Council floor, guarded resistance was made: the matter was more serious than a superficial examination would warrant, there was serious unrest among a large segment of the bishops, the majority of the Council Fathers had not understood what they were voting for on October 30, there was an inherent threat to the Pope's own primacy of jurisdiction, their consciences as the watch-dogs of orthodoxy and pure doctrine must be respected. Besides, the Pope was aware of the intimate connection between the mood prevalent in the Council and the delicate political situation in Italy. This was the thin end of the wedge; the tempered steel had been barely uncovered and brandished. But sufficiently. The delegation of three had forced Paul's gaze downwards to contemplate willy-nilly a revision of his position.

Nevertheless, he received the impression that they had given in; the Theological Commission met on Monday the 11th. John Courtney Murray spoke on religious liberty, dazzled, convinced, and silenced. The voting was 18 to 5 in favour of printing the text. A feeling of euphoria swept over the American bishops and Council *periti*. Things were progressing.

Another form of pressure was used on Paul. Charles Boyer, S.J., confidant of Ottaviani as well as of Paul, a stout defender of traditional theology, published an article in *L'Osservatore Romano* inspired by his friends in the Vatican directorate. Boyer's simple message, clad in the language which Paul understood so well, was: 'Only to Peter did Jesus address those words: "To you I give the keys of the kingdom of heaven." The Church has always taught that only to Peter has been given the government of the universal Church.' Boyer's article was bad theology, bad exegesis, bad history, but excellent tactics. It was full of ecclesiastical resonances. It exalted the Pope. Here was no turgid German or irritating Frenchman, but a solid Roman theologian talking – such was the impression the article conveyed.

On Saturday, November 9, Siri saw Paul again. This was the confrontation planned for the clash of Paul's mystical weapon with the hard metal of Siri's pragmatism, the inner collision of Vatican power-centres, the realistic stock-taking of all that the Vatican meant, all that Italian Catholicism meant, all that the juridical and the Romanist and structural connoted. Byzantine worldliness was matched against Pauline aloofness. It was the *jus romanum* pitting itself once more against Germanic unrest, Gallic perception, Anglo-Saxon tribalism, Semitic instability and confusion.

Siri had a very simple message to convey: neither as President of the Italian Bishops' Conference (and therefore, by implication, the whole Italian episcopate), nor as intimate collaborator of the traditional Catholic political centres in Italy, nor as cardinal of the Holy Roman Catholic and Apostolic Church, could he sanction the present trend of affairs. Paul was consciously and deliberately fomenting collegiality, thereby unconsciously promoting *sinistrismo* in the ecclesiastical and theological order, thereby furthering political *sinistrismo*, thereby strengthening the hands of those who were pushing Italy towards the political Left.

Did His Holiness think that President Segni's efforts to get a workable Centre-left government going under Aldo Moro could be viable under such circumstances? Even if some government under Moro could be formed, how long would it last? Until general elections in the spring? And then? Did His Holiness know that the Communists were ready to send goon-squads down into the piazza right now? And what would they be prepared to do if their 25 per cent vote in 1963 increased to 29 per cent or 32 per cent in 1964? Did His Holiness forget that there was unrest among the Right-wing elements in the Demochristian party and that a group of about thirty members were thinking of breaking away under the leadership of Scelba? And was this not tantamount to smashing any sort of political unity on the Demochristian front?

Besides, and this was the ultimate stab at all resistance on the part of Paul, he (Siri) did not think that His Holiness realized the fears and apprehensions of loyal Italian Right-wing segments in the political, financial, and social fields. Faced with the possibility of a drastic further drift to political *sinistrismo*, these segments would react violently for self-preservation.

The Genovese cardinal, with his stature as papal chaplain to northern Italy's industrialists and financiers, his easy entrée to their counsels, and his intimacy with their reading of the financial and economic horizons, could, as such, assure His Holiness that furtherance of *sinistrismo* in the Council was so abhorrent to their mentality that their reaction might endanger the financial equilibrium of Vatican monies; and, after all was said and done, the sinews in the huge administrative machine of the Vatican were, as elsewhere, its financial resources.

There was a further point. Was His Holiness forgetting the dim but quite definitely emerging outline of a European unity? And the possibilities it would offer to the Church for penetration in hitherto barren areas like Norway, Denmark, eventually even East Germany? Was not this the reason why the Holy See was in favour of European unity, was not all real hope of this unity based on concord among the big financial interests of Europe, and was it not the duty of the Holy See to cultivate these interests so that the Vatican would not be excluded or hindered once the unity had been forged? And was not this the reason why Adenauer had, perhaps rather impetuously but with a point to his remark, called Papa Giovanni *ein alte Idiot*, because of his penchant for

Gaullist viewpoints and his *sinistrismo*? In sum, did His Holiness realize that the only alternative to the agreed-upon policy of his advisers was to shift the weight of Vatican financial and economic resources away from Europe, to appeal to the New World, to establish there the solid economic foundations of his own household, his administration, the *Curia Romana*, and shift for the first time in two thousand years the balance of religious forces away from the Mediterranean basin, from Rome with its Petrine apostolic associations, and jeopardize its dogmatic importance?

Prior to these representations and immediately after them, Paul received some intimate friends. Yes, it was true: the people were losing faith in any hope of political stability. It was true they were withdrawing money. It was true the Vatican could not count on their undivided support, on their expert advice, to maintain its finances in order. President Segni, wrestling with the problem of picking a likely prime minister for a government yet to be formed, sat gazing out of his office-window in the Quirinal Palace, and instructed Ambassador Migone to keep Paul VI abreast of his difficulties and the turmoil beneath the surface of Italian parliamentary life. Apart from the threatening influence of Siri, it is known that the two other people most intimately associated with Paul in these days were Ambassador Migone and Vittorino Veronese, bosom friends, both admirers and intimates of Paul.

Paul was now in a delicate position. A sizeable number of Council Fathers were waiting for the major speech by some cardinal proposing the conciliar *Votum* for a 'Senate' of bishops. The one picked for this was Cardinal Silva Henriquez of Santiago de Chile. On Sunday, November 10, the latter was in Milan, expected back in Rome about 6 p.m. His private theologian, a Chilean Jesuit, had already spoken with the cardinal on the telephone and won his consent to the plan for the major speech. Immediately on returning, the cardinal was to go to Via Aurelia to see Cardinal Bea who would iron out the last details with him. In the meantime, five other bishops had been contacted and had agreed to support Silva's effort in speeches of their own. Cardinals Suenens and Doepfner, Moderators, had been consulted and were in agreement. In addition, Bea was already preparing his important speech on the Jewish chapter. It was to be translated into five languages and released to Press and radio. Paul had once spoken to Migone about feeling himself in a vice; he truly was now.

But more pressure was to come. A delegation of Spanish bishops and another of Italian bishops arrived to plead with the Pope as loyal, frightened sons. The tenor of their plea: the final implications of collegiality are not clear; we cannot vote in public against religious liberty but neither can we vote for it, for it compromises our position in Italy and Spain; the chapter on the Jewish problem is premature and its political implications could confuse the faithful. Had not certain Spanish Jesuit theologians written concerning the beloved John XXIII that his policies would lead the Church to destruction?

A visit from Cardinal Cicognani did nothing to diminish Paul's anguish and forebodings: he could assure His Holiness that the Jewish chapter would have unpleasant repercussions on Christians living in Arab countries. Cardinal Bea had gone too far; he may have been called *pater ecumenicus* by Henry Van Dusen during the *agape* celebrations in New York earlier in the year, but His Holiness was the divinely appointed *pater ecumenicus*. And Bea's treatment of Orthodox churches not in communion with the Holy See conflicted with some of the tried and true formulas of the Secretariat of State and the Oriental Congregation, two dicasteries of the Curia.

Another meeting with the three, Ottaviani, Antoniutti and Siri, brought further lessons home to Paul. They seemed to be taking a truly global view of things. A commentator might put it that they were in possession of all the facts, but their interpretation of these facts was very one-sided. His Holiness was well aware of the explosive situation in South America where the Church was literally bursting at the seams, where there was an acute lack of priests, where North American Protestant missions were making alarming headway, where Communism and Castroism were rampant, where the masses were bound to the Church by the thin thread of an almost superstitious devotion to the Madonna.

There was also a rising dissatisfaction among the intelligentsia of the Old World, especially in France and Germany, and social workers, the professional classes, university circles, scientists, technicians. The tide of European discontent had even washed the shores of America. The recent controversies at Catholic University were proof of that, harbingers of a change in the old American tradition of chancery fidelity.

Did His Holiness want to provoke a global explosion? The way things were going in the Council, such an event could not be headed off. In fact, the first rumblings were audible in the Holy City itself: Oscar Cullmann, a prominent Protestant theologian, it had been suggested, might speak at the Gregorian University or the Biblical Institute. If such an explosion were inevitable, the Church would certainly weather it out, as She had weathered the East-West Schism in the ninth and eleventh centuries, as She had weathered the Reformation in the sixteenth century, the Piedmontese persecution in the nineteenth century, the Fascist and Nazi onslaught in the twentieth century. But His Holiness was not called upon by historical destiny to be the *agent provocateur* of such an explosion.

Siri's insistence, the pressure of Ottaviani and Antoniutti, Boyer's reasoning, the larger issues of ecumenism at stake, all this seems to have had a definite impact on Paul. Competent authorities assert that at this stage he did have a certain feeling that the idea of collegiality threatened to jeopardize his own primacy. When he entered the basilica of St John Lateran on Sunday, November 10, he proceeded to dispel any doubts in the minds of his hearers on this score: 'We are,' intoned Paul solemnly and deliberately, 'the Bishop of Rome; therefore successor of St Peter, therefore Vicar of Christ, Pastor of the Universal Church, Patriarch of the Occident and Primate of Italy. Brethren and Faithful, have understanding and sympathy for the one who must present himself to you thus, to Rome, to the Church, and recognize in Our personal figure the grandeur of our sovereign and pontifical mission.' Furthermore, he affirmed that the sole right to enter here as 'master and lord indisputably belongs to him who has been canonically elected Bishop of Rome.' There is marked insistence on his position and dignity in these words which it would be difficult to parallel even in the words of Pius IX or Pius XII. Paul was afraid of the dangers at which Siri hinted.

Towards the end of his speech, Paul turned to Rome and apostrophized the City in the following terms: 'We salute thee, Rome, seat of our honour, with a grateful and affectionate soul. How shall we extol thee? We simply do not know whether you call for love rather than for admiration, since you are amply worthy of both ... Let the cultivation of what is just and upright, let flawless faith, let solicitous charity for the needs of others, let the modesty and the glory of purity be thy ornaments, so that the guests who come hither to see thee, may have abundant cause to praise thee and to find in thee models to imitate ... Realize thy dignity ... and we in our duty to the Universal Church and to thee will strain all our strength and spare no labour that thy greater spiritual good be obtained ...'

Such words in praise of Rome would have been more suitable coming from a medieval Pope than from the lips of a twentieth-century

Pope midway through the second session of Vatican Council II. There seems to be inherent in these words a spirit alien to the modern world, a provincialism. Man today, in his global development, had got past the point of local religious patriotism. The doctrines of the primacy and infallibility of the Pope could remain quite intact without having to apostrophize the place where Christ's Vicar lived as the place where God lived. This was a sign of the contraction of Paul's whole spiritual outlook in those tense days, his return to the tried-and-true, his Roman orientation.

Paul then gave orders that the conciliar *votum* for which Bea and others had been working was to be dropped. He allowed them to collect signatures, but there was to be no major speech in the Council, and no public vote on the proposal. By Monday night, the document circulated by Bea had obtained over 200 signatures. The feeling was general throughout Rome that big issues were being fought out behind the scenes. The American delegation was split. Cardinal Spellman had clashed with Cardinal Doepfner of Munich on the 11th on the issue of papal authority, Spellman maintaining a position which was tantamount to saying that the Pope had all the power but could use the bishops if he wished, Doepfner saying that the conciliar vote had declared as doctrine of the Church: the bishops share by divine right in the government of the Church together with, and under the leadership of, the Pope.

Contacts with representatives of the American hierarchy did not help much. Some were lukewarm to the implications of collegiality. Others hinted that any statement on religious liberty or on Church and State might be construed as unwarranted interference in American political issues. The bishops from satellite countries, in general, threw cold water on the theses of collegiality, religious liberty, and the Jews, as well as on any statement about Communism.

In the Council itself, organized voices reminded Paul that the hated Central European bloc did not speak for all. On Monday, November 11, the 74-year-old Aurelio Del Pino Gómez of Lérida, Spain, told the Fathers that the Roman Curia was staffed by men 'remarkable for their sanctity, wisdom, prudence, and charity ... I am filled with gratitude and admiration for them, composed as they are of men drawn from all nations ... We must be wary of the present concept of collegiality which tends to stifle the power of the Supreme Pontiff.' These remarks, he said, 'had been meditated on at length, in the presence of God.' On November 12, Ignatius Peter XVI Batanian, the Armenian

Patriarch, admonished the Council: 'The primacy of the Pontiff must not be limited in any way . . . We must proclaim to the world that the Church is passing through a glorious era . . . The First Vatican Council decided the question of the immediate, full, and exclusive power of the Pope over the whole Church.'

Consultation with the four Moderators of the Council and, in particular, with that favoured tower of strength, Cardinal Suenens, did not help in any way. The ultimate responsibility lay with Paul himself. The personal differences between Suenens and Doepfner, the negative attitude and sensitivity of Agagianian, the purely pastoral reaction of Lercaro and his personal veneration for Paul, were of no help to Paul in fashioning a strong policy. The four could not rid him of his fears. They could only voice their own hopes and differences. But decision there had to be. We will never know, completely and in intimate detail, the intricate involutions of Paul's path to decision between Friday the 8th and Tuesday the 12th of November.

Paul was now at the very paroxysm of his painful reassessment, in the agony of having to make his own decision. Up to this point he had worked on the summits of darkness. Now he had to descend into the valley of fateful decision and tread a path beset by spectres, the blocs of conservative and progressive Fathers, Jew and Muslim, Europeans and Americans, whites and Negroes, nuns and priests, laymen, chancery bishops, missionaries, cardinals, the *risorgimento* and *aggiornamento*, of Papa Mastai and Papa Roncalli. Beyond, at the end of the valley, shrouded in the mists of history-to-be-made, Paul could dimly perceive the darkened summits of another crag, its slopes awaiting his pilgrim's steps. For the present, Paul suffered deep agony, disappointment, and foreboding.

It was not the burden of decision which weighed on Pope Montini. For decisions as such had always come easy to him bathed as he was in the aureole of his mysticism. It was the *type* of decision which bothered him. It was hard to have to admit that he had committed himself as Pope to a retreat from positions already verbally occupied. It meant that verbal indulgence, reliance on lofty vision and the power of language, was ruled out. He had to decide on an action, impose an attitude in the concrete, divorced from the protective garments of words. *Verba volant*. It would be a decision that was rigid, stiff and stark, foisted on him both by his own inability to model history and by the unleashed forces of an ancient order of things at bay, unyielding and infinitely resourceful.

Another form of pressure was exercised. Two pamphlets appeared at this time: one entitled *The Council and the Assault of the Central European Bloc*, the other, *The Jews and the Council in the Light of Holy Scripture and Tradition*, the former signed by 'Catholicus,' the latter signed by a certain 'Bernardus.' The cardinal and the monsignor of the Curia who were responsible directly for the production of these two pieces remained in the background. They had adopted this means to influence public opinion. The *Assault*, by 'Catholicus,' echoed the line preached to the Council by such people as Cardinal Ruffini and Bishop Carli: collegiality was not only against Scripture and Tradition, it was anti-Catholic and destructive of Christ's Church. In particular, Bea's doctrine of *verità nella carità*, the honest search after truth with love in one's heart, was attacked violently as an assault on the age-old doctrine of the Church: error had no rights. It blamed the entire concept of collegiality on the Nordic bloc of central European bishops who were accused of wishing to rend the seamless garment of the Church.

The *Jews and the Council* is the most rational presentation of the Jewish question from the standpoint of official Church conservatism and anti-Semitism. Its message: Scripture states quite clearly that the Jews were voluntary deicides, the Fathers of the Church supported this doctrine, St Thomas Aquinas wrote in that sense, the attitude of the Roman Pontiffs can only be interpreted as an affirmation that the Jews partake of a world-wide plot to destroy the Church. Hence, all should be wary of the Jew and not destroy a fundamental *dogmatic* stand of the Church. Bea, his doctrine and position, was the real target.

In the meantime, early on Sunday, November 10th, Paul was informed by President Segni that he had picked Aldo Moro, Secretary General of the Demochristian Party, to form the new government with the collaboration and participation of the Socialists Nenni and Saragat. Paul gave his blessing but the price he was to pay, in conciliar terms, was to be high. He had been thinking deeply and consulting with everyone. With everyone, that is, except the American bishops. At no stage did a delegation of American cardinals go to him and insist on the discussion of religious liberty and the Jewish document. 'The Holy Father must not be pressured,' declared one American cardinal flatly to an urgent request in this sense.

For Paul the political state of Italy was of paramount importance. But he was also swayed by ecclesiastical issues and the threat to his own primacy and authority. Finally on Tuesday, November 12, he took a certain step. His ecumenical approach to Orthodoxy must not be frustrated. Besides, the idea of being the one who detonated an inner explosion of Catholicism did not appeal to him. Perhaps, if authority were strengthened, there might not be any explosion at all?

Climax there was – the climax of different policies which he had thought ran horizontally, parallel, and to a final co-ordinated point, but which suddenly seemed to collide, criss-cross, and threaten to endanger the progress of his pontificate. Paul saw himself no longer as Roncalli, realized that *giovannismo* was not his child, might even be dangerous perhaps, and decided that he was only just in time to assert what he was and act according to his own dictates.

The framework of his decision was simple: no re-adjustment of *giovannismo* was possible, for conciliarism had unleashed forces in the Church which threatened to tear it to pieces. If allowed to go on, conciliarism would make it impossible for him to realize the central purpose of his pontificate, the formation of a third world force: for this he needed strongly knit forces at home. The personal motivation for this 'retreat' is to be sought in the peculiar balance of his character: *mystique* and order, will and mind, interiority and pragmatism. The *mystique* of adjusted *giovannismo* had been shredded; for it was substituted a *reditus ad domum*, a return to the only possible substitute, the paternal house of Romanism and papalism. Gone was the persuasion of *giovannismo* that both pontiff and papacy, bureaucracy and people, pyramid and plain, were to be transmuted into a third entity. Now, the pontificate, the papacy, the bureaucracy and the people would transmute the plain. The difference was subtle; its immediate effects were and are obvious and disturbing.

By Wednesday, November 13, the opponents of his former policies had guessed his decision, had foreseen the probable outline of his solution. They instructed Bishop Luigi Carli, of Segni, Italy, to stand up in the Council and repeat all the provoking statements which Ottaviani had made on Friday, November 8. 'It is clear,' said Carli confidently on November 13 in full session of the Council, 'that collegiality is not fully approved or discussed. The whole thing was contrary to the procedural rules of the Council and therefore illegal. No elements of collegiality derive from divine law. Collegiality in the sense used by some Council Fathers is contrary to the divine law concerning Bishops.' This was the final straw. Carli was not contradicted: no cardinal called him to order; only silence greeted this *tour de force*.

The same day, Ottaviani granted an interview to the Divine Word News Service, and declared that he was opposed to any obligatory consultative body to assist the Holy Father. The word 'obligatory' was his own addition to and refinement of the current ideas. 'This would limit the supreme power of the Pontiff,' said the Secretary of the Holy Office. 'And the vote of October 30 was merely an indication of what the Fathers of the Council thought.' He added: 'Bishops could govern *under* the Pope, not *with* the Pope.' He then gave his own exegesis of Scripture: 'The college of the Apostles never existed, and therefore the bishops cannot succeed the apostles ... There is not one instance of collegiality among the apostles, except the Council of Jerusalem. There the apostles acted as one body.' To oppose him there was only Bishop Eugene D'Souza, 46 years of age, of India, who said: 'Is it not an act of derision for the Council to say that there is no need to take into account the opinions clearly manifested by that vote?' But at that stage his was a voice crying in the desert.

By the 13th, Paul decided that the document on religious liberty (Chapter 5 of Bea's Schema on Ecumenism) and the other one on the Jewish question (Chapter 4 of the same) could not, on any account, be submitted for a vote in principle much less go on for conciliar approval. He and his advisers of course, had to take into account the reactions both of the Council members and the waiting world: the decision would not be announced in those terms or in a sudden brutal or shocking way.

There would have to be a careful phasing of the disclosure: first of all, it would be announced that the schema on Ecumenism would be presented to the Council after the present discussion on Bishops was finished. After the general discussion, each chapter would be taken up. This was the tenor of the announcement made by Felici on the morning of the 13th. The next phase would consist in dividing the vote on principle: it would be proposed to Bea by Cicognani, in the name of the Holy Father, that only the first three chapters (dealing with Christian bodies) would be submitted for a vote, but with a promise that the other two chapters would come up for a similar vote in due course, before the end of the Council, with sufficient time to allow for discussion on them. The final phase would be to deliver the judgement that 'there was not sufficient time' now at this session to put the documents to the Council Fathers, who had only received Chapter 4 on November 8th, and Chapter 5 on the 19th. But since they had been distributed, Council members were invited to submit their emendations in writing to the Council Secretariat before the 31st of January, 1964. Thus phased, it was hoped, the two dangerous documents could be postponed *sine die*.

It is extremely doubtful that Bea was informed about the plan Paul had formulated to deal with the crisis over Chapters 4 and 5. But it is certain that the Old Man from the Black Forest read the portents accurately from November 12th onwards. His 'conciliar' contacts and exhortations and discussions outside the basilica were cut down. He communicated this policy to his immediate subordinates.

It is certain that no leading member of the American hierarchy was informed of Paul's decision concerning Chapters 4 and 5, as certain that Suenens and Doepfner at least were excluded from the inner counsels during these days. Paul was said to have found Suenens too insistent, too pugnacious and, besides, he and Doepfner did not see eye to eye on several points of policy. The net result was that the vast number of American bishops, theologians, experts, and Press representatives continued on blithely in the belief that this session 'must adopt Chapters 4 and 5 or else we cannot return to the States,' as one member of the U.S. Press panel kept repeating. One can judge of the trust and naïveté involved here when it is remembered that even as late as Monday, December 2, Cardinal Meyer was predicting that the desired vote would come.

During that seventh week of the session, there had been much expectation. The *New York Times* had spoken of 'a coming showdown between the conservatives and progressives.' All knew that something vitally important had taken place behind the scenes, but no one moved, only the row upon row of conservative speakers. And the saddest commentary on the situation is to recall the last session of the week, on Friday, November 15th. At 11.45 a.m. there was nothing else to say: no one, Silva, Bea, Suenens, Meyer, Ritter, Frings, De Smedt, not one of the supposed pillars of progress had anything to add or any pertinent questions to put. The Council members were let out at three minutes to twelve, one half hour before the customary closing time. The quiet of complete defeat; the assurances had been stilled; the voice of the Council trailed off into silence.

Yet Paul had still to implement his decision; and the implementation involved several delicate moves and important consequences. These moves would not be fully played out until November 22. The finality of his decision would not be apparent to some even on December 4, when the session formally ended.

Paul's close counsellors quickly formed a revised plan. It was clear that the movement to canonize the already approved doctrine of collegiality would have to be stifled. Likewise it would be impossible to allow the documents on religious liberty and on the Jewish question to be brought to a vote. This would mean deep disappointment to two influential bodies: the American hierarchy and the Jews. For the American hierarchy, it was sufficient for the Pope to call in the most influential members and explain that the circumstances were unfavourable. For the Jews, however, something would have to be done to ease the disappointment – at least temporarily. Why not include a visit to Israel in his Near East itinerary? In this way Paul could seem to acknowledge indirectly yet publicly the existence of the Jewish State and the disappointment would be lessened.

In deciding to stifle the movement for collegiality, Paul decided to act brutally and ruthlessly; this was an inner Catholic issue, and the bishops would listen to him. Besides, the success of his projected contact with Athenagoras and the theatrical setting of his meeting would blot out other considerations, at least temporarily. Time had to be bought.

On the evening of November 15, there was a meeting at which the four Moderators, the twelve cardinals of the Council Presidency, and the chairmen of the Council Commissions were present. The Pope wished to communicate to the leadership of the Council the main lines of his decision: to promulgate the two documents on the Liturgy and Communications. He wanted to sound them out also on some way in which the present procedural impasse could be resolved. Above all, he urged the need to effect two things before the Council's end: it must reveal some tangible results to the world and make sure that the principles of ecumenism at least would not suffer too much. He did not communicate to them the news of his decision to make a pilgrimage. He listened to some comments on Chapters 4 and 5 of Bea's schema. The amended draft of the decree on Communications had been approved on November 14. The final text of the Liturgy decree would be approved on November 22 by 2,158 votes to 19.

Paul's personal secretary, Monsignor Pasquale Macchi, and Monsignor James Martin, Vatican Secretariat of State expert for the Near East, left for Jordan and Israel. The former betook himself to the Apostolic Delegation in Jerusalem, and then visited the Holy Places, the other departed to inform other persons of Paul's intentions. Neither the Royal Government of Jordan nor the Government of Israel were informed, in advance, of Paul's intention. The arrival of Macchi and Martin was noted both by Egyptian and Israeli intelligence. The

Egyptian Press, under the guidance of Nasser who had learnt about the visits to Jerusalem and Tel Aviv, suddenly broke out in a furious storm about a secret mission sent by the Vatican to Israel.

A few days later Paul received the Latin patriarch of Jerusalem, Monsignor Gori, and questioned him closely on the inter-faith situation in Jerusalem, Israel and Jordan. Gori came away with the impression that the Holy Father certainly wished to have very detailed information about his patriarchate, but without any knowledge of Paul's purpose.

Soon Macchi and Martin returned to Rome, their mission accomplished: they had a clear idea of the itinerary Paul should follow, and a few authorities had been alerted. One Vatican expert commented at this stage that Paul was preparing his visit excellently from the ecumenical and ecclesiastical point of view but that rather fatal mistakes were being made diplomatically: neither of the interested governments had as yet been contacted. No effort had been made to offset the possible reactions of the Cairo government, although the Internuncio at Cairo, Monsignor Brini, had been consulted.

Things were arranged this way by Paul and his advisers in order to avoid unnecessary publicity. One chief reason was that it would have been a highly compromising situation if, on the one hand, the Pope had consented to pass through Israel (and thus acknowledge *de facto* the existence of Israel) and on the other hand still blocked the conciliar document on the Jewish question on the grounds that Arab opposition to the document would be unbearable. A moment's reflection serves to show us that the fundamental reason was not the possibility of Arab opposition, but rather vested interests – theological and/or economic.

During these days Paul's biggest achievement was that concrete arrangements were made with Athenagoras as regards a meeting in the Holy Places, the time, the place, the circumstances, the consequences.

Cicognani and Testa (head of the Oriental Congregation) who were 'in' on Paul's plans for a trip to the Holy Land, were insisting with Paul on several conditions for the meeting with Athenagoras: first of all, it was Athenagoras who should visit Paul, not Paul Athenagoras; secondly, it was unfitting that Paul should receive Athenagoras standing, and if they sat down, Paul should occupy a seat slightly more elevated – even by a few centimetres; thirdly, the Pope should, of course, be flanked by his top officials, Cicognani representing the Secretariat of State and Testa the Roman Congregation specially concerned with all contacts with the Oriental Churches. Lastly, Cicognani and Testa urged Paul to think now, and not later on, what channel was to be chosen for the permanent relations which he expected to establish with Athenagoras and the dissident Oriental Churches. It would be only right, they argued, that a new Commission for Extraordinary Affairs should be created, attached to the Curia as a permanent body under the Pope's direction, and that its personnel should be drawn from the two existing curial bodies which had already much experience in the affairs to be treated; the two referred to were of course the Secretariat of State and the Oriental Congregation.

Cicognani had very good reason to make these proposals to Paul. The Secretary of State was in possession of the gist of Athenagoras's letter to Paul which only reached Paul's hands on November 22. As a demonstration of how Bea's Secretariat was treated in all this, it should be noted that no copy of the letter was forwarded – as courtesy required – to the Secretariat. By chance, Willebrands and Duprey, the two top officials of the Secretariat, heard about it after Paul's visit to the Holy Land. Dell'Acqua then allowed them to have a copy. Cicognani's tipster in Constantinople, an ecclesiastic with access to the patriarch's decisions through more than one member of the latter's immediate entourage, informed Cicognani of the tenor of Athenagoras's letter before it arrived in Rome: Athenagoras greeted Paul's desire for a meeting, it corresponded closely to his own desires; he would expect Paul to return him a visit in Jerusalem; he insisted that the entire meeting should have an evangelical spirit and avoid anything that savoured of the juridical, institutional, let them meet as two patriarchs and not as the head of a state with a foreign potentate; it would be well to greet the Greek Orthodox Patriarch of Jerusalem, Benediktos, and to return his visit of courtesy – which Athenagoras could guarantee; finally, Athenagoras envisaged his meeting with Paul as merely the starting-point for a permanent contact leading to re-union, he was thinking of some way in which the relations between himself and Paul could be put on a firm basis.

Big issues were at stake here – ecclesially and ecclesiastically. We can pass over the rather pathetic recommendations made at one stage, such as that the *sedia gestatoria*, the Pope's mobile throne, should be transported to Jerusalem for the occasion: Paul did not want, he said, to ride on the shoulders of perspiring Christians down the *Via Dolorosa* which His Divine Master had trod on foot, bleeding and carrying a heavy beam on which he would shortly be nailed for all men's sins. This would make the journey a comedy, not a pilgrimage. Paul would carry a symbolic cross and would go on foot. It was not, however, such esoteric flights of Roman imagination that mattered at this moment; certain Vatican officials, who had never been in Jerusalem in their lives, were merely being carried away by the exuberance of their own triumphalism. The deeper issues concerned Paul's plans for a *third force* and the ecclesial and ecclesiastical form this was ultimately to take.

During the preceding weeks of the second session, the World Council of Churches had made an effort to have all contacts between Rome and other Churches (especially Orthodoxy and the Anglican Communion) channelled through the World Council. Bea and others made it clear that the Holy See could not operate through the kind offices of the World Council of Churches. The Secretary-General of the WCC appealed to Archbishop Ramsey, as we have said previously, but the latter merely acknowledged the correctness of the Holy See's attitude.

Now, however, it appeared that this fear of the WCC – whether the officials of that organization realized it or not – had some grounds. This was the first big issue at stake: true to the traditional line of the Vatican, the policy favoured by Cicognani and Testa would be one of *divide et impera* (divide and conquer). If the permanent relations between Athenagoras and Paul were to be maintained, on Rome's side, by a body composed as Paul's closest advisers suggested, then it was inevitable that, first of all, these relations would be institutionalized from the beginning, and, secondly, an effort would be made to achieve the 'submission' of non-Catholic bodies individually. The matter had many ramifications: in the minds of Athenagoras and Paul their contact was to be but a beginning, the opening of a door that would lead to relationships with all the churches, of Orthodoxy, Anglicanism, and Protestantism. It is typical of the hardhead administrative ruthlessness of these men that they were able to contemplate the alienating of certain elements in the WCC, relying no doubt on Bea and his Secretariat to heal wounds and maintain cordial relations as best they could.

This was the chief ecclesiastical consideration. There was also the ecclesial aspect. If events followed the pattern desired by Paul's advisers, the concept of the Church which Rome would present *officially* to the other Christian bodies seeking re-union would be primarily Roman and juridical. But this particular concept of the Church would preclude from the start any realistic hope of achieving a satisfactory union, of course. Apart from this, it had been demonstrated on the Council floor that it was not patristic, did not belong to the deposit of

G

revelation, and needed severe revision.

By November 23, Paul VI had agreed in principle to two very dangerous elements in the proposals made to him by Cicognani and others: he would be accompanied by Cicognani and Testa when he went to the Holy Land (and this in itself was the beginning of a certain institutionalization), and the envisaged channel of communications between Paul and Athenagoras would be along lines suggested by his advisers. Paul was to regret these concessions afterwards.

The future of Bea's Secretariat, therefore, became a matter of conjecture to the cardinal's immediate entourage. Bea had no doubt about the Pope's good-will. Nor did he doubt the good-will of Athenagoras: he was the first to establish relations with him on the Roman side. But Bea guessed that the life of his Secretariat was at stake. It is said in Rome that the greatest mistake one could make with regard to Bea would be either to underestimate his power of regaining positions of influence, or to allow him the *last* word. Antoniutti, the previous summer, had wished to do away with Bea's influence. Bea had had an audience with Paul *after* Antoniutti. What happened? Bea had merely been appointed to the Holy Office *with* Antoniutti, though Antoniutti had asked for the contrary. Cicognani and Testa had all had their say with Paul on the proposed visit to the Holy Places. Bea had his say last. Paul did not adopt their suggestions. He followed Bea's suggestions, even went so far as to put Duprey, one of Bea's top aides, in complete charge of all contracts, interviews, ceremonial, in connection with the Orthodox and others the Pope would meet. Yet when all this is said and done, there comes a time in the life of any man when the wheels of life slow down. Only the coming months will reveal the truth or falsehood of persistent rumours that he will step down. 'Bea has gone too far,' was the indignant remark of Cicognani at one nerve-racking stage during the Council. 'This cardinal does not make up the Council,' Paul VI himself is supposed to have said of Bea. Signs of impatience or passing moods?

As Paul contemplated the state of things on November 23, he had much to worry about, a little to console him, and a good deal of practical difficulties to iron out. He had, above all, much to think about.

The progress of things in the Council worried him. The audiences with the Consultors of the Oriental Congregation on November 14 and the meeting with the Council leaders on November 15 had amounted to nothing. The *malaise* persisted in conciliar circles.

The outbreak of anti-Semitic sentiments among the Council

Fathers had been disturbing; the *New York Herald Tribune* came out with headlines about such anti-Semitic statements. Bea's introduction of Chapter 4 (on the Jewish question) had been *pianissimo*, in low-key, a remarkable performance in understatement and restraint of expression. It was on the whole disappointing even for those who did not know that his speech had been vetted before delivery. Bea guessed that the gentleman's agreement made by Cicognani on November 20 to have a split vote on Chapters 4 and 5 was merely a time-buying device.

Paul also knew that his address to the French bishops on November 18 had gone badly. He told them that, in spite of their intellectual dynamism and penchant for new methods, they must nip incipient error in the bud so that no intervention from Rome would be necessary. To add insult to injury, he had departed without greeting them individually – a normal custom when a national group of bishops are received. The French commented sarcastically on the whole thing, recalling the laudatory remarks he had made to the North American bishops on November 17 and the handshake he had given each one afterwards. 'Evidemment, nous n'avons pas, nous autres, ni les sous ni les bombes,' commented one, somewhat irreverently.

Then the Oriental prelates let loose veritable streams of criticism directed at Bea's document on the Jewish question. Paul, like everyone else, knew that they were making sure that they would be welcome back in Egypt, Syria, Jordan, and Iraq. De Smedt complained bitterly to his colleagues about the utter lack of good faith and charity in the whole procedure. The reception of the schema on Ecumenism had been rather favourable so far, but voices were already being heard in the Council criticizing the basic concept of ecumenism. On November 18, Cicognani officially reported on the first three chapters to the Council in the name of the Mixed Commission of which he was president but which had had nothing to do with the composition of the chapters. Cicognani had insisted on his right to do so, promising Bea that the latter would be allowed to supply him with a text. Cicognani wrote his own speech.

Then Archbishop Martin reported on the opening part of the schema, and (at Cicognani's insistence) Bishop Bukatko, a Ukrainian Uniat, presented the part concerning the Oriental Churches. No Uniat bishop was acceptable to the Orthodox Churches, and the Ukrainians in particular were particularly distasteful to the Russians. Yet the same Romanist and traditional policy was at work again. Bea himself presented Chapter 4, as we said, and De Smedt Chapter 5, using a speech prepared for him by John Courtney Murray, the American authority on Church-State relations. In addition to the hamstringing of Bea's movements on his own ground (he was not allowed, by Paul's order, to introduce his own Ecumenical schema), voices in the Council turned out to be highly critical of the ideas of ecumenism and religious liberty. Their supporters were not vocal or courageous enough.

Paul, in short, felt that the old contours of conciliarism as he had seen them during the summer months were melting in the heat of the blind disorganization of the progressive movement among the bishops. More and more, he shook the former concepts from his mind, and turned to his Holy Land visit. It was while he was in this frame of mind that the assassination of President Kennedy occurred. *Giovannismo* was dead. Now another landmark of the Joannine era was dead. There was no causal connection between these two extinctions: yet, the shocking end of John F. Kennedy, as Paul knew and remarked to his entourage, would signify the end of a certain *élan* in American foreign policy and in the American presence throughout the world. Again, the concept of the third force loomed up in discussions and in Paul's thoughts. With Kennedy gone and Kennedy-ism dead, there was a vacuum in world forces which could not be filled, even by De Gaullism at its most magnificent. And Paul's attention was once more turned to the significance of his meeting with Athenagoras and its potential for a re-grouping of all Christian bodies. Beyond this sphere he began to see an ever-widening circle of influence exercised by the great non-Christian religions. Again, the idea of the Secretariat for non-Christian religions came up in discussion. With these orientations of his thought, Paul's new *mystique* began to evolve. It would take some months, fresh experiences, to reduce it to practical terms.

FIVE

THE PILGRIM

We are now going to review the period from the end of November to the opening of the New Year, 1964. From one point of view, it is a sad time – conciliarly speaking. From another, it is a time of intense interest, in that it marks the first period of the Pauline era properly speaking. It is characterized by the public act whereby Paul deliberately wished to indicate its importance to the world at large. The period helps to dispel certain doubts about Paul himself. Because he had decided that Joannine conciliarism was not for him, it might be thought that by a *contre-coup* he would adopt a contrary line of action. This, of course, is simply not true. What happens now is that Paul forms his own outlook. He is no longer the successor of John XXIII carrying on the work of Roncalli. He is Paul VI, Papa Montini. This is to be his work and his choice.

We still have to review the end of the Council. However, we are not concerned with mere recording; and so, in order to interpret what happened and how the Council *was ended* (for it did not simply *end*) by Paul, we must briefly sketch the outlines of the new vision and the basic convictions he formed. First, an account of his outlook. Then, a description of how he ended the Council in harmony with this outlook. Finally, some short considerations as to the future and Paul VI himself.

1. The Third Force

The basic change in Paul's outlook had to do with the role of Roman Catholicism and of Christianity in the international world which Paul now saw prefigured in outline. As for all other master-players at the chess-board, Paul's world consisted, primarily, of two mighty world blocs: the 'western' bloc composed of two loosely aggregated segments, the United States of America – with its commercial, economic and military interests throughout the world, and the slowly crystallizing bloc of Western Europe; and the Soviet bloc with its gaggle of dependent satellites held in the mailed grip of economic, military and ideological chains. Side by side with these two definitively marked segments of organized and ideologically oriented human beings, there operated two catalytic elements: the large uncommitted area represented by the newly-born nations of Africa and Asia, and the keystone element in the entire pattern, mainland Communist China.

Papa Montini was not influenced by any outdated post-World War II concept of these complicated elements. Nor was his thought conditioned as to geographical and geo-religious terms by what Walter Lippmann rather aptly described as a post post-War mentality. Originally, in the cold-war period, Europe and America stood together as the 'West' over against the Stalinist Soviet Empire in the East. Neither Africa nor the Far-East had at that time any definite configuration. As Bismarck remarked towards the end of the nineteenth century, the most important fact of the twentieth century was that the people of England and America spoke the same language. Then as Europe started to regain stature, both economically and nationally, the post post-War mentality began to emerge. An economically restored and militarily re-equipped Europe stood side by side with America, dependent on her for its military muscle – especially in the domain of nuclear weapons – and facing the increasing threat of Soviet Communism now increased six times by the addition of China's 700 millions to its arsenal of human labour, military potential and ideological resources. The newly modified 'West' and Soviet East fought for exclusive place in the awakening lands of Africa.

But the post post-War mentality no longer adequately explains the most recent development in the world situation, which has once more radically – organically – changed. We have to note here a curious fact apparent throughout, whether we are considering Russian Communism and the geographical and ideological territory over which its *imperium* extends, or Roman Catholicism and the area under its socioreligious control both in Europe and elsewhere, or Western Europe with all its national structures, economic systems and political legacies. This fact is relatively easy to describe but difficult to categorize or classify under one heading.

First of all, the Soviet Empire has undergone the dissolvent effect of the nuclear age. The age-old Marxist principle of war, local or general, between classes or ethnic groups, has lost all meaning in an age when a general war, or, indeed, a local war, would mean the death and burial of both Communism and Capitalism. The realization of this and its implementation are the main characteristics of the recent phenomenon of Khrushchevism and have found ready formulation in his well-known phrases: 'the peaceful co-existence of Capitalism and Communism,' 'the peaceful victory over Capitalism,' etc. The deeper effects of this are to be noted throughout the Soviet Empire in Poland, in Hungary, in Czechoslovakia, both in the big cities and small villages, throughout Eastern Europe. In addition, there is the brute fact of the economic precariousness of the Soviet economy in contrast to an undeniable boom in the West. France, West Germany, Italy, Spain, instead of foundering, have prospered. But, in the last analysis, what precipitated the new world configuration was the rising red star of China.

From 1949 onwards, until recently, Russia has built up China as its biggest satellite: credits have been extended for the purchase of tools and food supplies, industrial and economic equipment, factory and technical installations; specialists and technicians have been trained in all branches of industry and commerce; Russian scientists, instructors, skilled workers have all been sent there, with a view to building up the vast potential of this tremendous ally under the hegemony of Moscow. These were the days when Russia's door to the whole of South-East Asia was open. Moscow even started the Chinese on the road to nuclear capability.

It will remain a mystery for a long time why Mao Tse-tung took the apparently irrevocable steps of breaking with Russia and of throwing overboard the sincere, if naïve friendship of Nehru's India. At one blow, by driving a bayonet through northern Indian defences and becoming a military threat to the whole North-Western plains area, Mao Tse-tung not only deprived himself of the active and at times irritating support of Nehru and his followers, he also produced a revulsion among the Indian peoples themselves. He also instilled such fear into his original masters in the Kremlin, that not only were essential supplies of technicians and nuclear development withdrawn, but Russia intervened in an active way to aid India in its war-effort against the Chinese invasion. Doubtless, the inscrutable master of China's millions, together with his theoreticians and experts, had decided that the time had come to 'go it alone.' Their reasons were obvious.

A new situation was apparent in Europe. Europe was emerging as a new world bloc. It was clear that, ultimately, Soviet Russia and its satellite countries would have to be associated with this new Europe. 'Europe,' said Charles De Gaulle, 'stretches from Calais to the Urals.' More important, the Communist ideal represented by Soviet Russia no longer corresponded to the actual state of things in Cuba, in South America, in certain parts of Africa, for in those areas the brand of Communism which suited the mentality of the masses was the old Stalinist, militaristic, pre-Khrushchev brand. Here was a fertile field to be cultivated. It would afford China and Maoism an ascendancy which Soviet Russia could no longer afford to grasp.

In Roman Catholicism, an analogously identical phenomenon was taking place. With the rise of mass education and mass civilization, with material prosperity and progress, with the leavening effect of inter-communication between nations and groups, on the political, religious or social level, the old hide-bound divisions between right Church and wrong Church, the true Christian and false Christian, began to dissolve. We have noted time and time again with astonishment the similarity in the way a 'liberal' Communist theoretician will speak about Communism and the way a 'liberal' Christian will speak about Christianity. The similarity exists also for the 'conservatives' in both camps.

In Europe, a dissolving of ancient barriers has become evident. In the early years of the fifties, it was quite obvious that in spite of differences of a political, industrial, agricultural and cultural nature, this huge delta had decided to move towards unity. In the early years, a quick solution to the difficulties was ruled out, and the earlier plans proposed by Monnet and Schumann: the Coal and Steel Community, Euratom, the European Common Army, would not be capable of forging the necessary unity. Similarly, the attempt of England to be associated with a half-formed Europe, on its own terms, was foiled by De Gaulle who rightly saw that the only unity possible, ultimately, was a unity built on already existing economic and industrial unity and with the existing governments as its architects. His Europe of the Fatherlands never meant any more than this. He saw accurately that there were already two axes running across this incipient Europe: the Bonn-Paris axis and the Rome-London axis, both non-traditional, both based on contingent necessities, both preludes to a greater merger.

In America, and the American Commonwealth, the same crisis has revealed itself, clothed in garments peculiar to America. The advent of John Kennedy seemed to set off a chain-reaction among the groups that made up the pluralistic society of America. Again, the phenomena of 'liberal' and 'conservative,' of 'right' and 'left' appeared. Again, the same analogous similarities of language and behaviourism. It would seem that if there was any deep, essential meaning to Kennedy's concept of a New Frontier, it went far beyond such things as economic structures, civil rights, socialization, urbanization, industrial controls, etc. For the New Frontier concept seemed, at heart, determined to add a new dimension to the American optic: to create a consensus around the figure and policies of the youthful President who would help lead America to abandon the policy of staticism it had so long practised in national and international affairs, help it to give up immobile positions as a fixed target, and to revamp its concepts both of military force and diplomatic offensive. It is almost certain that if Kennedy had lived, he would eventually have 'unfrozen' the static position taken up in the straits of Formosa, have introduced flexibility into American policies in Europe, and finally escaped from the rigid positions taken up in South-East Asia.

With his death, the intense differentiation taking place in America lost its tautness and tenseness. The lode-stone of his political personality and the lines of his policies which evoked both negative and affirmative responses in America and throughout the world, would never again draw the public eye. A period of flux, of immobility, was destined to intervene, no matter who became President in 1964.

Paul, faced with the corpse of *giovannismo* and watching on television the casket of the 34th president of the United States being lowered into the earth of Arlington Cemetery, knew in his heart that an era had ended. Before his eyes, in clearer and more definite outline, loomed the shape of a third force. This was his conceptualization of post-Joannine conciliarism, his interpretation of post-Joannine ecumenism, his answer to the enormous question: where is the world of the mid-sixties going?

There can be no doubt about it, the coming recognition of China by France (he had been informed of this near eventuality before Christmas 1963) was the first step towards a normalization of a *de facto* situation. Mao Tse-tung's dictatorship existed, whether or not we liked its iron-clad regime, its ruthless obliteration of the four freedoms, its ghastly mess of economic errors, industrial miscalculations, rampant militarism, creeping subversion in the Far-East, in North Africa and in the southern hemisphere of America. China represents an ascendant force in the delicate system of world equilibrium. No amount of non-recognition will do away with this fact. On the other hand, no one – not even a De Gaulle – can accurately foresee the train of events in the near future. But, non-recognition implies an ostrich-mentality, a renouncement of all possibility of effecting any change in Chinese Communist attitudes and the preclusion of any sort of penetration into the opaque mass of its tightly closed ranks – of a kind that was eventually possible in the case of Soviet Bolshevism. In January, while Paul was patiently labouring on the first step of his new synthesis, *L'Osservatore Romano* and *L'Osservatore della Domenica* (Feb. 2, 1964) both echoed his new attitude towards the Chinese situation.

Relying on the full power, influence and leadership of the Roman Pontiff, Papa Montini envisaged a structurization of a new policy in three or four stages, a laborious operation carefully calculated to set in motion still another piece on the checker-board of international life, and which in time might remove obstacles, be a solvent for bottled-up passions, a cement for loosely coagulated kindred forces, a pole of attraction for centripetal forces.

The meeting with Athenagoras was but an initial step, but it involved, microcosmically, not only the structurization which Paul wished now to impose on events, but the external act by which Paul signified that he was turning his face to another goal. In this sense, his pilgrimage to the Holy Places was replete with implications: it was, at one and the same time, a diplomatic action and a seeking for the light, a walking of the *Via Dolorosa* and a foretaste of the great banquet of reunion. It was Peter in the chains of his historic dilemma and Paul journeying among the Gentiles. It denoted his desire for light and guidance, and, at the same time, was the first act of Papa Montini as himself rather than as the successor of John XXIII. It reflected his basic conviction that the Church he headed was on pilgrimage – again.

Through Athenagoras, Paul initiated the first step of his policy: the establishment of a permanent relationship with the great Catholic communions, Greek Orthodoxy, Russian Orthodoxy, Anglicanism, and the other major dissident Oriental Churches, Armenian and Coptic. The relationship itself, its nature, and the structure that would maintain and foster the relationship were the two central problems. We will have more to say about this later.

The next step involved the intermeshing of Roman effort and the united effort of this larger Christian grouping. This was why we said that the keystone of Paul's thought was his insistence on Romanism, on the Roman structure *as it is now*. For he envisages a Catholic grouping on a patriarchal basis with an evangelical spirit (as opposed to an institutional or juridical spirit), welding several juridical and already institutionalized groups into a single dynamism: Christianity led by several leaders who would resolve themselves into one kind of leadership.

Later on, Paul then projected the co-operation of non-Christian religions, Judaism, Islam, Buddhism, Shintoism, Hinduism. Of these, two, Judaism and Islam, had certain characteristics – the possession of The Book, a form of ethical monotheism, and certain elements – in common with Christianity. But the common denominator of all was the profession of religious values and aspirations which could not be satisfied with the merely material, social, political or nationalistic.

2. The Pilgrimage

We shall now cover the events from November 22 to December 4, and then those during the remainder of December and the opening days of January, 1964. Paul's days in the latter part of November were full of activity: planning his Holy Land visit, receiving groups of bishops, and working out the concrete applications of his new outlook. The North American hierarchy was received on November 21, the Irish, South African and Rhodesian bishops on the 22nd, the Japanese bishops on the 24th, and so on. If Paul had wanted to work up a common mentality among the bishops he had magnificent opportunities to do so.

The Moderators of the Council had audience on the 23rd to discuss the procedural rules of the Council once more and iron out certain difficulties. Even at this stage, they did not fully realize that a vote on Chapters 4 and 5 was ruled out. The Lebanese Ambassador was received on the same day and Paul once more faced the problem of the Jewish document. He also wanted to sound the ambassador out on the repercussions of his visit.

Within the Council things were going in a see-saw direction, between the conservatives and progressives. As the days rolled by and the victory of the conservatives seemed clearer, the more stubborn the progressives seemed to be that 'the vote will be taken,' 'Chapters 4 and 5 will certainly be voted upon, perhaps even promulgated.' And even when Felici announced on November 25 that December 3 would be devoted simply to a commemoration of the Council of Trent, and December 4 would be the closing day on which the business of the Council would consist solely in the ratification and promulgation of the Liturgy and Communications documents (followed by the 'suspension' of the former so that its provisions could not be applied immediately), the progressives still clung to their conviction that 'this cannot happen,' 'we have been promised by Cardinal Cicognani that there will be a vote,' 'this cannot happen, the Pope will not allow this to come about.'

But the iron control of conservative forces was everywhere apparent, and dominated by a single-track pursuance of one objective and one objective only – to tide things over, to let nothing get out of hand, until the end, then everything would be all right. Speaker after speaker rose in the Council to hammer away at ecumenism and Bea's schema. The best example of how things went during these days was the abortive attempt to protest the badly bungled text of the Communications decree.

The document suffered from very serious defects. Its preparation by a special commission had been haphazard. Not all the commission members had read the final text which they, nevertheless, voted to approve. On the floor no organized attempt was made to look at the document critically. On November 16, three journalists produced a one-page critique and distributed it to the bishops. They also secured the signatures of four eminent theologians of the Council (including John Courtney Murray and Bernard Häring), who recommended the critique as worthy of consideration.

This critique declared that the text on Communications 'could one day be cited as a classical example of the way in which the Second Vatican Council was incapable of facing the world around it.' It spoke quite clearly: 'This text seems to give the State authority over mass media, and this is dangerous for political liberty everywhere. It is also forbidden expressly by the Constitution of the United States.'

The action of these journalists as journalists was questionable: they were in Rome to report, not to take sides. But it served a good purpose in bringing out the one-sidedness of Archbishop Felici and resulted in a photographic reportage of his zeal. On the 25th, some priests and laymen were distributing a related document (containing an urgent request to the Council members to reject the text of the Communications decree). It bore the signatures of several Council Fathers. Felici came out into the square, looked at the situation, and saw that it was getting out of hand. He called the Vatican police who confiscated the offending papers. One German bishop, Reuss by name, refused to surrender his copy to Felici. The Archbishop made a swift lunge at the paper, but was repulsed by Reuss. In disgust, Reuss then threw the paper at Felici, remarking something in German as he did so.

Afterwards Felici spread the story that some of the names affixed to the document were falsifications, hoping thus to discredit the whole venture. This is interesting, when we remember the behaviour of Felici in the case of Balič. Not only was Balič allowed to distribute his booklets in the square and in the basilica itself but his documents were printed by the Vatican press. But Balič was voicing the opinions of the same masters whom Felici served. The latter's quick lunge at Bishop Reuss in St Peter's Square on the 25th of November, 1963, is preserved for ever in the photographs which some quick-witted cameramen snapped on the spot. It remained for the bearded Tisserant to stand up in the Council the same day and to concentrate all his Gallic ire and curial dignity on the perpetrators of this incident. Tisserant had raised no objections when Balič distributed his tracts on the Blessed Virgin – within the basilica itself. The Communications decree was approved by a majority of 1,598 votes for, and 503 votes against.

The same day, November 25, Cardinal König of Vienna, in an interview with *L'Osservatore Romano*, voiced his opinion that the Church must prepare to meet not only with Christians but with non-Christians. For this purpose the Council should provide, he said, a set of principles which would make unequivocally clear the Church's attachment to the principles of religious liberty. 'Without a declaration from the Council on religious liberty,' said Cardinal Ritter of St Louis, 'mutual confidence will be impossible and serious dialogue will be excluded.' The same day also, Bishop Vitus Chang told the Council that the notion of ecumenism should be enlarged to include not only the other Christian confessions but all religions and all peoples everywhere.

On November 27, the Council heard sounds from Stephen A. Leven, auxiliary bishop of San Antonio, Texas, which they not only never dreamt of hearing, but some did not consider either necessary or fitting. He spoke out first of all against the paternalistic attitude adopted by curial members and their followers when speaking to the Council:

'Why not put an end, once and for all, to the scandal of our mutual recriminations?' asked the Bishop. 'Every day it becomes clearer that we have a real need of a dialogue not merely with the Protestants but with ourselves as bishops.' Furthermore, he added, 'We have certain Council members here speaking as if the only text in the whole Bible was the Matthean text: "You are Peter and upon this rock I will build my Church" (*Matt.* 16:18). And they preach at us as if we are against Peter and his successors, or as if we wished to weaken the faith of believers and to promote indifferentism.'

He then turned to the question of ecumenism and religious liberty. There are people, he went on, 'who prefer to blame non-Catholics whom they have never seen, rather than instruct the children in their own parishes. And, on the other hand, why is it that they fear lest the effects of Ecumenism not be good? Why are their people not better instructed? Why are their people not visited in their homes?' Everyone knew that the bishop was referring to Italy and Spain. 'The prelates who desire a sincere and fruitful dialogue with non-Catholics are not those who show dissatisfaction and disloyalty to the Holy Father. It is not our people who omit Mass on Sundays, who refuse to partake of the sacraments, and who vote Communist.'

It is a measure of the liberty allowed to bishops who wish to speak bluntly in this fashion that Bishop Leven went time and again to the Council leadership and enquired when his turn would come for speaking, only to be put off. He had made the mistake of handing in a copy of his speech (required by Council rules) and there was no intention of allowing him to get his remarks off his chest. However, by chance one day, he found Archbishop Morcillo González of Saragossa, Spain, in charge at the Secretariat table, and spoke to him in Spanish. This flattered Morcillo so that he moved Leven's name up near the top of the list and he was finally allowed to speak.

It is also a measure of the 'clerical' attitude of certain American and other bishops that Bishop Leven was the only one submitted for additional membership in the Council commissions who was not elected. He had violated the cardinal rule: the bishops and hierarchy must not be criticized.

During the final days of November, one does not know which to wonder at most, the well-planned tactics of the conservatives or the trusting, bumbling, naïve, pessimistic behaviour of those who wanted Chapters 4 and 5 put to a vote. There were only ten more days to go. The mood of deliberate procrastination was as follows: from November 23 to November 28, the answer to all enquiries about these chapters was: 'Yes, of course, the vote will be taken.' From November 28 to December 1, the response was: 'No, we really have had no time to discuss these chapters, but they will be first on the agenda at the next session, and the Council Moderators are going to announce this firmly and unequivocally.' From December 2 to December 4, there was a bald, bland statement: 'We have had absolutely no time to get at the vote, really. Will the Council Fathers please submit their emendations and remarks on these two chapters in writing and before the 31st of January, 1964?'

The story now takes on a more ludicrous aspect. It was all being played out according to the plans of Cardinal Cicognani: he had blocked the originally promised vote on the chapters with the promise that 'they would come later, before the end of this session,' and had also prevented these chapters from being printed for a long time.

As the days went by and distrust mounted among the progressives, rumours started to circulate that seemed to come from the top-level of the Council leadership and to state categorically that no vote was envisaged. Meyer and Ritter approached Agagianian courteously and asked him whether there was going to be a vote. 'Why, of course, there is going to be a vote,' was the Armenian's answer. This was on November 27. On November 28, Spellman and Ritter and Meyer were with Paul and learned definitely that there would be no vote. All three had an innate dislike of 'pushing the Pope to do anything,' as one of them expressed it afterwards. The same day, Bea entered his own Secretariat wearing a deadpan face and told his colleagues that there would be no vote. But, he said, he had been promised that the Council Moderators would state quite clearly that Chapters 4 and 5 were on the agenda for the next session. Suenens told Ritter and Meyer on November 28 that there would be no vote but that the Moderator of the day, on December 2, would announce firmly that Chapters 4 and 5 were on the agenda for the third session.

This new gambit – no vote because of lack of time but the definite allocation of Chapters 4 and 5 to the agenda for the third session – lasted a short time. Rumours to the contrary also circulated: there would be no vote and there would be no confirmation of the place of the chapters in the third session. Meyer of Chicago, for once, appeared furious, and promised to go to the 'highest level' in order to get satisfaction. There was still hope, he and his advisers thought, to get the Pope to impose some sort of general approval on the two chapters. Suenens, speaking on Sunday, December 1, before the Canadian bishops, said that at least a statement of approval and confirmation would be made by the Council Moderator on the following Monday, December 2.

On this Monday Bea was scheduled to speak. Already the old man had been battered by continual warnings from Cicognani and by imperious demands that the text of his speech be vetted by the Secretary of State. This he had submitted to with as good a grace as possible. Then at 7.30 a.m. on Monday morning, he was telephoned and told that it would be essential for him to state to the Council members that only time had prevented the Council from coming to a definitive vote on Chapters 4 and 5. He was to impress on his hearers that a mechanical and material factor, and not the machinations of wilful men, had stopped the Council from proceeding as it would have wished. Even before Bea rose to speak, the observant bishops could have sensed in advance the change in atmosphere. Meyer was silent and depressed. He was no longer manifesting anger or impatience at the way things were going. Over the week-end word had reached him that all attempts to change things were 'against the will of the Holy Father.'

As Bea spoke, Agagianian was Moderator for the day. The German cardinal repeated all his former statements about the two chapters. He reiterated the statement that there had been no other cause, definitely no other cause, for the failure of the chapters to come to a vote except the insurmountable difficulty of time. There had been no time. Before he arrived at the end of his speech and when he had just started the passage where John XXIII was mentioned in laudatory terms, Agagianian cut off the microphone deliberately, so that Bea's voice trailed off, and he was merely to be seen, standing in relative silence, his mouth moving, his hands emphasizing, his eyes travelling over the rows of bishops. Agagianian explained lamely afterwards that he cut Bea off in order to avoid the rather inevitable applause that would have followed Bea's effort. Whenever Bea made a major speech it was applauded. But this was merely an excuse for bad manners and bad taste. Agagianian was acting on instructions.

The tenor of Bea's speech was not encouraging. In particular, in the last part he spoke in such a way about his Chapter 4 (on the Jewish problem) that it was quite unclear as to whether this chapter would be in the hands of his own Secretariat or entrusted to a new Secretariat for non-Christian Religions. The latter had not yet been established by Paul. Cardinal Bea is a man who weighs his words carefully. In actual fact, he had been told by Paul that the best way out of the difficulty caused by Chapter 4 would be to entrust it to such a Secretariat. But Bea was too cautious to assert this and too providential-minded to omit all indirect mention of it. As was to be expected, the Moderator of the day, Agagianian, did not issue any statement confirming that Chapters 4 and 5 would be on the agenda for the third session. He had been told to omit such a statement. The tragedy had been played out to the end. Bea made one addition to the censored text of his speech that day, however: looking up and speaking *ex tempore*, he assured the Fathers that Chapters 4 and 5 *would* be on the agenda of the third session.

Bishop Helmsing of Kansas City, Missouri, had asked one very simple question on November 29: 'I have one question to ask,' he said. 'When we were asked to vote separately on Chapters 1–3 of this schema on Ecumenism we were assured that we would have an opportunity to vote on Chapters 4 and 5 in this session. When will we have this vote as promised?' This was the simplest and most direct request made on the Council floor during the twisting days of late November, for it presumed good faith and a fidelity to a promise given. Nor should the good bishop have been allowed to stand alone in his efforts. If the American cardinals had taken the initiative, if they had spoken in the Council and brought pressure to bear equal to the pressure from the enemies of Chapters 4 and 5, the story might have ended differently.

To understand the turn of events, one must recall that on December 3, a petition signed by 300 Council Fathers was handed to Cicognani that the Council condemn Communism in very clear terms. This had been preceded by several speeches, notably that of Edward Mason, a bishop located in the Sudan, in which the same theme had been insisted on. Now if the Catholic Church admitted the principles of religious liberty as set forth in Chapter 5 as proposed by Bea, this would mean that not only could anyone – with the blessing of the Church of Rome – choose whatever form of religion his conscience dictated, but he could go even further: he could choose atheism. And atheism has one very virulent form today, Communism. The chapter on religious liberty, therefore, in the view of certain people was considered as a tacit approval of anyone choosing to be a Marxist.

The reasoning behind this view is, of course, distorted and amounts to a perversion of Bea's principles, yet bishops from over forty-six nations signed the petition. Furthermore, the backers of the petition were allowed to distribute unmolested a sixteen-page memorandum to the Council members, which argued that it was against Catholic principles to admit that the Church could enjoy unrestricted freedom in a Communist state. Tisserant did not inveigh against this act as he did on an earlier occasion. There was no need. Tisserant and Felici were both believed to be behind the entire project.

For the American public and the American mind, the issue of religious liberty and the Council's attitude to it is of great importance. And the true bearing of the attitude of the conservatives at the Vatican Council can be understood rightly, if we reflect on the case of Daniel Seeger of New York, a conscientious objector who professed atheism but refused on grounds of conscience to accept the draft of the Selective Service authorities. The Selective Service Act states that 'no one is to be exempted from the draft as a conscientious objector unless he holds to a belief in a relation to a Supreme Being.' Now Seeger stated that he believed in 'goodness and virtue for their own sakes' and that he opposed war as unethical. The U.S. Court of Appeals, to which Seeger had recourse, ruling in his favour, stated clearly that 'we here respect the right of Daniel Seeger to believe what he will, largely because of the conviction that every individual is a child of God, and that Man, created in the image of his Maker, is endowed for that reason with human dignity.' In the mentality of those who opposed Chapter 5 on religious liberty and its principles, the decision reached by the U.S. Court of Appeals is blasphemous.

As for the schema on Ecumenism (Chapters 1–3), the discussion revealed that there was fundamental disagreement about the ideas proposed in this document as a whole. Nothing definitive was achieved in the matter of ecumenism. Paul had decided to let this hope of his drop for the time being. On November 27, he let it be known that he was going to augment the powers of the bishops in a special document, which was read on December 3, during a personal appearance at the Council. The bishops henceforth could exercise forty powers (faculties) which till then had been reserved to the Holy See. There were also eight new concessions or faculties. If one reads the language of this document, carefully, one finds that the Pope neither states nor excludes the idea that he *granted* the bishops these rights. The point is this: the bishops as bishops, as successors of the Apostles, as pastors of the Church, have certain inalienable rights by divine right. However, the subtlety of the situation seems to have escaped the bishops in their joy at receiving the authorization to exercise new faculties. It was Paul's way of offering a superficial satisfaction to the vast majority who had voted for collegiality, a woefully inadequate and pitifully poor ending to the debate on collegiality and the weakest response Paul was capable of giving to the straw vote of October 30. But it was worthwhile psychologically Again it bought time for Paul.

The December 3 meeting of the Council was devoted to commemorating the Council of Trent. This was one of the fruits of plans laid during the summer recess by the conservatives. As an epitaph on the second session it was most fitting, and Cardinal Urbani's discourse, in the presence of Paul, contained resonant tones of the old voices that had been dimmed, for a short while, during the session. They were again heard clearly, triumphantly and satisfyingly. Urbani insisted that the session just finished had confirmed the primacy and solidity of the pontificate of Paul VI. The Romanist line. There had of course never been any question of debating either the primacy or pontificate of Paul VI during the second session. What Urbani meant was that these had emerged strengthened from the struggle to minimize and tarnish them during the discussions on collegiality.

Drawing a parallel between the Vatican Council and the Council of Trent, Urbani then spoke of the 'usual zealots' who would have distracted the Council from its proper course. He appealed to the Fathers to admire the 'dogmatic canons' of Trent and the reforming disciplinary decrees adopted then. He praised the liberty of speech allowed in the council, and pointed to the extensive fruits of the reforms introduced by Trent. His speech was the signing-away of *giovannismo*. This was not an effort to translate the substance of the ancient doctrine into a modern language; it was the very thing John XXIII had explicitly ruled out as an objective for his Council. But John could rest in peace.

On December 4, Paul delivered his final address to the members of the Council. The speech was a masterpiece of understatement and showmanship. Paul knew that the majority of bishops were disappointed over his failure to sustain them in their conciliar desires, and had to gloss over the glaring gaps in the list of final achievements. After a long introduction in which he praised the fact of the Council, he enumerated the two chief fruits of the session: it had approved two important documents, the Liturgy constitution and the Communications decree. These were proof, he said, of the fruitfulness of the session. It is difficult to see how Paul could congratulate the Fathers on the Communications decree. However, the important point was that the façade of achievement had been preserved. The Council had actually finished *two* documents. Numbers are impressive.

Next Paul enumerated the objectives for the next session: a clear, definitive statement concerning the sources of revelation, the nature of the episcopate and its relation to the Pope, the position of the Virgin Mary in the Church, and, finally, shorter schemata on a variety of subjects, including revised codes of law for the Oriental and Western Churches. He did not affirm that either the Ecumenical schema or the chapters on religious liberty and the Jewish question would come up for discussion, and he made no appeal to the Council bishops to prepare for the discussion of them, as he did in the case of the above-mentioned subjects. His placing of the schema on revelation at the head of the list served a definite strategic purpose: it would frighten the conservatives (who had been badly mauled in the first session over this document) and make them less disposed towards a third session. At this point, it appeared, Paul was not enthusiastic for a third session.

If Paul had ended his address here with the usual pious and laudatory remarks about the zeal, enthusiasm and fidelity of the Council Fathers, the speech would have been a failure. But he had up his sleeve a theatrically staged announcement which by the surprise it caused, swept everybody off their feet.

After due prayer and reflection, he said, 'We have decided next month to make a pilgrimage to the Holy Land.' The purpose? Twofold: to pray and ask for light, and 'to call back to the one Holy Church the separated brethren.'

The reaction was as expected. Some of Paul's hearers heard the words but did not understand them. The material words did not convey any semantic meaning of their content: the thing was so unexpected. No one had ever suspected that Paul would visit the Holy Land, or imagined the Holy Father in an aeroplane. The others understood but could only emit a breathless 'ah!' Then, in one simultaneous rush of perception, all understood.

Hand-clapping started down along the rows of seats like wavelets lapping against a pebbled beach. The lines of peering faces and immobile shoulders suddenly lost their rectilinear, monotonous, motionless form and broke as Council members turned around to look at each other, to sit up straight in amazement, to wave to friends on the opposite side, to glance at those seated in the tiers above and behind them. 'Long live the Orient!' cried the young auxiliary bishop of Antioch, and then embraced his neighbour, an older man, whose mitre toppled off in the process. Amid the surge of appreciation, handclapping and occasional cries of approval, Paul had paused in his speech, gazing over the top of his glasses at the Fathers and smiling quietly, confidently, thankfully, in great relief. At least this action of his had called forth universal approval.

He had managed to keep some of the good wine until the last. An iron secrecy had kept this project from the general public until the correct psychological moment. When it was produced, he had all ears. He did not make it the heart of his allocution. His disquisition on the achievements and the remaining work of the Council was banal, disappointing. Having led them to a point where spontaneously the question would arise: 'And now what?' he gently announced his voyage in a matter-of-fact voice. It was a careful bit of rhetoric and very skilfully staged as to its emotional effects, a performance that would be hard to surpass. '. . . the happy result of the Council . . . after mature consideration ... after the fashion of a pilgrim ... to that region, the native country of Our Lord Jesus, we shall go.' Only after the 29th word (*peregrinatoris*, pilgrim) did ears prick up. But in Paul's periodic Latin, the all-important verb came at the end.

Outside the hall, in the bars of St Peter's, in the Press offices, the radio station, on television, in magazines, the wave of enthusiasm began to mount. His remarks were hailed as historic, epoch-making, a stroke of genius, the action of a pioneer in Church leadership. It seemed to be all of these things. Its chief purpose in the actual circumstances of December 4 and the aftermath of the Council had been brilliantly fulfilled.

All at once Paul had acquired the centre of the stage in contemporary thinking. At his immediate disposal were the huge complexes of television, radio, journalism, news agencies, interpreting, presenting, forecasting, praising. There would be over a thousand journalists in the Holy Land to report on his trip. Italian television authorities would send a team of over two hundred men to cover the journey. *Paris-Match* would charter a plane complete with radio and other facilities. Every step of the trip would be photographed in still and moving film.

Within the confines of the Council, Paul had achieved one thing: when the froth and the spume of enthusiasm had volatilized, he had succeeded in glossing over skilfully the disaster, conciliary speaking, that had overtaken the Council. No one is insensible to public reaction. When this public interest amounts to a tidal wave of wonder, it becomes impossible not to share in the general enthusiasm. In addition, it opened up possibilities. Perhaps this could be the start of a new initiative on Paul's part.

In fairness to the Pope's motives, it must be said that he did not decide to make this pilgrimage merely in order to provide a smoke-screen, a *coup de theâtre*, to distract attention in a very critical audience. But, in the concrete circumstances in which he announced the plan, this was its immediate effect. The session had ended badly, on the surface, after approving two decrees the execution of which seemed somewhat uncertain at the time. Deeper down, worse had happened. Paul had decided to put off any voting or discussion of the religious liberty document. He had decided also that the document on the Jewish problem would be entrusted to a new Secretariat for non-Christian Religions, and that Cardinal Marella, a member of the Curia and a staunch supporter of the curial line, would be in charge of it. More significantly, he was uncertain at that moment whether to have a third session at all. In fact, the probability of a third session was much less than anyone suspected.

Felici had announced on November 29 that the date of the next session would be officially communicated to the bishops in the New Year 'at the proper time,' and, he added, the period between September 14 and November 20, 1964, represented 'the most likely dates.' They did and still do.

The reasons for this are obvious. First of all there is the political state of Italy. No one knows whether the present government will last. The political, ecclesiastical and financial Right are against it. The Communists are against it. The power-centres of the Vatican are against it. Secondly, Paul VI does not want a repeat performance of the second session: he could probably not stand again the strain between two irreconcilable factions, one entrenched in ancient centres of power, a minority to boot, and the other a vast majority hammering at the Bronze Doors and demanding in the name of the universal Church and revealed Truth, a reformed outlook and liberating of pent-up forces within the ecclesial body. He can apparently not satisfy the latter nor dislodge the former – unless he takes a step far more earth-shattering than merely taking a jet plane to the Orient. He must detach Rome from Rome, and this would mean the end of Romanism. But he could hardly do this morally, intellectually, ecclesiastically, or in terms of power. He scarcely has the power to do so. 'Have sympathy and consideration for the successor of Peter who stands before you,' he once pleaded to an audience.

The conservatives frankly do not want a third session. Paul has spoken of discussing the sources of revelation at this session. But this was the question on which their strength snapped like a twig during the first session. Nor do they want to discuss collegiality again; on this issue they were definitely defeated by overwhelming votes. The progressives want a third session for obvious reasons: to press home their partial victories in the first and second sessions. A third session holds out the possibility that the basic questions will be finally treated. But if progressive-minded bishops come to believe that it will be impossible to treat of subjects like religious liberty in a third session, will they be so enthusiastic for another bout?

When faced with an impossibility in one direction, Paul VI tends – like all human beings – to turn his gaze to other more feasible directions. Paul's choice, as seems clear from his address on December 4, is for ecclesiastical problems. His decision to go to the Holy Land in order to meet with Athenagoras was the starting-point for new ideas and a new synthesis. If Paul decides ultimately not to have a third session, he will explain it to himself and his counsellors as something positive, and not as a reaction to a list of negative reasons.

In his newly adopted outlook, Paul VI seems to have decided that no Council could ever change the *status quo* at the Vatican, that no Council would be capable of changing the mentality of the holders of power or of wresting that power from their hands. He found this out in November, 1963. Then he decided that the endeavour to push through documents like Bea's schema on Ecumenism or the theses on collegiality was putting the cart before the horse. In December and January he found that this was true of the Liturgy document. Voted and solemnly promulgated with almost theatrical seriousness by the Council in plenary session on December 4, the document was first of all subjected to a juridical sequestration known as *vacatio legis:* the new law would not apply until the 'Holy See' decided how and when and where. Then when he had prepared his *Motu Proprio* (which we have mentioned previously), the Holy Office castrated both it and some of the original provisions contained in the Liturgy constitution itself.

This is what happened. Published in January the *Motu Proprio* provoked severe reactions among the progressives. An article actually appeared in the *L'Osservatore Romano* criticizing the *Motu Proprio* of the Pope! It was signed by a Benedictine, Dom Marsili. At the same time, the right-wing Press reported that the French bishops had violated the rulings by flagrantly acting on norms which the 'Holy See' reserved to itself. Then Bishop Carli of Segni and another bishop went to Paul and complained about the matter: you see, Holy Father, there is nothing but revolution and disobedience abroad. It is not possible to apply the Liturgy schema and its provisions. Give them an inch and they take a mile.

Paul had foreseen this. No. The centres of power in the Vatican are too powerful for anyone, Pope, cardinal or bishop to change. The whole history of his contacts with Athenagoras has provided him with a fresh set of possibilities, a new *politique* in ecclesiastical matters. We shall touch on this in the third section of this chapter. Meanwhile we must notice in passing the main events connected with the Pope's visit to Jordan and Israel.

Hardly had Paul announced his visit to the Near East when Athenagoras came out openly for a meeting of all the leaders of Christendom.

Athenagoras had been deluged with letters from all over the world telling him that his meeting with Paul was a heaven-sent occasion and assuring him of prayers and moral support. Paul dispatched Father Duprey to Constantinople to see Athenagoras, not to ask him whether he would be willing to meet with Paul, but to draw up the main lines of the protocol for the meeting already decided upon. On his return to Rome, Duprey made such an excellent impression on Paul that he was put in charge of all arrangements for the proposed meeting and any ecumenical contacts it might lead to.

Paul hesitated about some of the proposed arrangements. He found it hard to resist the pleas of Cicognani and Testa that the Pope must not visit Athenagoras, but Athenagoras must visit the Pope. It was pointed out, however, that the Good Shepherd in the Gospel did not hesitate to go out of his way to meet any of the sheep who might be wandering. Why could not Paul act evangelically in this as well as in many other matters? Paul decided to go and pay a visit to Athenagoras.

Then there were the other visits. Benediktos, the Greek Orthodox Patriarch of Jerusalem, would visit Paul and must be visited by Paul in return. Paul would also receive the Armenian Patriarch. For all these meetings and contacts, detailed instructions and plans were worked out involving salutations, the exchange of gifts, ceremonial, actions bordering on what Canon Law called 'communicatio in sacris.' Every action, Paul knew, would be loaded with significance, for men, for history, for Christianity.

Paul had definite ideas about his visit to Israel. He knew that security arrangements and ceremonial would be correct and reliable. But none of his advisers had the least inkling of the potential in this visit, it appears. Paul would take the opportunity to remind the Jews of how much Pius XII had done for them – to offset the effect of Hochhuth's play. Neither Paul nor his advisers gave thought to the essential element in the situation: the first time that the successor of Peter had been received in a friendly and cordial fashion by a state composed of the people who had so long suffered throughout the lands leavened by Peter's message and who belonged, as an integral part, to the Revelation of God which Christianity professes to teach and interpret.

Athenagoras decided to send two emissaries to consult with Paul and his counsellors in Rome so that discussion of the final arrangements could be rounded off. He sent a telegram to Bea telling him that two high metropolitans, Athenagoras and Meliton, would arrive early on Christmas morning. They did not arrive, because the Turkish government refused to grant Meliton a passport. He is a Turkish citizen. Athenagoras (he was quickly dubbed 'the little' to distinguish him from the Patriarch Athenagoras who was called 'the big') being an American citizen, had no trouble in departing. He was met at the airport by two officials of Bea's Secretariat.

The patriarchal envoy was received at the Vatican with full ambassadorial honours and introduced into Paul's presence with his gifts from the Patriarch. He spent five minutes alone with the Pope, and then – to the chagrin of Cicognani and his aides – Paul called in Duprey and the three discussed all pertinent matters for the next forty minutes. After this, he was whisked over to see Cicognani and Dell'Acqua at the Secretariat of State and spent about a quarter of an hour with them: Paul had telephoned over, while Athenagoras 'the little' was on his way, and instructed them carefully about how to treat him.

The arrangements were, in brief, that Paul and the Patriarch would meet at the Apostolic Delegation in Jerusalem, Jordan. Tisserant, Cicognani, and Testa would greet the Patriarch at the gate of the Delegation, while Paul stood at the door of the house and welcomed Athenagoras in. Paul would make a return visit to Athenagoras at the residence of the Greek Orthodox Patriarch Benediktos. They would spend only a short time alone together, but there was no intention of discussing important matters. The meeting and its symbolism were all that mattered now. Even at this late stage, attempts were made to sabotage the essential lines of this symbolism. On December 29, Paul's official representative in Jerusalem, Monsignor Zanini, told the Patriarch of Jerusalem, Benediktos, that 'there is no question of a return visit by His Holiness, the Pope, to the Patriarch.' Zanini knew Paul's wishes, yet he went against them. A letter to Zanini informed him that Duprey was in exclusive charge of all arrangements; while another letter to Benediktos warned the Patriarch that he should believe only what Duprey told him.

One source of trouble for Paul came from the Egyptian Press. Nasser's organs of propaganda started denouncing the visit to Israel as a violation of Arab rights. Israel did not exist and does not exist for the Arabs. It is unlawfully occupied territory in the centre of Palestine, according to them. The visit of Paul to Israel where he would be received by the government and the president was tantamount to an act of recognition of Israel as a state. The Nasserist machine uttered veiled threats, suggested that no Arab government could possibly protect Paul from the threat of assassination. Besides it would have a direct effect on the delicate relations between Arabs and Christians.

To his credit, Paul refused to be influenced. At one stage, arrangements became complicated, and he thought of calling off the visit to Israel. Yet, once he had made up his mind, he set about staving off any further action by the Arab nationalists at Nasser's command through diplomacy. He used diplomatic channels to convey his firm resolution to Nasser. He addressed the diplomatic corps at the Vatican and reiterated that his was a purely spiritual journey with no political overtones, asking them to inform the world that the Pope was merely a pilgrim like any other pilgrim, and that any attempt to read politics into his motives or to capitalize politically on his action, should be received with disdain. Paul also used the channels of Italian diplomacy to impress the same lesson on Nasser. He succeeded. The tone of the attacks dwindled away and finally disappeared. Nasser turned to another pet project: a meeting of the Arab summit to consider reprisals against Israel who intended to divert the waters of the Jordan for irrigation purposes.

The details of Paul's visit to Jordan and Israel are so well-known, that there is no need to repeat them here. Evidently, Paul took the whole thing in his stride. There were ludicrous moments, for instance, when Paul offered to take President Segni's hat while the latter fumbled for the papers of his speech at Fiumicino airport the day Paul departed. Or when Cardinal Tisserant was hit over the head with an umbrella and cried out: 'I am a Cardinal.' Or when both Tisserant and Testa had to take refuge in a small shop and leave Paul to be carried along by the sea of shouting, cheering, enthusiastic Jordanians through the streets of the Old City. There were critical moments also, when Paul gave his blessing in *Italian* at the airport, not in the traditional *Latin*, or when King Hussein sent his Minister of Foreign Affairs to protest to Paul over his speech in Israel: Paul had seemingly implied that only Israel was the Holy Land. But on the whole nothing serious marred the trip.

Paul's first meeting with Athenagoras took place on the Mount of Olives at the Apostolic Delegation, where he met the patriarch and exchanged with him the Kiss of Peace. The moment has been immortalized in photographs. Paul addressed Athenagoras as 'Your Holiness.' Athenagoras addressed Paul as 'Your Holiness.' Paul: 'We must bring our Churches together. Nothing is insurmountable in our effort to unite mankind. But we must unite first of all.' Athenagoras: 'This moment is one of the most significant for mankind. Humanity at its highest spiritual level has the opportunity at last to guide the world

towards peace.' After more words, they and their retinues recited the
Lord's Prayer together.

At his second meeting (in the residence of Benediktos), the two
leaders spent five minutes together, then at Athenagoras's suggestion,
they recited the Lord's Prayer and read the text of Christ's prayer at
the Last Supper according to the Fourth Gospel. The scene here was,
by far and away, the most symbolic of all the memorable things that
happened during the trip and outweighs in ecclesial importance even
the Kiss of Peace. Duprey stood between the two leaders and held a
Protestant edition of the New Testament in front of them (Nestle's
edition). The edition has the Greek and Latin texts on opposite pages.
Paul recited the Latin verses while Athenagoras recited the Greek
verses, alternately. They then both read the passage on unity and, the
prayer of Jesus for unity, each in his own language. Both thought of
that unity in different terms of course. The only point of contact was
the inspired word of the Gospel. It was an evangelical meeting. Paul
was to be heavily criticized for this fraternal action when he returned
home to Rome. Yet what fair-minded person can fail to realize the
significance of what these two men did: their difficulty in understanding each other, their desire to fulfil the unity prayed for by Christ,
the distance that separated them.

Paul's speeches during his visit to the Near East were generally warm
and gracious, well thought out and well-written. They were marred
by reference to the 'Roman Christ' and to Roman Catholicism as 'the
one, true Church of Christ.' In his Bethlehem speech he actually
reminded the Orthodox Greeks that the gate of the true fold was
open and waiting for them to enter – evidences of Paul's irradicable
Romanism.

His speeches in Israel were rather impersonal and lustreless. Avoiding
any reference to Israel as a State, he praised warmly the efforts of Pius
XII in aiding Jews during the Nazi terror and indirectly repudiated
Hochhuth's play, *The Deputy*. Shazar, President of Israel, in his farewell
speech, quoted the traditional Jewish reply to any Christian missionary:
'And we will walk in the name of the Lord our God for ever and ever.'
But this also Paul could not know or realize.

3. The Pilgrim

On his return to Rome Paul greeted the members of the College of Cardinals. To Bea he said: 'I have followed in the footsteps of John XXIII and in yours, and see how far I have gone already!' To the other cardinals, he said: 'Something has happened; I need your advice.' Soon Paul sent Cardinal Lercaro of Bologna off to the Near East for further talks with leaders of the Orthodox Churches. The plan now was to gain the adherence of all the eastern patriarchs to a summit meeting. Athenagoras of Constantinople and Paul had decided on this.

Paul's advisers drew up a report on the results of his visit, weighing the political, ecclesiastical, ecumenical, and ecclesial aspects. The only two aspects of the visit not treated adequately were the conciliar and the Jewish. Paul then turned his attention to certain concrete problems. At one stage in his talk with Athenagoras, the latter had referred, both affectionately and in a complimentary way, to Jan Willebrands and Duprey and had told Paul that he got on well with these two. It was true. Duprey had been extremely useful to Paul during his entire visit. Paul therefore told both that he wished to see them often during the coming months, and that they should feel free to come to him when they thought it advisable. The problem of what to do with Bea's Secretariat now came up for consideration. In the end, the Pope resolved to deal with this problem in the light of his new outlook.

His new strategy was quite simple in concept but difficult of execution: there must be created within the existing Vatican apparatus some juridical and institutional means whereby the relationship with the Orthodox Churches could be fostered and maintained at the highest level; this could not be Bea's Secretariat for several reasons. Firstly, it was not a curial office. It was a conciliar organ. Secondly, Bea himself was probably not the best man for the job as he was a stumbling-block and an apple of discord to the opposition, who would not be able to obtain the adhesion and co-operation of other curial members. Thirdly, Paul had practically promised Cicognani and Testa that the new organization would be made up of existing curial units. Fourthly, he must find some way of controlling the existing curial organization.

Paul basically wanted to set up a new creation of his own. The spirit in the Secretariat for Christian Unity did not quite fit into his ideas. But, he knew, Bea's Secretariat was most valuable; it had already done most of the ground work for ecumenical contacts, had reaped a rich harvest of experience and had created an atmosphere of cordiality and good-will with non-Christian bodies. This must be used to the full. Paul even saw a way in which the Secretariat could be adapted to his final purpose.

It is necessary to keep in mind, at this point, the implications of Paul's choice made in November, 1963. The choice concerned that new phenomenon called conciliarism. Conciliarism, in effect, is a very definite thing. It is no longer the mere idea that some two thousand bishops met in the basilica of St Peter's, that they talked to each other for a certain number of hours during a certain number of days or weeks, and then, having congratulated and thanked the Holy Father and the Roman dicasteries on their magnificent job, they returned to their homes and the accustomed calm returned to the Vatican. Things had gone far beyond that. The difficulty is that conciliarism had reached the point where words no longer sufficed, either for progressives or conservatives. It is no longer a question of an abstract doctrine only remotely connected with the hard facts of daily life. It was now the very stuff and substance of the thing called Rome.

He had seen also during the two sessions of the Council that words sufficed only up to a certain point, after which actions were not only desirable, they were necessary, if conciliarism was to progress on its road, if anything was to happen. And he also knew that what dissatisfied ordinary men with the Council and Church was not whether there were one or two sources of revelation, whether a priest recited prime, terce, sext and none, whether the Council of Trent had been duly and magnificently commemorated, or whether the Council should adopt the Latin expression *jus primatiale* instead of *primatus* to express the concept of his primacy and satisfy the purity of Cardinal Bacci's Latinity, or whether the bishops should wear a *mozzetta* in his presence, or Roman clerics be forbidden to carry parcels in the streets or to ride vespas or bicycles or look at television. The problems ordinary men faced would have to be faced by the Church. Conciliarism was the way to tackle these problems. Without conciliarism there was no getting at them.

Conciliarism is a new principle, made up of two elements which in themselves could go a long way towards adjusting the basic antinomy we noted earlier in the historical structure of the Roman Church. These two elements are: collegiality and the de-Romanization of the Roman Church. It may appear to some that only collegiality is typical of conciliarism. But a little reflection will suffice to show that one must come to the conclusion Paul reached.

The application of collegiality to the government of the Church would mean the diminution of the Roman element – necessarily, because it implied the internationalization of the Curia. It would mean that there would be let loose in the ancient corridors and secluded offices of the Vatican all the intellectual acid of Gallic analysis and doctrinal individualism, the easy familiarity and no-nonsense administrative 'know-how' of shrewd, hard-headed Americans, the brooding *Angst* of the Germanic mind, the suave British way, sense of justice and objectivity, the fire-eating passionate Oriental love of solitude, the intangible, imponderable recesses of the Eastern mind.

Again, the application of ecumenism and its principles would mean the eventual diminution of the same Roman element, because reunion would eventually be achieved with the patriarchal Churches of the East and the various independent-minded bodies of the West, and no one could be so foolish as to think that either Patriarch Alexis of Moscow or Patriarch Athenagoras of Constantinople or Archbishop Michael Ramsey of Canterbury would agree to be subject to a mere college of Cardinals, or even settle for equal status with churchmen whose rank was entirely a papal creation, not corresponding to any actual position or predominance in the Church. The cardinalitial system replaced the earlier primatial or patriarchal system in the West. Any way one looks at it, we end up with an immediate threat to Romanism and specifically the Romanism of the twentieth century, if one opted for conciliarism.

Then, again, over and above the conceptually clear elements contained in conciliarism, there was the mysterious element which fascinated Paul as it fascinates all of us. If one considered the bishops individually at the Council, one would probably be appalled at their lack of knowledge of the concrete issues, their obvious lack of any real awareness of themselves as bishops, pastors, or successors of the Apostles. During the debates, the speeches were preponderantly conservative in tone. Speaker after speaker from the Latin or Mediterranean world stood up and discoursed in fluent Latin on many topics. Yet when it came to an important vote, the majority always voted progressive. How can this be explained? By ascribing it to the effective oratory of the Middle-European bloc, as the conservatives alleged? Or to the cloak-and-dagger machinations of certain progressive cardinals, suspect Jesuits, with liberal lay-auditors, a few journalists and lay Catholic thinkers thrown in to boot? These elements account for something, to be sure, but not all. There was a *residuum quid*, a communal instinct that gripped these ordinary men once they came together in Council, and only ruses and tricks were able to get past them in the second session. What was this 'something'? The Holy Spirit? A twentieth-century version of glossolalia? Or a genuine, Christian, ecclesial instinct, authentic collegiality?

The choice before Paul was a concrete one: follow conciliarism (because there was no question of preceding it) or abandon conciliarism. To follow conciliarism would have meant 'war' with the Curia, for the members of that body were not going to be evicted wholesale or piecemeal without registering their opposition to any such plan. It would also have meant *aperturismo ecclesiastico*. But he could probably not control the end result of all this. The proximate results of such action would be quite clear. Non-alignment between Vatican home and foreign policy and the corresponding governmental policies of Italy. Relaxation of the bonds of authoritarian control and doctrinal rigidity hitherto regarded as an anchor. Probably, also, chaos for a time. Chaos under his own roof. But Paul was not willing to receive Brother Chaos – even for a time – in his household.

On the other hand, to abandon conciliarism and all that it meant opened up an unpleasant prospect. Not so much that he feared an explosion. Explosions were always occurring. The explosion of irrelevancy. The explosion of revolt – of individual or group. The explosion of the intellectual asking too many questions and cramming so many answers into his brain that it finally burst the seams and carried away much that was good. It was like that in the time of Jovinian and Photius, Abelard and Luther, Renan and Döllinger. It would always be like that.

Paul feared and fears that the Church will not be in tune with the modern world and able to take its lawful place as leader of a genuine moral rearmament, as a clearly apparent rock-bound foundation for all human happiness, as a universally accepted rallying-point for the ethical, moral, and authentically Christian forces that are being driven underground in our times. He had seen this in a small but significant way towards the end of January 1964. At issue was the thorny theme of religious liberty. During the second session, he had finally condemned Bea's document on religious liberty to outer darkness. There had been weeping and a certain amount of gnashing of teeth. This might have ended the matter – if the Church had been living in a vacuum or in the times of Gregory VII or Innocent III. This is the twentieth century, however, and there are movements abroad that cannot have any other origin than what John XXIII called the 'marvellous providence of God that is leading the human family to its destined unity.' A bishop long resident in Rome remarked on this occasion: 'We have just missed the finest chance in the twentieth century to be the only body in the world who could provide a set of principles on religious liberty acceptable to all men of good-will.'

The words were prophetic. In January, Arcot Krishnaswami, Indian expert on religious discrimination and member of the U.N. Subcommission on the Prevention of Discrimination, presented to the U.N. Human Rights Commission a text on this very subject. He had based his text on draft-texts submitted by Morris Abram (U.S.) and Peter Calvocoressi (Great Britain). The reaction to the text of Krishnaswami was not favourable among Jews, Catholics and Protestants: they found that his text did not safeguard or underline the supranational character of certain religions. The matter was complicated by the bland proposals of the Soviet member of the same U.N. Subcommission, Victor Titov; the document, he said airily, does not make atheism and religion equal. He had other objections also: parents, for instance, should not be allowed to decide the religion of their children. This implied two things: children should be reared as atheists until they could 'decide' themselves what they wanted to do, and it meant explicitly naming one particular 'ism,' atheism, whereas no other outlook (any of the great religions, for instance) got any explicit mention. There are some interesting parallels, by the way, between what Titov said and some of the conservative speeches at the Council on religious liberty: the Catholic religion must be kept as the one true religion to which all men were bound to be converted, otherwise they were in error; Bea's document was not sufficiently 'Catholic' in tone – it could have been written by a Protestant, according to one bishop; only a very limited liberty should be allowed other religions and none at all to those who profess atheism or agnosticism.

The Catholic Church in America and elsewhere has no charter on the principles of religious liberty or non-discrimination in religious matters, because as a matter of record, Paul VI and his counsellors permitted a document along these lines to be blocked in the second session. If any member of the U.N. Subcommission in question or of the U.N. Human Rights Commission had heard Cardinal Browne speaking on the theme of Bea's document, he would have been appalled. The cardinal stated quite openly that non-Catholics have only limited rights because they are in error from the Catholic point of view. Boiled down to essentials, there was a striking parallelism between the guiding principles of Victor Titov and this conservative cardinal at the Council: both maintaining that their own points of view should prevail over all others. This is the basis of the frequent charge that the Church wishes to proclaim religious liberty wherever and whenever she is not free to act, and refuses to proclaim religious liberty wherever and whenever she is predominant.

In January and February of 1964, there was a wave of statements in the United States on the subject of Chapters 4 and 5 of Bea's schema. Cardinal Meyer of Chicago expressed the belief that both Protestant and Catholic ecumenists are convinced that 'the ecumenical movement cannot be securely founded until a clear statement on the subject of religious liberty is fully developed.'[1] Monsignor John Tracy Ellis said in San Francisco that the Catholic Church 'must make an authoritative and unequivocal declaration of its support for religious liberty.'[2] Father de Sales Standerwick, S.A., speaking at Washington, said that Catholics must pray for themselves that they may be free of anti-Semitism.[3] Speaking on a somewhat broader plane, Bishop Charrière of Lausanne declared that 'Roman prelates who at the Ecumenical Council opposed the principle of episcopal collegiality, actually undermined the moral authority of the very entities they direct.' He expressed his sorrow 'at this attitude of a minority which attempts to defend the Pope against the Pope while showing hostility to the Council Moderators who did but act in unanimity with the Holy Father.'[4] And Bishop W. E. Doyle of Nelson, Canada, declared that the Catholic Church must speak out on the question of religious liberty to remove suspicions that it speaks with two tongues. It is important and timely, he said, 'that the Roman

[1] NCWC News Service (domestic), 1/24/64 – F, p. 4.
[2] Ibid., page 6.
[3] Cf. 1/25/64 – S, p. 12.
[4] Cf. ibid., 1/24/64 (foreign), 1/24/64 – F, p. 4.

Church is considering the Religious Liberty schema at the Vatican Council.'⁵

'Avoiding anti-Semitism isn't enough,' said Father Eugene H. Maly, professor at Mount St Mary's. 'Catholics have an obligation to develop a real love for the Jews. Moreover, not one of the bishops was against the chapter itself (Chapter 4) ... We are especially open to this (the charge of over-simplification in levelling charges at any group) in our relationship with the Jewish people because of their close attachment to us in their religion.'⁶ Bishop Paul F. Leibold said that the ecumenical movement was 'a religious dialogue carried on in the spirit of charity, and it seems clear that a first necessary step in this direction, especially here in the U.S., is that a wall of mistrust, created by doubt and misunderstanding of our stand on religious liberty, be removed.'⁷ The national director of the B'nai B'rith Anti-defamation League said that the idea of Jewish responsibility for the death of Christ 'is still distressingly alive and a cruel, critical factor in perpetuating anti-Semitic prejudice.' The statement on Jewish-Christian relations pending before the Ecumenical Council is 'a significant development which could, if adopted, presage a major and more positive change in attitude throughout the world.'⁸

Having opted not to follow conciliarism, Paul found it difficult to abandon it nevertheless. For one thing, there was the question of the third session. It was not so much that a third session *had* to take place: the affair could always be put off, and perhaps it would have to be. But there was the mountain of work done already by the conciliar commissions. There was the wave of expectations raised and the flood of apprehensions at home. Perhaps, some solution to the problem of conciliarism could be found along the road of Ecumenism, Paul's particular brand of ecumenical development, that is.

When the subject of a reform of the Curia was first broached during the second session, a whole gamut of proposals was offered. Most suggestions boiled down to a rather crude reckless: 'abolish the Holy Office,' 'get rid of Cardinal Ottaviani,' or similar ideas. More refined proposals, of course, gradually came to the surface. There was the principle of *smantellimento* (dismantling), which amounted to this: take away from the Holy Office everything that the other congrega-

---

⁵ Cf. Information Service of the Canadian Catholic Conference, January 27, 1964, p. 6.
⁶ NCWC News Service (*domestic*), 2/6/64 – Th, p 1.1.
⁷ *Ibid.*, 2/3/64 – M, p. 4.
⁸ *Ibid.*, 2/4/64 – Tu, p. 5.

tions or the bishops could do quite well themselves and so cut it down to a manageable size. Actually, it will be necessary to institute some kind of *smantellimento* if affairs ever reach that point. There was also the concept of *fossilizzazione* (fossilization) – actually only a refined *récherché* version of the preceding concept: the Holy Office should be allowed deliberately to become as effectual in the life of the Church as the Beefeaters are in the life of the British Army, or the residual eye on the skull-top of a healthy two-eyed bull-elephant. This had a certain Rabelaisian or *trahison-des-clercs* touch about it. The Holy Office also came in for a lot of good-natured ribbing (as well as serious criticism). Thus the oft-used initials H.O. (Holy Office) were said to stand for 'hold on' – the policy of the Holy Office during the first session. On his birthday, Christmas Day, Cardinal Ottaviani was supposed to have said to a cringing subordinate, Parente: 'Today, pizzas for all the prisoners in the dungeons! – except for Küng, Rahner, de Lubac and our Venerable Brother'; the Venerable Brother being of course Cardinal Bea who was under severe fire from the Holy Office at the time for his *agape* talk in January 1963. Some young students of Rome University actually had prepared a huge sign reading 'Apartments to let' (*Affittasi*) and intended to tack it up on the façade of the Holy Office in late November, 1962.

The only plausible element in these proposals was their pinpointing of the central role played by the Holy Office. But to take on the Holy Office by oneself (even for a Pope) would be as futile as trying to lift the Abu Simbel temple and statues without first cutting them out of the solid rock in which they are embedded. In our case, the rock was the entire curial system. It was the system that had to be changed.

Paul had many ideas, and many were proposed to him, about how this change could be effected. It could take the form of various possible reorganizations. The existing curial organs (Holy Office included) could either be regrouped around a new parent organ or an already existing one. The parent might be either the Secretariat of State (if a choice were to be made amongst existing organs) or it could be an entirely new body of international complexion. Alongside existing curial organs, a completely new, independent, supreme organ might be created of international character. In that case, it would probably not be logical for the parent organ to be international. On the other hand, if the parent organ were merely a re-activated College of Cardinals, it would of course be international.

There was definitely need for some new regrouping and reorganization. A lot would depend on Cicognani, whether he would graciously consent to step down from his post as Secretary of State. As part of the plans Paul made with Athenagoras there was one item concerning the holding of theological discussions to iron out the differences between Roman Catholicism and Orthodox doctrine. Nothing in the entire Roman scene was more difficult to solve. It is as clear as the statue of Michael the Archangel on the Castel Sant'Angelo that such discussions will be impossible if the Holy Office is to do the vetting, the censoring, the passing on documents, personnel, requests, norms of thought or action. The Greeks might as well stay at home and Paul give up all hope of furthering ecumenism. Yet, technically and canonically speaking, at the present time, it is the Holy Office's *right* to exercise these powers. During the second session it asserted these rights over an Ecumenical Council. More regrettable, its claim was not only not opposed by Paul, the Moderators or the bishops of the universal Church, but it was acquiesced in by Paul, accepted with difficulty by three of the Moderators (Suenens, Doepfner, Lercaro) and acquiesced in by one (Agagianian). The bishops were not consulted.

Any new set-up, therefore, must be accompanied by a regrouping and a curtailment of powers. If such were possible, then a new body would be able to enter into some sort of fruitful discussions and relationships with the Orthodox and other non-Catholic churches.

Early in February Paul became aware that the opposition to his plans was hardening. He called a meeting of the cardinals resident in Rome, delegated two of their number to comment on the results of the Holy Land visit, and asked all to speak their minds on the results and on his plans for the near future. He was not present because it was urged that the cardinals would be freer to express their opinions in his absence. Afterwards, the minutes of this meeting were sent to the cardinals abroad. The reaction of the cardinals at this meeting was not as enthusiastic and whole-hearted as Paul could have desired. He was now up against one of the many difficulties he would have to face and overcome. By opting to work with this organism, apart from the Council, he had decided to go ahead without taking into account the authority and moral prestige of the Council. The first fruits of this policy were disappointing. In time, perhaps, Paul VI would come to appreciate the fundamental reason why John XXIII called a Council in the first place, and why, once the Council was in session, he came down at the right moments on the side of the majority. It was to be a hard schooling for Paul VI.

To Paul's way of thinking at present, should it be possible to re-organize the Vatican, then the calling of the third session in the Autumn of 1964 would not be so urgent. It might even be premature, for func-tions and relationships might not have matured to the point where he could present concrete results to the bishops of the world and seek the approval of the Council. This must be numbered among the funda-mental reasons for the doubt, at present, about the holding of a third session. On the other hand, if the present plans of Paul are frustrated, he may decide to go ahead with the third session anyway, although new difficulties may arise if he does so. But by then the Pope may have learnt the lesson which John XXIII learnt in his own way.

Thus, while facing trouble at home within his own household, Paul is also facing mounting expectations abroad on the key issues of the second session: ecumenism, religious liberty, the Jewish problem, and collegiality. He has set as one of the goals for the third session, a dis-cussion and decision on the thorny question of the sources of revelation. The matter is of importance in relations with Protestants. But, one can hardly argue that this is going to bring the Church more up to date or help it solve the problems of a shortage of priests, the intellectual stifling in Catholic circles, population control, nuclear disarmament, world peace. Perhaps by the time the third session of the Second Vatican Council is held, the present chain-reaction of disturbances around the globe will have resulted in something bigger and uglier. Perhaps the leaders of this great organization will perforce have their eyes turned to more fundamental questions.

Returning to the main lines of our thought, we can easily see that any charge of *amletismo* with regard to Paul is a gross exaggeration. There is a single thread running through Papa Montini's career up to this point: he is determined to assert the leadership of the Roman Pontiff and the potential of his leadership. At the beginning he adapted *giovannismo* to this purpose, and even thought that it would work. But Montini was counting on a different kind of second session: he did not envisage the ferocity of the conservative reaction, he did not under-stand the innate weakness of the bishops, and at the crucial moment he failed to take the calculated risk – which John took in the middle of the first session when, against the united opposition of the Curia, he sided with the large majority who had voted down the Curia's outmoded document on the sources of revelation. The majority on that occasion was not a procedural majority; yet Roncalli *imposed* its will on the minority. The one time that Papa Montini gave the bishops a chance to reveal their desires (in the straw vote of October 30), they showed him what they thought and what support he would receive *if* he showed his hand. But he failed to do so.

After November 23, he forged a new outlook no longer based on *giovannismo* but his own, completely his own. At its core lies the same principle, the leadership of the Roman Pontiff as Roman Pontiff. There are subtle differences of emphasis and phrasing, finer shadings and more studied colorations in his words and actions, yet the principle remains the same.

No one dared criticize Paul VI for his decision, for the simple reason that no one else works on the fourth floor of the Vatican and occupies the Chair of Peter. No one, therefore, is in a position to gauge definitively the impact of the forces with which he had to deal last fall. In strict justice and fair judgement, the accusation of *amletismo* cannot be urged. But the impression remains that by giving in to the forces working against him, by choosing to collaborate with the Curia in its present state, Paul has fallen into a trap. Sooner or later, a definitive confrontation must come. His present position is even worse: the bureaucratic and conservative forces, which were driven into the Cloaca Maxima, as it were, in the Joannine era, have apparently emerged once more in triumph, stronger than ever. True, they bear the traces of their trial. Papa Montini must now face the bland, reassured smiles of men who have come through it all and are back again at their old game, more convinced than ever that it is but another instance of the age-old lesson: the gates of hell shall not prevail against the Institution.

To revert to the Pyramid, then, we can see that the very principle on which Paul acts is now slightly ambiguous: on the one hand, he now has the task as Roman Pontiff (John had the task as Bishop of Rome *with* the bishops of the Church) to rid the Church of those elements which hinder its proper expansion, growth, the fulfilment of its ideal. On the other hand, he has chosen to work with elements which are incompatible with such a purpose. Figuratively, the Pyramid cannot be 'de-pyramidized,' cannot be dismembered and still have a cornerstone. More pertinently, we cannot remove the framework or body and still hope to have the apex-stone in its place – Romanism without Romanism.

As regards the Plain, the task is even more difficult. Paul has certainly mapped out his approach to the streams flowing over its surface. First of all, he wishes to channel the Christian elements, to fuse all Christian

influences into one thing. He wants reunion, or at least some kind of
unity which would lead ultimately to reunion, to a making-one of the
whole. No person can say how long this will take. Yet, in the meantime,
there are influences and currents mounting in force. A tide of opportunity is in the making. It will not always be at full flow, may even
start to ebb, suddenly or slowly, back from the walls of the City. And
Paul's schematic reduction of the ecumenical possibilities to the phased
process: *Orthodox first – Protestants second – non-Christians third*, is a
somewhat dry, abstract, unrealistic approach to a living problem involving living people, the result of intellectual processes, not born of
immediate intuition. It lacks emotional appeal. If we remember that he
is also working on another schematic programme: *Romanism-reformed
Curialism*, we can appreciate the difficulties he has undertaken to solve,
and we can get some glimpse of the crags he has chosen to climb during
his pontificate.

Within the City there are still tensions which he has not as yet set
about solving. Any system in conflict with its own fundamental
principles eats away at its vitals. The tensions within Catholicism, a
burgeoning intellectualism, a conservative leadership, increasing
restrictions on lawful expressions of opinion, the continuation of un-
Christian attitudes towards those of other religions, a refusal to adapt
laws and practices to modern conditions – without touching the substance of ancient doctrine, of course – all remain. And Paul seems to
have no plan to cope with them.

This is the trajectory followed by the pontificate of Paul VI thus far,
since his coronation as Pope to the present day. It was not a wavering
path dotted by burnt-out flares or leaving a wake of trailing failures,
but a strongly pulsating ascent as it soared to its first zenith. It has been
subtle in its search for a newly-oriented path, yet one clearly ascertain-
able and definable in its scope: Paul has been caught up in the inexorable
workings of history and history's law applies to him: 'You think that
things are not moving fast enough? Be patient! True, we could make
many reforms immediately, but they would all come to nothing if the
minds and the personalities had not changed. For this one needs time.
Such is the law of history.'[9]

To some it may seem that the *élan* and dynamism of Paul's pontificate are still alive: his Romanism tends to confirm the impression.
Yet Paul VI, as a man of his day – which he certainly is – knows that if
this were the case, his own pontificate would merely be an inter-

[9] Paul VI to a group of Eastern bishops. Cf. *Le Monde*, December 7, 1963.

mediate phase between the *giovannismo* of his immediate predecessor and the full flowering of the dialogue with a world increasingly in need of dialogue. He would be a pope of transition, a *papa di passaggio*, as Vaticanologists called John XXIII in 1958. This would be the greatest irony of contemporary history.

But no innate, compulsive reason dictates this as an ironclad necessity. Paul is certainly as intent on the ultimate goal as John was. At present, he may be merely holding a glass up to folly and anachronistic behaviour. Shrouding his actions and his figure, there will always be the pathos of his isolation, his aloneness as architect of a new structure. As the fulfiller of a supernal mission in faith and in word, he is never motivated by a desire to please for the sake of pleasing, and is always provided with an ultimate refuge from the bite of men's tongues and from disappointed hopes, in his *mystique* of office: 'One must not be measured by the plaudits either of men in general or even of one's immediate associates, but by the mission one fulfils, by the faith which animates that mission, and by the word which formulates it.'[10]

Ultimately, unless a tide in human affairs overtakes him and by-passes all his efforts, it may be due to him and him chiefly that 'all nations of the earth do praise the Almighty,' that the living Word once more vivifies, that Jacob's ladder is pitched between heaven and Charing Cross or Times Square, that Christ is seen walking on the waters of the world, and the Petrine privilege of primacy amongst the brethren is the focal point for unity, indicating to men where God has chosen to dwell on earth among His children.

[10] Paul VI to an audience of parish priests and pastoral workers, February 11. Cf. *Il Tempo*, Feb. 12, 1964.

APPENDIX

The relative strength of the chief Christian denominations, according to statistics given in L'Osservatore Romano, December, 1963.

WORLD
Christians:	974,489,630
Catholics:	584,869,340
Protestants:	256,457,440
Orthodox:	133,163,850
Other Religions:	2,094,917,170

EUROPE
Population:	646,805,000
Christians:	498,424,850
Catholics:	256,958,950
Protestants:	128,993,400
Orthodox:	112,532,500

ASIA
Population:	1,714,493,000
Christians:	61,094,400
Catholics:	42,757,150
Protestants:	15,371,250
Orthodox:	2,966,000

AFRICA
Population:	263,799,200
Christians:	64,009,630
Catholics:	27,137,790
Protestants:	22,444,390
Orthodox:	14,397,450

AMERICA
Population:	428,114,600
Christians:	338,691,150
Catholics:	254,651,450
Protestants:	80,872,400
Orthodox:	3,167,300

OCEANIA
Population:	16,206,000
Christians:	12,280,600
Catholics:	3,364,000
Protestants:	8,816,000
Orthodox:	100,600

INDEX